Rethinking Design and Interiors

Human Beings in the Built Environment

Shashi Caan

Laurence King Publishing

Published in 2011
by Laurence King Publishing Ltd
361–373 City Road
London EC1V 1LR
Tel +44 (0)20 7841 6900
Fax +44 (0)20 7841 6910
E enquiries@laurenceking.com
www.laurenceking.com

A catalogue record for this book is available from the British Library

ISBN 978 185669 756 9

Designed by Laura Tabet

Printed in China

Contents

PICTURE CREDITS

AUTHOR'S ACKNOWLEDGMENTS

The architectural truism of "it takes a village to build a building" very much applies to the actualization of this book. The simple yet poignant questions asked by my students inspired me to search for a deeper understanding and to investigate some of the fundamentals of both human needs and design criteria. At the end of the project, I would like to acknowledge all those who have contributed to its completion. These contributions include many discussions, advice, research, and reviews of ideas and various versions of the manuscript. Apart from those people with whom I have interacted, there remain others who have worked to help transform the manuscript into the physical reality of a book. I express my heartfelt thanks for your effort.

As a teacher I must first and foremost thank all my students. I have learnt a great deal from them. It was their curiosity and persistent questioning of a need to understand design that forced me to seek comprehensive explanations for complex matters. The concepts in this book are born out of their quest for clarifications, and, in the process, it has enormously enriched my own comprehension.

I am grateful to Philip Cooper, Editorial Director at Laurence King Publishing, who not only encouraged me to commit these ideas to paper, but also patiently guided me through the intriguing process of writing and publishing. Indeed, my thanks go to the entire Laurence King Publishing team, who helped with the myriad aspects involved in the publication of this book. Without their support and help, my ideas would still be the subject of verbal debate.

To develop these initial ideas more fully, a broad and theoretical research effort was required. I am fortunate to have had assistance from a group of wonderful and smart researchers, who helped to expand the inquiry and give its content substance and depth. I am most appreciative of the support from Mikel Ciemny, Heidi Druckemiller, Olivia Klose, Karla de Vries, and Tara Rasheed for their perseverance in helping to locate the right sources, illustrations, and references. Their help was instrumental in providing a foundation and coherence for my thesis. The overall hypothesis and text would not be quite as reflective or cohesive without the profound help and support of Patrick Ciccone, whose dedicated research helped to give shape to the core argument. The final manuscript would not be complete without the attention to detail and dedicated effort of Annabel Barnes, who helped to ensure that all material came together flawlessly.

My mentors, colleagues, and peers, Susan Szenasy, Ruth Lynford, Madeline Lester, Denise Guerin, Beth Harmon-Vaughn, Jennifer Busch, Danielle Galland, Cheryl Lim, Ian Pirie, John Rouse, Phillip Abbott, Brad Powell, and Drew Plunkett all provided comments and insights throughout the writing and at the various stages of the manuscript. They were instrumental in helping me to dissect, examine, and reassemble the core arguments and content. My faculty colleagues at Parsons the New School for Design—too many to mention individually—all contributed with expert opinions and insights which, directly and indirectly, led to my conviction of the necessity of this exploration.

My more recent exposure to the world at large and the global community made me realize that many of the issues discussed here reach across countries and cultures. This experience was made possible through my involvement on the board of the International Federation of Interior Designers/Architects (IFI), both as a member and as its president. The various individual board members and member organizations worldwide have greatly contributed to the breadth and depth of my insights. The editorial expertise and discernment provided by both Kristi Cameron and Liz Faber was crucial for reaching lucidity and precision in a message that is near and dear to my heart.

Finally, I must thank my role model and sage advisor, Theodore Prudon. Without his unconditional support and encouragement this project would not have been possible. His consistent probing for substance gives this book its depth and his intellect is equally embedded in these pages.

In the end, *Rethinking Design and Interiors: Human Beings in the Built Environment* provides a series of connective ideas. They are shared with the intent to broaden the debate and to bring greater attention to the importance of designing environments for human occupation. Having articulated these thoughts, with enormous help and support from those mentioned here and many others involved in the process, I am optimistic that we are on the cusp of new opportunities for exploration, which will, by design, lead to better and more sensitively designed interventions.

Preface: Rethinking Design

Susan S. Szenasy
Editor-in-Chief, *Metropolis Magazine*

It is no secret to any observant person today that every profession and every process is in crisis. Approaches that were invented and then matured in the previous centuries feel hopelessly out of date. And all signs indicate that we are not yet prepared to meet the crisis. In many parts of the industrialized world the quick-fix mentality trumps the deliberate, systematic approach that could create long-term policies befitting a democracy. What brings this ineffectuality to crisis proportions is that we operate in a global economy characterized by the instant movement of capital while the people on the ground–with their local needs, wisdom, and material resources–are left to fend for themselves.

To understand this new context, we must expand our thinking to include the overarching needs of our time: dramatic and catastrophic environmental degradation worldwide, rapid and voluminous global communication, and unprecedented and life-changing technological innovation. These developments call for a new way of thinking about our world at every scale, in every culture, in every geographic location. Like other endeavors, design, that thoughtful human act which gives shape to all cultures, must be recast to embrace systems thinking.

You hold in your hand a book that points the way for the design of interiors in our newly complex world. It offers a deep dive into the things that make us human, our most intimate surroundings–our interiors–being one of these things. It explores our deep-seated and evolving relationship with our rooms, be these in our homes or any other interior where we spend a majority of days and nights. It traces this intimate relationship from the cave, where the first humans escaped from danger, to the high-rise corporate office where we carry on complex, yet invisible, electronic transactions in ergonomically sophisticated spaces.

While we graduated from the ancient cave to the modern office, we seem to have forgotten the very things that make us human: our basic need for shelter, for well-being, for social interaction. As you will learn here, each one of these topics, and many others subsidiary to them, have been and continued to be studied by social scientists through observation, documentation, and analysis. Now, this scientific approach must become the underpinning of design thinking. The art (beauty, emotion, intuition) of interiors needs a scientific foundation (observation, research, analysis).

Even as the profession continues to develop its ever-higher standards for the environmental footprint of interiors–through its demand for non-toxic, healthy material–it has yet to dig deep into the research on behavior and feeling, comfort and experience. While those who design interiors can document the relative greenness of their designs, their intuition tells

Preface

them that this is an incomplete approach to their work. Holistic design, or systems thinking as Buckminster Fuller used to call it, pays attention to all our senses – smell, sound, temperature, touch – as well as the natural and designed environments that support them.

You are about to embark on a fascinating journey of how art and science can come together for the benefit of those who inhabit interior spaces, for the natural environment in which we have all evolved, and for the profession that creates the inner space. In the process you'll reacquaint yourself with such basics of the human condition as trust, dignity, and satisfaction.

September 2010

Introduction

As working professionals, designers of interiors do not question enough what their discipline really is or wonder about how what they do is perceived by the public at large. They exercise the skills they have so carefully developed, solve the problems immediately at hand, and have the gratification of seeing satisfied clients. But spend time with thoughtful young people who are studying design with an intent to shape meaningful environments, as I did while serving as the chair of the interior design program at Parsons The New School for Design, in New York, and you will quickly find they are seeking a more comprehensive definition of that expertise: How, exactly, does it relate to the other design disciplines and what is unique about it? Why do we need design for the interior?

As someone trained in architecture, industrial design, and interiors, I know all too well that, at their core, all design disciplines share certain skills. But I am also very aware of the fact that what they are concerned with is not necessarily interchangeable. Yes, architects deal with interior volumes when they design buildings, and they think about how the shape of those spaces will affect the occupant. And industrial designers think about the comfort and functional requirements of the individuals who will spend hours sitting in their chairs while at work or traveling, and the surrounds of these products. Designers specializing in interiors think about how people occupy and experience spaces, and how to arrange and use the objects that fill them in a way that enables us to recognize who we are as individuals, and how we relate to others, as well as creating the many other intangible qualities that make us successful through the success of our environment. This is not only limited to single rooms (of any scale) but also to the narrative of the experience created in the transition between interconnected volumes (with or without literal walls or ceilings). At the core of interiors is an understanding of abstract qualities of shaping this negative space or void. All these complex parts need to come together to form a cohesive whole.

Shaping the spaces we inhabit is human nature. Since we first abandoned sleeping under the open sky for shelters with roofs and walls, we have been modifying our surroundings by adapting and shaping all the components intended to support and improve the quality of our lives. Interiors and design, therefore, are intimately connected to who we are as a species. Interiors most closely define human beings, our behavior and emotions, within our built world in a way no other discipline does. This answer did not satisfy my students; they needed one that more clearly and better defined the parameters of the discipline and thus the career they had chosen: interior design.

After leaving my position as chair at Parsons to pursue the international commissions my firm had acquired and to assume the presidency of the International Federation of Interior Architects/

Designers (IFI), I began to realize that there was an even bigger issue at stake. Not only do we not understand the role of design for interiors as it exists today, but we are on the cusp of extraordinary global and societal changes that will profoundly impact requirements for how we live and thus the places where most of our lives are spent: inside, which will affect, for that matter, all design. We are fighting to survive on a planet whose ecosystems our very success as a species has thrown out of accord. As we struggle to accommodate our growing numbers in increasingly dense cities and buildings, we are becoming ever more urban dwellers. In the not too distant future, we will inhabit structures so large and so complex that they constitute entire neighborhoods and communities. This will present us with new challenges for creating interior spaces. It will force us to remember why we began to design in the first place: to improve the human condition and provide ourselves with a measure of physical and psychological comfort. So facing all of those challenges, what will this discipline have to become?

We are at a critical moment in the history of the world but also in the evolution of design disciplines. To meet the challenges we face, these disciplines need a better foundation upon which to build, which will require the development of a scientific understanding of how the built environment affects us. Designing interiors will also mean embracing a much broader engagement with, and responsibility for, our societal and environmental actions and making certain this knowledge is embedded in both education and practice. This book endeavors to outline how today's practice developed and why the discipline is perceived as it is. How it must change by gathering the data—phenomenological and sensorial—and must include a greater understanding of human behavior and how it can be influenced through the language of design. Once we can better quantify and qualify the human experience of objects and spaces, we can align this new design knowledge with our educational and design processes. This new knowledge will finally foster a greater appreciation for, and connection between, the built environment and its occupants. It will engender and promote well-being and facilitate human advancement.

The need for this design research is not limited to any particular design discipline but will form part of a common language, and will allow for ever more collaborative practice even while specific disciplines grow more specialized. But of all the design disciplines, interiors have an important role to play in leading the way toward developing the core body of knowledge that will inform all design practice: the interior fulfills, and always has fulfilled, our most basic need for shelter. While the future of humanity is tied to its past, the history of this past is expressed not in stylistic periods but in how we have evolved as human beings. This comes from within us. And thus design has to come from within to envision and craft a sensitively responsive and responsible future built world.

Shashi Caan
September 2010

Chapter One

The Search for Shelter   11

Man was first a hunter, and an artist: his earliest vestiges tell us that alone. But he must always have dreamed, and recognized and guessed and supposed, all skills of the imagination.

Guy Davenport
The Geography of the Imagination[1]

Chapter One

An early human painting in a cave. While the purpose of prehistoric cave painting is unknown, examples are generally found in areas that were not easily accessed. Although many theories exist, the popular belief is that they were done for a greater purpose than mere decoration. The earliest interior was created when our ancestors discovered the inside space of the cave. That environment created a space that was safe from the dangers of the outside world, and one where new forms of self-discovery and delight could flourish.

Human evolution and design shape each other. Design, always a search for appropriate solutions to problems, has evolved from utilitarian and indigenous applications into the formal practice we know today. It springs from the wells of our own nature –to create, through imagination, the means of human betterment–and has become ubiquitous in all facets of life. There is nothing we encounter that is devoid of design.

To design well, however, we must take essential human needs and behavior into account. While we have some comprehension of our functional and stylistic requirements, we have not yet developed a necessary understanding of our visceral and psychological needs. To fathom what these are, it helps to consider the very first habitable environment–the cave–for that is where humans originally dealt with their most basic need, shelter, through conscious intervention. By taking up residence in that first interior, they uncovered design as the means by which our longings for safety and security could be realized. The cave allowed them to feel protected from harm and free from anxiety or doubt, and the minute they went inside, they gained a very different understanding of who they were and began to evolve in a way that was quite different from what would have happened if they had stayed outside.

The story of the evolution of the interior is thus a reflective history of us and our intrinsic need to improve our experience of the world. This is the reason we design. Exploring the deep past of the human habitat is, then, not solely a look backward but part of the view forward. Knowledge of the built environment's humble beginnings enables us to start to understand more clearly the impact it has on people. Only once we recognize this connection can we begin to build the comprehensive body of knowledge that is essential to move design forward. The design profession(s) necessarily must deal with our fundamental sensory, cognitive, and bodily needs as we embrace

The Search for Shelter

Evolution of building	Periods in time	Formation of types of shelter
Realization of need for shelter	Foraging	
Discovery of building process	Hunting	
Development of building process	Early agriculture	
	Farming	
Refinement of building process due to technological and material evolution	Machine age	
	Electronic age	
	Global network age	? ?

ever more sophisticated and elusive technological and industrial advancements that threaten to further distance us from our basic humanity.

Shelter's Human Roots

Initially there was no inside space and the world, inviting or hostile, was nothing but the outside. There might have been something in the way of limited refuge—a bower of trees that provided shade from the sun, a cluster of stones behind which to hide—but it was of fleeting utility. Even when primitive humans could find temporary respite from the danger of the world, they remained outside. This presented a dichotomy. Natural pleasures —like taking delight in the beauty of greenery, enjoying the warmth and comfort of the sun—coexisted precariously with the fear of animals, weather, and other humans. The discovery of the interior (of found shelter) presumably would have stimulated an awareness of the need for a more intimate, protected, and controllable environment, which in turn allowed for a newfound modicum of comfort and delight. Crawling into that first cave may have been an instinctual flight from the hostility of the exterior world, but the decision to remain there is evidence of an awareness of the benefits of shelter. That moment of intention was an act of design that would change us forever.

The first attempts at building—tents and huts—were appropriated from the shape of the cave. Like the cave, they provided shelter and security from other humans, animals, and nature, but these man-made constructions also allowed people to live in environments where they would have perished without a protective barrier. Though essential in the discovery of shelter, the cave was not an adequate long-term solution, and the lessons of that found space were quickly adapted in newer forms.

Archaeological and anthropological evidence points to the emergence of these artificial replicas nearly simultaneously to the discovery and inhabitation of naturally occurring caves. The noted American anthropologist J. Walter Fewkes describes the structural influence of the cave: "Two lines of architectural evolution reach back to the cave as the original form: (1) growth of a building within a natural cave, and (2) evolution of a building from an artificial cave."[2] The experience of the cave—natural and man-made—was inseparable from our expectations of the qualities of inside space. Thus, our awareness of design and of the interior was coterminous.

While early man-made shelters may have been portable, and consequently ephemeral, they were no less important to the creation of habitable interior space than the more permanent cave. "By their very nature, portable shelters such as tents do not leave lasting imprints for archaeologists to study."[3] Nonetheless, tents and huts, which were a primary form of habitation for early humans, survive today in a few nomadic cultures and can teach us what some of the early development patterns were about.

That nomadic lifestyle and the limitations of materials, structural technologies, and labor, would have meant that early shelters were basic. They often took on a circular shape, which is both easy to construct and responds to the outward radiation of the fireplace. These centralized volumes, made by leaning branches against each other and then tying and covering them, were constructed easily and quickly, and constituted the fundamental profile of all housing. Dome-shaped huts were the most basic form of habitation for hunter-gatherers, who until 15,000 BCE comprised almost all of the population.[4] Even today the plan of the traditional Navajo hogan, with a stove in the center of a domed space, resembles that basic circular form. The idea of shelter that the cave offered was not lost or forgotten, but survives in trace form, as recreated and adapted in other types of dwelling when people spread across the world.

A brief depiction of the evolution of shelter from pre-history into the future. Lao-Tse said: "The reality of the building does not consist in roof and walls but in the space within to be lived in." The shape of the shelter we inhabit directly reflects our way of life, but our progress in creating human habitation has not always been linear. Instead, the fundamental qualities that interiors must address have lain dormant during the technological evolution of architecture. As a species we have historically sought to understand and rationalize our physical universe and being. With this focus, even though found shelter promoted progress, the focus on environmental insides—physical and psychological—appears to have remained secondary since as far back as the hunting phase. At that point, if a building and its insides had been recognized as equally important entities, perhaps today we would have a respectable and equal development recognizing the importance of the insides of the built environment. Finally, our attention has turned inward as we focus on understanding DNA, genetics, and our extended built environment.

The traditional Mongolian yurt represents human ingenuity in creating shelter in a variety of settings through minimal means. The yurt's simple circular form is easily demountable for transportation; once installed, it creates a supportive interior in contrast to the sparse Mongolian steppe. Traditionally used by nomads, the yurt–more home-like than a tent–is a portable, felt-covered wood lattice structure. Made by stretching a felt cover over a circular frame, the lattice consists of wall sections, a door frame, roof poles, and a crown. Mostly self-supporting structures, some styles have one or more columns to support the crown. Viewed primarily as a nationalistic symbol among many Central Asian groups, the yurt is often used for the serving of traditional foods and as cafés, museums, and shops, especially for the sale of souvenirs.

Thinking About Interiors

While cave dwellings were more permanent, they were not necessarily continuously occupied, since early humans remained transient following the migration of animals and the changing seasons. Anthropologist Lawrence Guy Straus: "Caves are not necessarily the most comfortable of places in which to camp at all seasons; many are cold, wet and draughty. Some, for instance, may have been strategic vantage points for seasonal hunting, but were too windy, cold or high for long term or winter occupation. Some caves may often have been used, therefore, for fairly specialized activities, for short, albeit repeated, occupations."[5] Indeed, the experience of the cave was a prelude to what only much later would become permanent shelter, once the practice of agriculture provided a stable food source. At that point, the fundamental lessons of the cave and other temporary or seasonal shelters had already been transformed by generations of adaptation.[6]

The *Oxford English Dictionary* defines shelter as follows: "A structure affording protection from rain, wind, or sun; in wider sense, anything serving as a screen or a place of refuge from the weather."[7] The definition also suggests a sensory or emotional experience: "The state of being sheltered; the state of being protected from the elements; security from attack...To seek, find, take, etc. shelter. Under the shelter of = protected by."[8] These feelings of protection were captured in the first built environment and must continue to be addressed in the spaces we build for human habitation.[9]

Reconstructed Navajo temporary summer dwelling, Canyon de Chelly National Park, 2009. Traditional Navajo shelters were and are constructed to provide protection in open fields from the sun and weather in the Arizona desert. The hogan, another archetypal form of early shelter still assembled today, represents the ingenuity of early designers, who from the most basic means were able to fashion habitats for protection from the elements.

This page:
The rock overhang was, along with the cave, the first found space. From the division between outside space and inside shelter, humans created the interior. The photograph, interior elevation, and plan on this page show cave dwellings in Cappadocia, eastern Anatolia, Turkey. Though these caves date from the fourth century CE, they evoke the same primal need for shelter that the earliest interiors accomplished. Cappadocia, used primarily as a hiding place by early Christians, was built by carving into the mountains and contains several underground cities. Often with elaborate churches, houses, and other structures, which showcase the lifestyle of entire communities, the spaces also clearly exhibit details such as customized storage areas for grain and beautiful murals. These sites illustrate the fundamental human need for a protective shelter when under attack from external forces –in this case due to religious intolerance.

Opposite, top:
This four-story house in Montezuma, Arizona, is thought to have been built by the Sinagua tribe, and was most likely abandoned due to the exhaustion of water supplies in the region. The Sinagua, a pre-Columbian cultural group, occupied parts of Arizona between 500 and 1425 CE, with the earliest sites consisting of pit houses and later structures evolving into the Puebla architecture.

Opposite, bottom:
Cave dwellings with granaries, Ireland, late nineteenth century. The earliest forms of shelter maintained a delicate balance with the natural world, sometimes literally, as in these dwellings nestled in a cliff side. Early designers were cognizant of the role that human interventions had on natural surroundings, a sensitivity that has perhaps been lost as the world we inhabit has been transformed into one entirely of human design. The archaeological label "cliff dwelling" is generally used to describe prehistoric habitation making use of niches or caves, especially in high cliffs. These often included more or less excavation or masonry additions.

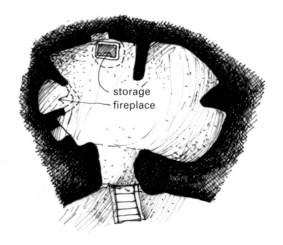

storage
fireplace

Cliff dwellings at Gila National Monument, southwestern New Mexico, fourteenth century. Looking out from the protection and security of the cave's interior at the landscape framed by the opening simultaneously provides a sense of serenity, peace, and beauty. These qualities are intrinsically necessary for human well-being and progress.

Early humans sought a place for personal safety, but the ability to enjoy sensory pleasures privately and without fear of danger gave rise to a new range of experiences, chief among them comfort. Finding the cave was the beginning of making void space habitable for discovery, nurture, and well-being, not simply survival. The paintings in the earliest caves – regardless of their original purpose – were an intentional change of the wall surface, possibly for the purpose of adornment or to claim the territory, but certainly beyond any basic functional requirement. The paintings are evidence that the need for physical control and sensory delight exist simultaneously; they could not then and cannot now be separated. One is necessary for the expression of the other.

The main protagonist in the story of interior, then, is not the discovery of habitable space, but the human being. The essential qualities that provided succor in those earliest interiors are just as relevant today, because our essential nature remains unchanged. Recognizing that is imperative, not just for designers of the interior but for all design disciplines, since the improvement of the human condition is at the core of all design. Design is the deliberate intervention in our environment to ameliorate the conditions of our existence. Sadly, this critical component of human identity has been insufficiently acknowledged. We continue to view the relative success of civilization primarily in technological terms, to perpetrate the myth of progress mainly through mechanical–technical means, rather than by the measure of human advancement and self-knowledge.

Chapter One

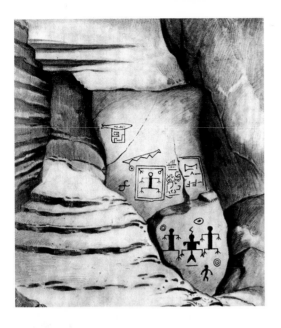

Top:
An illustration of cave paintings in Mexico. While their intent and function is debated, cave paintings provide a decorative element as well as being a vehicle for self-expression, visual recording, and the possible marking of territory. The painted element of the earliest caves points to the inseparability of the human need for mental and sensory stimulation from the need for shelter. Decoration, art, and design existed at once in the cave—there was no reason to separate them as different experiences.

Center:
Consisting of a series of rooms and passages, the Altamira Cave in Cantabria, Spain, dates back some 15,000 years to the Magdalenian period in southern Europe. The lifelike yet simple depictions of animals such as bison, horses, and boars are extremely well preserved.

Bottom:
While the caves of Cappadocia were occupied from the fourth century, many of the frescoed churches date from the period between the tenth and the twelfth centuries. The fractured side of this small cave shows the man-made replication of the prehistoric cave and of the Byzantine church interior carved in the hillside and without an architectural edifice. The Cappadocia dwellings also show the inherent human need for the familiar and the recreation of visual and sensory environments, which stimulate and provide a vehicle for ritual. Ultimately, these environments provide and satiate the need for human comfort and delight.

Dune House, Jacksonville, Florida, William Morgan, architect, 1975. The earliest shelter, the cave, continues to influence us even if it has largely been superseded. Literal attempts to revive the cave, though outlandish, still evoke a subliminal association that humans feel with cave forms.

The Lost Origins of Building

In historical accounts of the development of architecture, the original search for shelter is often treated as pre-history. While such accounts point to the primal need for protection as the catalyst for the creation of buildings, they routinely neglect to credit these same motivations in the subsequent development of building. Eliminating the search for shelter from the standard history of the built environment obscures a fundamental part of the narrative of human experience.[10]

The physical record is invaluable as raw material on early habitation, but it alone is not enough to reveal the evolution of shelter. Making matters more difficult, that archaeological information has long since been absorbed into a well-rehearsed mythology about the origins of building and architecture, a story that extends from Vitruvius to the present. The cave is important in the central narrative first and foremost as a guiding concept of the first interior, rather than as a material reality that can be recovered intact from the historical record. We can give it a state of completion and connection to human nature not present in the physically fragmented records and, by doing so, restore to design a fundamental concern missing from our thinking today.

Primitive humans, having discovered the cave, would have set about improving their level of comfort by using available materials, such as fur for added warmth. The first-ever rug may very well have been an animal skin on the cave floor. Eventually, our ancestors either intentionally contrived or consciously sought other conveniences, using niches for storage and ledges for seats or sleeping above the cold floor. In later archaeological examples of the occupied cave—dates vary from site to site—the interior was zoned, with areas designated for specific functions, such as cooking, sleeping, and gathering. Various small objects were crafted, among them carved stone bowls and

An illustration from 1902 depicting the lifestyle of a shaman and his wife surrounded by crafted tools and objects in their cave dwelling in Mexico (precise location not documented).

wooden spoons, tools that today are basically the same as they were in the cave, indicating our long-ago reaching out for something beyond a life of subsistence.

But the counterevidence of archaeology and historical anthropology is not, on its own, enough to revise architecture's intellectualized myths of origin, which have lasted so long because they have been told with an absolute certainty that precludes negation. This accepted history virtually altogether extracts the human being from design, preferencing formal concerns over our innate ones. Untangling the facts will produce a historically and academically sound account that establishes human needs as the fundamental criteria for design and helps to provide more meaningful parameters for the built environment going forward.

The story of the first building is found far back in writings about the built environment. The search for shelter is also acknowledged, at least in passing, in many of these canonical histories, and many of today's myths were born in this material.

A few examples are in order. The opening sentence in the 1867 *Encyclopedia of Architecture* by Joseph Gwilt, a nineteenth-century English writer and architect, is: "Protection from the inclemency of the seasons was the mother of architecture."[11] It should have read shelter, not architecture, since later Gwilt does not ascribe the origins of architecture to this motive. For him, architecture came into existence only with the creation of another layer of sophistication and rules that make building an art form: "If the art, however, be considered strictly in respect of its actual utility, its principles are restricted within very narrow limits; for the mere art, or rather science, of construction, has no title to a place among the fine arts."[12] Gwilt, like so many in his time, categorically dismisses all early building as primitive and thus not part of the art of the evolution of architecture, a common perspective even to this day.[13]

Sir Banister Fletcher's 1896 *A History of Architecture*—for many decades in the twentieth century the standard reference book in architectural schools across the English-speaking world—opens with a declaration similar to Gwilt's, though more nuanced: "Architecture had a simple origin in the primitive endeavors of mankind to secure protection against the elements and from attack."[14] Primitive humans then learned how to create other habitats: "The 'savage' hunter sought shelter in rock caves, the earliest form of dwelling, and learnt to build huts of reeds, rushes and wattle-and-daub or tents of saplings sheathed in bark, skins, turves, or brushwood."[15] And like Gwilt, Fletcher's history makes a distinction between this early history of shelter and the later stylistic development of architecture, thereby focusing exclusively on formal, aesthetic aspects; an understandable concern for art historians but one that has little to do with basic human needs: "The above-mentioned prehistoric remains show little constructive development or sequence. Historic architecture … while waxing and waning in virility, yet followed a continuous evolutionary course."[16]

Fletcher's history acknowledges the critical role of the search for shelter, but ultimately sees it as taking place in a self-contained and resolved era, with no real correspondence with later human interaction with the built environment. This leaves the history of the interior, which began in the cave, discarded as irrelevant to the present and future.

The distinction drawn between a mere building and a work of architecture is now orthodox.[17] But in rejecting early forms of shelter, whether a building, hut, or cave, this view overlooks the fact that the design originated before the advent of building or the art of architecture. Art and utility were one. The cave was painted before it was "rebuilt" and filled with the tools and objects that supported living (today we would call this vernacular design).

Even though Fletcher is easily dismissed as outmoded and his book is no longer popular reading in architectural schools, his line of argument is relevant in exposing an enduring misconception: namely, that design and building can be categorized as conforming to the epochs of stylistic history, and that prehistory—the period before written records but with tangible physical remains—though an intriguing background, is ultimately irrelevant to the contemporary built environment. This argument also feeds a more endemic view of the built environment as primarily an external phenomenon, the manifestation of civilization, rather than a more internal, personal experience, which extends out from within. The exterior shape of buildings reflects the character of a culture, so the argument goes. Banister Fletcher's thunderous summation of this point of view influenced generations of designers and architects:

> Architecture, striding [*sic*] down the ages, was evolved, moulded, and adapted to meet the changing needs of

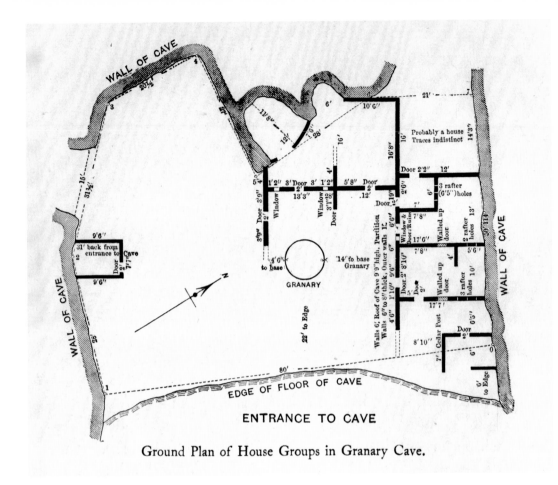

Ground Plan of House Groups in Granary Cave.

nations in their religious, political, and domestic development. A glance along the perspectives of past ages reveals architecture as a lithic history of social conditions, progress, and religion, and of events which are landmarks in the history of mankind; for as architecture is in all periods intimately connected with national life, the genius of a nation is unmistakably stamped on its architectural monuments […] Throughout the history of the human race, architecture, the mother of all arts, has supplied shrines for religion, homes for the living, and monuments for the dead.[18]

Plan of cave dwelling and granaries in Mexico. Though the cave is often thought of as a primitive shelter, many cave dwellings evolved into sophisticated interior spaces, with areas partitioned according to use. The interior unlocked a profound sense of human ability to manipulate the environments that we create and inhabit, exhibiting intention and desire—the fundamental elements of design.

It is worth quoting this passage at length to contrast it with the true narrative revealed through our ancient history: design springs from the experience of space. Continuing to view the designed environments we inhabit in the terms of style and form alone, almost devoid of human occupation (as depicted in so much contemporary photography), narrows our understanding of design.

One of the earliest references to shelter can be found in none other than Vitruvius' first-century *De Architectura*.[19] His story of the origins of buildings begins with the discovery of fire, which men harnessed from a brush set ablaze by lightning:

The Search for Shelter

Woodcut of the discovery of fire, from Cesariano's edition of Vitruvius' *De Architectura,* 1519. The human motives to create shelter can be found woven into the most familiar, canonical accounts of the origins of building. Here, a Renaissance-era illustration to the earliest surviving work on building shows how humans found mutual comfort and the means to communicate with each other through the accidental discovery of fire.

Drawing from Viollet-le-Duc's *Dictionnaire raisonné de l'architecture,* 1856. The first shelter or building is a familiar part of architectural mythology. The most familiar accounts point to a primitive hut as the origin of all future building, though they often overlook the human reasons for creating shelter after establishing this genealogy. Shelter, however, remains the most elemental reason that we inhabit inside space.

EX PRIMA MVNDI HOMINVM AETATE AEDIFICATIO · MVLTI ENIM AB ANIMALIBVS EXEMPLA VITAE CONSERVAM O̧ IMITATI SVNT & C̃

"After it subsided, they drew near, and observing that they were very comfortable standing before the warm fire, they put on logs and, while thus keeping it alive, brought up other people to it, showing them by signs how much comfort they got from it." In Vitruvius' vision, fire is what first brought people together, forming a community around the comfort of a controlled source of warmth. This, in turn, led to the epochal discovery of language. This first "gathering of men," he says, brought them into "conversation with another," whereas before there had only been "purely individual [...] utterance of sound."[20]

The origin of shelter, then, was for Vitruvius a shared enterprise: comfort, while experienced individually, was recognized as a collective good–one that humans soon learned to pursue more proactively. By his account, "coming together in greater numbers" enabled them to realize that, unlike animals, they could "do with ease whatever they chose with their hands and fingers, [and so] they began in that first assembly to construct shelters."[21] Note that Vitruvius refers to the construction of "shelters" –not buildings or monuments. The discovery of comfort was accidental, but, once made, humans realized that they could not do without it. The next step would be to design an enclosure to capture and maximize the heat of the flames and thus maximize the experience. Vitruvius' history shows that the instinctive need for security and ease is the essential reason why we build.

History tells us that design, defined simply as an intention, has

Woodcut of the first shelter, from Cesariano's edition of Vitruvius' *De Architectura*, 1519. In Vitruvius' account, the discovery of fire and language led men to create a more permanent form of shelter that could be replicated. The account should inform our own view of shelter: it was the product of human ingenuity. Designing collectively, humans could create shelter and comfort more effectively than they could alone.

The Search for Shelter

Chapter One

a dual heritage: one of chance—the fire and the cave that our ancestors stumbled upon, and another of purposeful application. Design is thus experiential (the desire for warmth) and practical (devising the means to fulfill that desire).[22]

This point was famously echoed by Abbé Laugier in the eighteenth century. His account, a product of Enlightenment interest in mankind's primitive or natural state, ties our primeval activities to the creation of all future architecture. "Such is the course of simple nature; by imitating the natural process, art was born," Laugier writes. "All the splendors of architecture ever conceived have been modeled on the little rustic hut I have just described."[23] Laugier establishes a common lineage between hut, shelter, and building: "It is the same in architecture as in all other arts: its principles are founded on simple nature, and nature's process clearly indicates its rules. Let us look at man in his primitive state without any aid or guidance other than his natural instincts. He is in need of a place of rest."[24]

In exhorting us to look at human beings' "natural instincts," the need for a place to rest, Laugier indirectly introduces the concept of comfort as a central motive for building the primitive hut:

> Man wants to make himself a dwelling that protects but does not bury him. Some fallen branches in the forest are the right material for his purpose; he chooses four of the strongest, raises them upright and arranges them in a square; across their top he lays four other branches; on these he hoists from two sides yet another row of branches which, inclining towards each other, meet at their highest point. He then covers this kind of roof with leaves so closely packed that neither sun nor rain can penetrate. Thus, man is housed. Admittedly, the cold and heat will make him feel uncomfortable in this house which is open on all sides but soon he will fill in the space between two posts and feel secure.[25]

In Laugier's account, man was seeking security, not the creation of a form. The fundamental DNA of the spaces we build today is the same as that of the crude shelter humans originally sought out or made.

If we venture to restate Laugier ever so slightly, we can easily tease out a latent meaning, which says that the principles of design in general (and the reason for interiors in particular) are based on a person's "natural instincts." Both mythological and anthropological accounts acknowledge this to some extent, but the design progress that has resulted from these instincts should be seen in the same praiseworthy light as the advancements made in the leap from building to architecture.

The true story of design serves as a counterweight to architecture's long-standing myths. As was the case with the very first interior, satisfying our innate longing for shelter, both physical and physiological, is still the vital reason we design today. This is the basis for all aspects of the built world and the practice

The primitive hut, as depicted in Abbé Laugier's *Essai sur l'architecture,* c. 1755. As described by Laugier, humans recreated the accidental comforts of found covered space as the motives behind the first building. Though fanciful, these motives are not far from the true impetus that led humans to create inside space.

The Search for Shelter

of all the design disciplines. If, as in Fletcher's famous formulation, architecture is the "mother of all arts," then the interior is surely the father of all design.

Reclaiming the Past

We cannot label the first humans, in the act of design, as being unaware of their motives. This all-too-common outlook has been deemed a logical fallacy by advocates of so-called folk or vernacular design. Thomas Hubka, who has argued folk architecture's significance as the underpinning for design practice, writes that the popularity of "primitive" design in the 1960s (the decade that produced Bernard Rudofsky's famous *Architecture without Architects*) failed to attribute design motives to nonprofessional designers, delimiting "the real accomplishments of vernacular builders by ascribing to their designs and buildings misconceptions about their purpose and method, such as the exaggerated notion of intuitive (divine?) methodologies amounting to mystical causation."[26]

The origin of design that is proposed here draws upon both myth and fact, but does not claim to evoke some mystical era, when design operated under a different, unconscious logic. Rather, it asserts that the primal drive for security and comfort led people to consciously create the means to better the conditions of their existence. Design was born as an act of common sense, then grew into a skilled craft and ultimately became a specialized profession. But design, the term that applies to all of these examples, is simply a process that describes how the human mind identifies and solves problems in a way that satisfies us functionally, psychologically, and aesthetically. Design has been there, it was just that no one spoke its name. Born well before its emergence as a professional practice during the past two centuries, design is, and will always be, intrinsic to human nature.

It is even possible—without moving too far into waters fraught with intellectual danger—to argue that design predates art, if only because it is rooted in survival rather than in expression. In fact, design may have been a necessary prerequisite to aesthetic enjoyment, allowing for pleasures beyond bare existence, although much evidence points to the almost simultaneous development of all of the arts far back in the early Stone Age.[27] Many recent assessments of cave art have dropped the epithet "primitive" and acknowledged early prehistoric works as art. A similar awareness should be brought to design: the adaptation of the cave constituted a design intervention that does not need to be qualified by the relative term "primitive."[28]

Hardly a crude, long-abandoned requirement, the human need for shelter remains with us today in memories of the environments that have supported and nurtured us. Spaces that have emotional resonance can be said to evoke a range of responses —in some cases almost an ancestral memory of a lost paradise, but also recollections of half-forgotten places we have passed through, as children or adults, that float somewhere in the back

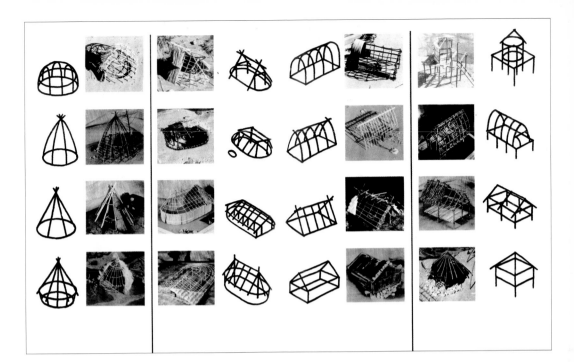

of our minds. The search for shelter, then, is universal, but also, by its intimate nature, deeply individual.

Some have taken this idea even further, and argued that one of those embedded memories is a recollection of the ultimate supportive environment: the womb. This buried memory, if it exists at all, is so remote as to be no more than a canvas on which our wider search for the perfect space is painted. The idea of the womb is intriguing because it suggests the comprehensive aspirations of design: to create environments that sustain us completely while offering protection from the outside world.

But even if its place in our collective memory remains unprovable, the example of the womb can serve as a metaphorical point of origin for the way we perceive our spatial surroundings. For example, James Marston Fitch argued, on largely physiological grounds, that the man-made environment–from our clothes to the physical volumes enveloping us–should support us in a manner similar to the way the womb does.[29] Designer Frank Alvah Parsons wrote that, "House and Clothes have answered the human requirement for shelter" along with their more evident aesthetic requirements.[30] But Fitch notes a psychological shortfall in the way we experience the built world: "unlike the womb, this external environment never affords optimum conditions for the development of the individual. The contradictions between internal requirements and external conditions are normally stressful."[31] Interior space must, therefore, serve as a bridge between the realities of the built world and the ideal conditions we seek.

Though driven by this same search, early attempts to create

The evolution of early forms of shelter. The development of these shelters shows the replication of elements of the cave in forms that were easily constructed from available materials. Nearly all these forms of dwelling use a simple round shape, which was the easiest to build with limited time and resources, and which best captured the circular thermal zone of the fire. This diagram also illustrates the evolution of architectural form from the round into square footprint. For centuries, these forms have expanded in plan size or upward. With the advent of new materials and representation techniques, organic forms are made conceiveable shelter did not always succeed, especially according to our modern expectations. Yet even in its most minimal forms early shelter satisfied—or attempted to satisfy—emotional and sensory desires that the outside world alone could not provide. Even today, human beings can just barely survive without the intervention of clothing and buildings. And our need for stimulation, perhaps even more pressing now than our need for shelter, also persists.

In the end, the distinction between our spaces and ourselves is not so easy to determine. As Stanley Abercrombie writes in *A Philosophy of Interior Design*: "When we enter a building, we cease being merely its observer; we become its content. We never fully know a building until we enter it."[32] His observation echoes Winston Churchill: "We shape our buildings: thereafter they shape us."[33]

This explains why we decorate spaces and don't leave them bare. Even cave paintings in the earliest shelters were an attempt by our ancestors to transmit something of themselves into a vessel that enveloped them. The interior is a buffer, a transition zone, between ourselves and the world at large.

So deeply ingrained is our longing for shelter that it does not occur at the level of consciousness and is understood even by children at play. The "passion for building enclosures, or for 'adopting,' for taking possession of an enclosed volume under a chair or table as a 'cozy place' for making 'home,' is one of the commonest of all children's games" writes Joseph Rykwert.[34]

Our expectations for the built environment are, then, both biologically ordained and based on knowledge accumulated as we grow older. "In every case they incarnate some shadow or memory of that perfect building which was before time began: when man was quite at home in his house, and his house as right as nature itself."[35] A somewhat similar assertion may be found in anthropological literature on human habitation:

> Human thought, as expressed by material culture, language, and beliefs, is modified to a certain extent by survivals of past environments. In early conditions this modification was strong, but later, when man had obtained greater control over his surroundings, external conditions lost some of their power. The character of primitive habitations is perhaps more influenced by environment than any other product of man's intelligence, but even in them we find surviving traces of former conditions.[36]

In order to realize environments that meet the full spectrum of our needs, the design profession must first develop a scientific understanding of the human mind and environmental aesthetics. This new design knowledge has to recognize our cultural expectations for buildings as well what is rendered in our genes, that distant memory of the cave.

Only with these factors in mind can design realize its full potential

−otherwise it will have a permanent blind spot. Design must find balance between the issues that technology and modern society have created while honoring primal desires, between the external world and the inner self, and between function and beauty. Good design is the result of a process that emerges from inside us and gives shape to what is around us.

Chapter Two

Being   35

Dwelling, however, is the basic character of Being in keeping with which mortals exist. Perhaps this attempt to think about dwelling and building will bring out somewhat more clearly that building belongs to dwelling and how it receives its nature from dwelling. Enough will have been gained if dwelling and building have become worthy of questioning and thus have remained worthy of thought.

Martin Heidegger
Poetry, Language, Thoughts[1]

As far as we can discern the sole purpose of human existence is to kindle a light of meaning in the darkness of mere being.
C.G. Jung, *Memories, Dreams, Reflections*[2]

Merely to exist is not human nature. Yet how the environments we create shape who we become is not fully comprehended in design. We need deeper research in order to understand our aspirations for improvement. Only then can we design for enhanced states of the human condition, states that happen at the delicate intersection of the psychological, sociological, and physiological.

To provide meaningful design solutions that meet human needs, we must first define the experiences and qualities that constitute essential parameters. Design must embrace the human being as more than flesh and blood in order to reintegrate the abstract and the esoteric. Because design for interiors is the most inclusive of the design disciplines, and has the most fundamental connection to human nature, it is the one best suited to lead an exploration that will produce new criteria for design, working from the inside out. This is a particularly poignant role at the beginning of the twenty-first century, when humanity is racing toward the adoption of megastructures as a means of coping with the sustainable and social issues we face. Designed to house activities as broad ranging as farming, industry, education, housing, and entertainment, megastructures represent interiors that are no longer small-scale, individual environments; rather they are entire neighborhoods under one roof, which share fully integrated and balanced environments and thus constitute new ecosystems. To cope with such developments the interior must be seen from an unprecedented vantage, where science and art once again converge.

The new criteria for design have to include a comprehensive understanding of how man interacts with the physical and the phenomenological world. Design must evolve to satisfy yearnings for the intangible, such as peace of mind and trustfulness. While the tools to quantify human needs (both physical and abstract) exist, thus far we have only the rudiments of the experience and knowledge necessary for the designer to be able produce well-designed, supportive objects and spaces.

Our existing verbal and visual vocabularies demonstrate a limited ability to address the qualitative aspects of interior spaces. Design terminology is specifically pragmatic (it consists of expressions such as function and circulation, and codifies physical safety), but such terms cannot describe the intentional emotive interplay between humans, objects, and environments. This interplay is necessary to stimulate elevated awareness and behavior, and so create environments that may, for example, be able to offer the occupant a sense of dignity, and foster greater trust as an outcome of the design process.

Most architectural theory has reduced the philosophical concepts of space, harmony, and balance to formal artistic criteria, and rendered the very people for whom buildings are created as lifeless abstractions, almost non-essential participants in the design process. If we are to achieve a better design methodology, there is an urgent need to develop more accurate means of addressing the emotive power of design.

For too long, designers across all disciplines have avoided delving seriously into the phenomenological aspects of design.[3] We have simplified our existence and have thought of humans in universal terms, as if there were a common denominator that can serve as the measure for everyone. In fact, the first design criteria that must be reviewed are the proportioning and measuring methodologies of the human body. This field needs a conceptual poetics based on the beauty of human diversity. Designing for being requires more than just measuring the body in its relevant parts; as for any building activity, it must start from the inside and work outward to incorporate all of the qualities of experience.

Interior Space and the Second Skin

The design of our environment reflects and shapes our understanding of the world, both through intellectual means and in primal, intuitive ways that reason alone cannot easily comprehend. Design is the mediation between an interior experience (within space and within ourselves) and the exterior world. Our physical surroundings are tangible only through the lens of human perception. The brain interprets raw stimuli, gathered through our senses, and from this we formulate our reality.[4]

This relationship between the internal and the external is central to human nature and is, therefore, essential to all design. It is best addressed through interior space, the intimacy and scale of which must relate to the human body, mind, and spirit. Whether it be a small-scale room, expansive atrium, or an irregularly defined volume (town square, plaza, or garden), an interior space connects to our being on multiple levels.

The interior, we have established, should be recognized as not only a zone of physical interaction but also one of psychological and emotional effects. We know intuitively that its tangible aspects – the shape of a chair, the temperature of a room, the size of a volume – can affect us on a physiological level. But above and beyond this, interiors also have an impact that is difficult to describe in strictly physical terms. Many people have tried to capture these intangible qualities.

The entry in Diderot's eighteenth-century *Encyclopédie* shows that historically the interior has been viewed not only as a physical container but also in ways that encapsulate both the physiological and psychological zones of human experience:

> INTERIOR, adj. The antonym is outside. The surface of a body is the limit of what is inside & outside. What belongs

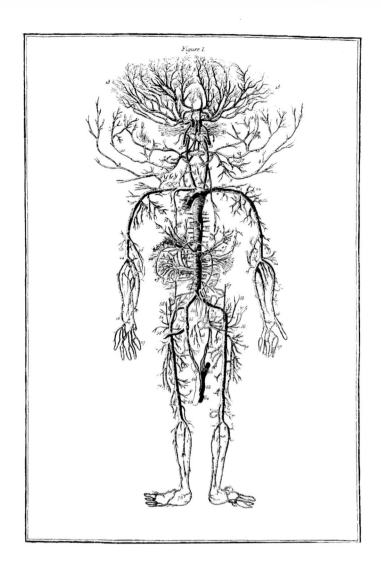

Anatomical cross-section of human arterial circulation and building section, Diderot and d'Alembert, *Encyclopédie,* 1751–1772. The *Encylopédie* offered two definitions of the interior: the first one as everything inside the human body, both physical and mental; the second one as anything contained and separated as an enclosure from the exterior world, like the insides of a building. These two plates from the *Encyclopédie*–one anatomical and one architectural– show attempts to graphically capture both meanings of interior.

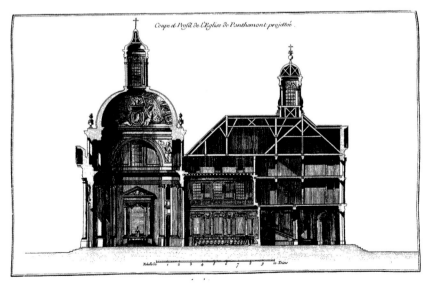

Being

to this surface, & all that is placed beyond where one looks at or touches the body is exterior. Anything that is beyond the surface, in the depth of the body, is the interior.[5]

Diderot's definition suggests a wider notion, perhaps still elusive in design, that combines both palpable surface effects and ones that touch the very core of our being. He offers two complementary readings of the interior: one that can be applied to buildings and another that applies to people. The interior of a building, as Diderot defines it, is merely the inside, or everything from the walls inward. But as the interior relates to the human being, it reflects both our outward personality and what we might today call our inner self. What is most interesting about Diderot's definition is that it begins to suggest that what is inside the walls and what is inside ourselves may overlap.

Accordingly, the interior is the best medium through which to address the interaction between human beings and design. The interior is not, as widely thought, the simple outfitting of a room but, rather, the manifestation of all qualities concerning the human occupation of space.

Diderot's definition also introduces the notions of separation and boundary in classifying what is inside and out. Any artificial barrier beyond our skin—clothing, walls, a building facade (and certainly the peripheral space surrounding the body)—can be defined as a *second skin*. Though it lies beyond the physical boundaries of our body, our second skin is nevertheless critical in defining who we are and how we are perceived; thus our identities extend beyond our physical perimeter. Design is the intermediate zone between our skin and what lies beyond. As our second skin, it is an essential extension of ourselves.

The argument that buildings and their interiors serve as extensions of human beings is not new. The function of a building has often been equated with the supportive environment of the womb, as discussed in chapter 1, while its walls have been likened to clothing.[6] Just as clothing extends the function of the skin, the building envelope expands our personal space into an area that is not limited to one that is in direct contact with our bodies.

We create progressive layers beyond the naked body for protection, function, and identification, and also to provide a surface area for adornment and fashion (see diagram on page 42). No matter how sophisticated the argument, our understanding of this zone has often remained literal, emphasizing the physical barriers that define interior space and ignoring the subconscious and interpretative possibilities created by the second skin.[7]

Humans do not view space distantly, as if through a frame. Rather, it is people who define space through the process of perception. Between our interior selves and the exterior world lies a series of literal and perceived boundaries that we establish. These barriers do not stop at the outer limits of our bodies, and comprise our second skins, while more distant boundaries define

urban space. Designers, therefore, must not limit their dealings with people to the physical environment; rather they must concern themselves with the dynamic flux of the self as it comes into contact with the built environment.

There is a large body of thought on space and spatiality in architecture and the built environment. However, the discourse still lacks a sense of the implications of human interaction in built space. While many conceptual and theoretical exercises have explored the abstraction and volumetric relationships of space, we do not have a clear understanding of the behavioral response of people to built space. Accordingly, we lack in-depth design knowledge of the experiential attributes of designed space.

The American poet Ralph Waldo Emerson eloquently stated the influence the body has over its surroundings: "The human body is the magazine of inventions, the patent-office, where are the models from which every hint was taken." Emerson believed every human creation was an extension of the body: "All tools and engines of the earth are only *extensions of man*'s limbs and senses."[8] For Emerson, the phrase "extensions of man" carried a purely technological interpretation of human agency, since it prized tools but probably did not extend to the built environment.[9] But the phrase can also be interpreted more

Woodcut from *Hypnerotomachia Poliphili,* by Francesco Colonna, 1499. This woodcut illustrates in a cutaway view, somewhat unintentionally, the critical importance of the zone beyond our immediate physical bodies in defining who we are. Clothing, furniture, furnishing, and the barrier to outside world–the wall–all create a notion of ourselves in a way that is impossible in the outside world alone.

Evolution of clothing	Periods in time	Secondary skins				
Realization of need for primary body protection						
Discovery of fabric-making processes						
Development of clothing from function to fashion						
Refinement of clothing due to technological and material evolution						
			?	?	?	

broadly—distantly echoing Marshall McLuhan's use of it in the 1960s—to mean that our immediate environment is an extension of our body and our internal self. Augmented with these qualitative criteria, the second skin is as much a psychological projection as it is a physical one. Human beings have a reciprocal relationship with their spatial environment. Our ever changing interaction with the space around us affects who we are and influences how we behave. This relationship is quite complex and is impacted from two directions. The first is in terms of who, what, and how we are, which changes from place to place, such as from office to home, from public to private, and from city to city. The second is how the intentional shaping of the environment—that is, by design—can affect the person occupying the space. Anthropologist Edward Hall makes this point in his classic work *The Hidden Dimension*: "Both man and his environment participate in molding each other. […] In creating this world he is actually determining *what kind of an organism* he will be."[10] While this truth is likely obvious to most designers, it is not sufficiently acknowledged or applied. The interior, our medium for engagement with the world, affects our self-perception and our designed environments must therefore optimally support us.

Despite its present ubiquity, the idea that space, rather than being a formal concept, is something that is physically occupied, used, and experienced, did not move to the center of architectural discourse until the last decade of the nineteenth century. Over the next half a century, architects began to talk about space in terms of abstraction—evolving from the context of modernism—and as it related to the need for more rational design.[11] As the practice of interior planning evolved, the role of space-making—the molding of habitable space not devoid of its functional or quantitative requirements and as related to the placement of specific functional zones, furniture, equipment, and objects—became clearer. This was in direct contrast to earlier interpretations of space-making that focused more on the formal presentation of the abstract design intent than on the use and experience of that particular space.

Philosophically, space is a projection or reflection of our consciousness into the physical world. Even in the earliest philosophical descriptions of space the interpretation is human-centered. Two quotes from the German philosopher August Schmarsow—one of the most influential figures in applying the term *space* to architecture—address our spatial relation to the world: "We perceive the spatial construct as a body outside ourselves with its own organization." Space is thus an "emanation of the human being present, a projection from within the subject, irrespective of whether we physically place ourselves inside the space or mentally project ourselves into it."[12] According to Schmarsow, our perception of the world and the space we inhabit flows directly from us; the world is nothing without human discernment.

An expression of this point of view can be found in the work of a number of writers. One of the more elaborate and detailed descriptions appears in H. Van der Laan's little-known *Architec-*

tonic Space: Fifteen Lessons on the Disposition of the Human Habitat.[13] His analysis, highly idiosyncratic, is offered with the precision of a mathematical proof. In the lesson "Space, Form, and Size" Van der Laan postulates that by placing walls within boundless space, humans created space that could be perceived from both the outside and the inside:

> Architectonic space owes its definition to the mass of the wall, which bounds the space from *without*. By contrast the space that we experience and relate to ourselves gets its definition from the activity of our various faculties, which determine its boundaries from *within*.[14]

The exterior form of architecture is shaped by the same barriers that create interiors within the shell of a building. By contrast, the human experience of space always emanates from within ourselves. Space is both the physical area of enclosure (as defined by walls, a distant form of second skin) and the volume of interior space *as we perceive it*. Van der Laan also proposes space as an opposition of metaphorical voids (what we carve out of natural space when we build) and metaphorical solids (the way we experience that built space): ..."We must imagine that architectonic space that comes into being artificially between walls as a sort of emptiness in relation to natural space." He continues: "Moreover the two space-images are opposite in nature. [...] By building an enclosure bounded by walls, we may take away the completeness of natural space."[15] Built space, then, reduces the fullness of space that exists in the natural world. This is space viewed empty of human occupancy. Viewed from the inside out, however, the solid and void are reversed:

> Parallel with this conception we must look upon the human space that we experience around us as a fullness surrounded by emptiness; in this case natural space is an emptiness in relation to a space that we experience as fullness −not like a bubble in water, but like a drop of water in the air.

> Thus with space-formation the fullness *surrounds* an emptiness, whereas with space-experience it *stands in the midst of* an emptiness.[16]

These two juxtapositions do not negate each other but exist simultaneously, as complementary notions that are inseparable from one another. Yet even an analysis of space as intellectually and conceptually rich as Van der Laan's takes us only so far in understanding how people perceive themselves in relation to space. The stripped-down nature of his argument, addressing the abstract blank wall as a barrier between inside and outside, treats the human being as an abstract entity with no physical connection to the exterior world. This points out the great defect in all theories of space. Even with those that claim space originates in the human mind−from inside to outside−there remains a disconnect between the space of internal philosophical cognition and the exterior space of sensory projection.[17] In these philosophical models space is

Chapter Two

always abstract, never habitable, and much less does it take into account human engagement and activity.

Yet, space is more than the void and air defined by four walls: it is something we take possession of and make our own; it is intimate and personal. What, then, does it mean to occupy space? Imagine a space without the built world, consisting only of the distance between people. If the discourse on space in architecture fails to recognize that people exist, then this proposition is exactly the opposite: it is space considered only as an empty plane populated by other humans. This, too, is a fiction, but one that lets us address human interaction before placing human beings in defined environments.

Edward T. Hall, the founder of the anthropological study of human space called "proxemics," proposed that it was divisible into four zones of distance:

1. Intimate space, which spans from direct physical contact to some 18 inches (45 centimeters) away
2. Personal space, a zone from 18 inches (45 centimeters) to 4 feet (1.2 meters)
3. Social distance, from 4 feet (1.2 meters) to 12 feet (3.6 meters)
4. Public space, from 12 feet (3.6 meters) to 25 feet (7.6 meters)[18]

These different registers of human interaction carry with them embedded social and cultural mores about what can and cannot be conducted in each zone. Though simplistic, Hall's divisions point to space as originating from the sensory information that can be transmitted between people at different distances (see diagram on pages 46 to 47).

Further, in his seminal book, *The Hidden Dimension*, Hall holds that: "No matter what happens in the world of human beings, it happens in a spatial setting, and the design of that setting has a deep and persisting influence on the people in that setting."[19] Hall notes the spatial quality of our environment, but he argues that positioning ourselves at the center of the built environment is radical in the discourse of architecture and design, given the long dominance of abstract interpretations of space. Even in cases where people are central to the creation of a space, that space is rarely designed to support a person's being but is more likely intended to impress him.

Before we can establish a human-oriented vision of space, we need to delineate the different zones of space in the area beyond our physical bodies that remains directly adjoined to us: 'personal space is defined as *the zone around an individual into which other persons may not trespass*.'[20] This affects the design of interiors, since our sense of self inevitably stretches into areas where we intersect with other people. Conversely, in the broader context of public space, the zone within which we expect to interact with many others, we consciously adjust our boundaries to accommodate the intrusions.

Thus the experience of interior space does not begin, as many

Informal Distance Classification	Intimate	Personal

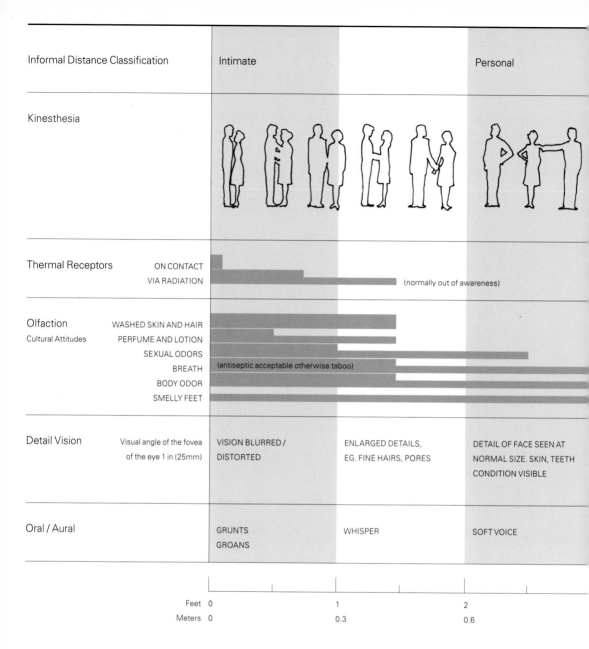

Kinesthesia

Thermal Receptors	ON CONTACT	
	VIA RADIATION	(normally out of awareness)

Olfaction
Cultural Attitudes

- WASHED SKIN AND HAIR
- PERFUME AND LOTION
- SEXUAL ODORS
- BREATH
- BODY ODOR
- SMELLY FEET

(antiseptic acceptable otherwise taboo)

Detail Vision	Visual angle of the fovea of the eye 1 in (25mm)	VISION BLURRED / DISTORTED	ENLARGED DETAILS, EG. FINE HAIRS, PORES	DETAIL OF FACE SEEN AT NORMAL SIZE. SKIN, TEETH CONDITION VISIBLE

Oral / Aural		GRUNTS GROANS	WHISPER	SOFT VOICE

Feet 0	1	2
Meters 0	0.3	0.6

Maximum extent culturally acceptable

Taboo

Proxemics chart of human interaction, originally created by anthropologist Edward T. Hall in the 1960s. Hall introduced the term proxemics to describe a theory that sought to define the spatial interactions and boundaries between humans. In this chart, the zones of interaction between humans are defined and analyzed in terms of the senses. Hall observed that the experience of a space is not just a matter of visual perception, but one that involves all levels of sensory necessity, perception, and interaction.

Social-Consultative

Public

SMALLEST BLOOD VESSELS
IN EYE NOT VISIBLE. HEAD
HAIR AND WEAR ON
CLOTHING CLEARLY VISIBLE

FINE LINES OF FACE FADE.
DEEP LINES STAND OUT. LIP
MOVEMENT / EYE WINK
CLEARLY VISIBLE

AT 16 FT (4.8 M) SHARP
FEATURES DISSOLVE

CONVENTIONAL MODIFIED
VOICE

LOUD VOICE FOR GROUP TALK.
RAISED VOICE FOR ATTENTION

| 4 | 8 | 9 | 10 |
| 1.2 | 2.4 | 2.7 | 3 |

Modernist furniture, as depicted in *Life* Magazine, 1950s. The outlines demarcated by the furniture form the general outlines of a room, but without walls, and express an articulation of inside and outside. These boundaries create a notion of volumetric space. Nevertheless, the furniture photograph reflects a common presumption that the interior is limited only to a single room, rather than an interconnected environment of support.

architectural definitions erroneously hold, at the threshold of entry from the outside. On the contrary, that entry experience is secondary. Instead, interior space begins within us and includes the surroundings in immediate proximity to our bodies. In the end, personal space is not a question of how we perceive existing conditions but, rather, how we express ourselves in a spatial context.[21]

The design process should begin with the individual and work its way outward. Our experience of the world necessarily takes place through the lens of the built environment. Recognizing this provides a fascinating new definition of the interior as a second skin, and as the mediator of all design.

Extensions of Self

Furniture is the most literal and direct extension of ourselves into space. Except for the air itself and the clothing we wear, it is what we make the most physical contact with each and every day. Indeed, we are often unconscious of the degree to which we rely on furniture in performing our daily activities. Apart from its stylistic elements (still one of the most familiar aspects of furniture design), it supports us physiologically and psycho-

logically. As Bernard Rudofsky wrote, a chair is "more than prosthesis, an extension of the human body; it provides a bolster for the mind."[22]

According to recent archaeological evidence, the first chairs were created in the late Neolithic period, which lasted from 10,000 to 4000 BCE. In her popular book, *The Chair: Rethinking Culture, Body and Design*, Galen Cranz argues that the upright position imposed by the first seat was a forced, unnatural position for the human body. She suggests that the chair was invented as a means of projecting social power. Her conclusion is not too different from the commonly held design assumption that chairs are stylistic creations first and functional objects second.[23]

However, there is an opposite, and convincing, anthropological view that the human body can be found in a fairly limited array of postures: standing, lying down, and in an intermediate position.[24] Though these can subsequently be broken into smaller (often minute) postural variations, it is more important to note that although it is possible to lie down and stand without the aid of furniture, it is impossible to retain an intermediate position for an extended period of time without support. So the chair fulfills a physiological need: it is a prop for human activity.

Interior, ECA Evolution House, Edinburgh College of Art, Scotland, Shashi Caan Collective, 2007. This project photo shows an interstitial space which functions as connector and mediator between two distinct functions and itself (functioning as a breakout and waiting space)—a complete and necessary entity. The intent was to convey and promote ECA's philosophy of open communication, accessibility, collaborative learning, clarity of thinking, and detail as the communicator of the whole. Visually, the space can be changed and transformed anew by using color and light and minimizing or optimizing transparency in all directions.

Being

Evolution of the chair	Periods in time	Supporting the human body in the intermediate sitting position
Realization of need for intermediate sitting position	Stone Age	
Discovery of chair-making	Bronze Age	
Development of chair-making processes	Iron Age	
	Early Middle Ages	
	Renaissance and early modern	
Refinement of the chair due to technological and material evolution	Industrial Revolution	
	Electronic age	
	Global network age	

Diagram of the evolution of the chair, which has remained remarkably consistent in function since its creation, despite changes in its appearance. As a functional object, the chair still fulfills its original purpose to create an intermediate position between standing or lying; it allows for a range of activities not possible for a human being without the intervention of this position.

Even if it has overt social and cultural functions, its fundamental purpose is to provide support.

The distinction between furniture for human use and portability, as opposed to an accessory within the space of the room, evidences its immediate ties to the human body. A similar division exists in the French language, describing real estate versus the internal inventory of buildings: *immeubles*–literally "immovables" are buildings–while *meubles*, or "movables," are furniture.[25] (An inexact English equivalent for *immeubles* versus

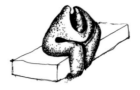

meubles would be appurtenances in contrast to the movable objects in a household.) This etymology reflects the fact that furniture was moved between upper-class households (a custom that occurred as late as the nineteenth century), and might also be read as evidence that furnishings were mobile extensions of the human body. A building is immovable space; by contrast, the outcomes of design, such as furniture, are direct extensions of human form and are–or should be–movable or adaptable by us and for us in space.

Design inherently encompasses both functional and stylistic roles. The tension between the chair as support element and the chair as stylistic element has never been resolved. Furniture, like all of the components of our second skin, always exhibits elements of functional support independent of, but in combination with, exterior stylistic appearance. The term second skin may prove to be too simplistic to describe design's intermediary role between the body and the physical space we inhabit. Still, it helps to combine those dual conditions, both of which design must address if it is to become a practice that caters fully to human needs.

The experience of space is, arguably, not solely visual; instead, vision acts in concert with other senses.[26] Smell, sound, temperature, and touch alter and change our perception of space. They are all contributors to our comfort and well-being and reach elements of our psyche and memory that cannot be reached by purely visual sensations. In contrast, many current design trends use a single, stylized image as a metonym for an entire project. We are expected to judge the merit and value of the built environment from a lifeless transposition onto the pages of magazines or in what flutters across television screens. This development is deeply troubling: the human being is often entirely missing from consideration, and the end result is an empty stylistic shell. Such an approach turns the designed environment into a depopulated space that more often succeeds only as an image. A human being cannot feasibly live in such an environment, at least not in comfort.

We need to design spaces in a way that takes human variance into account. Gaston Bachelard addresses the correlation between space and our internal selves in a magical passage in *Poetics of Space*, where he describes how our psychological

SENSE ORGANS SIMPLE PERCEPTIONS COMPLEX PERCEPTIONS ATTACHED ENTITIES

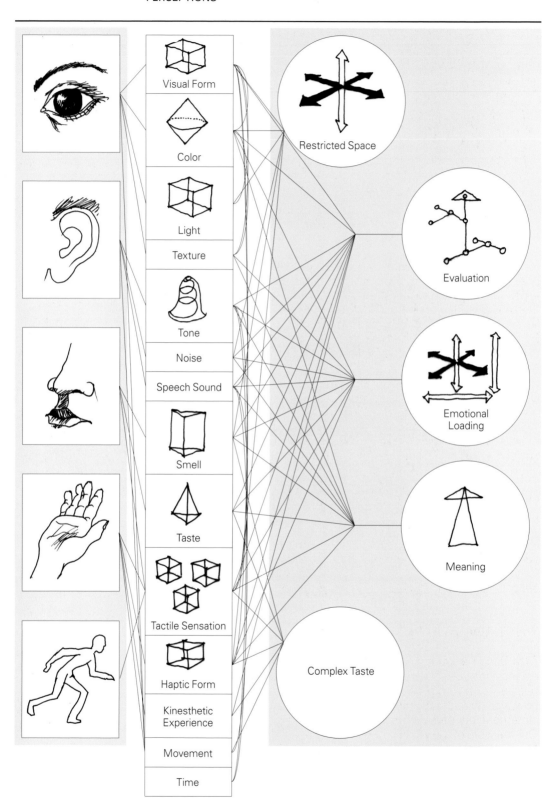

relationship to the same space constantly changes: "My house
is diaphanous but it is not of glass. It is more of the nature of
vapor. Its walls contract and expand as I desire. At times, I draw
them close about me like protective armor. … But at others, I
let the walls of my house blossom out in their own space, which
is infinitely extensible." The passage highlights the fact that
our second skin is protective yet malleable, and is capable of
rejecting or absorbing the outside world.[27]

Bachelard's passage also points to space's fungibility within
our own perspective. Space is both a reality and a perception;
it changes depending on our state of mind and our perception
of ourselves is always in flux. To best serve the human being,
design must take this variance—not just from person to person,
but also in our ever changing sense of ourselves—into account.

This renewed way of thinking about design depends upon an
equally reinvigorated concept of who the human being is. For
too long we have simplified our world and thought of man in
abstract terms, as if there were a single, universal human being
who can serve as the common denominator for all of us. And
for too long we have avoided delving seriously into the emotive,
sensory, and phenomenological impacts of design.

The Un-Universal Man

Man is the measure of all things. The phrase is a cliché and its
origins, in Plato's fourth-century BCE dialogue *Theaetetus*, have
been all but buried beneath constant repetition.[28] Its familiarity,
however, should not obscure the fundamental truth of the
statement: our perspective determines how we see the world.
Our measure of the world has, not surprisingly, been anthropic—
the way we record our surroundings is rooted in human terms.[29]
A good example of Plato's statement is very pragmatic and the
first unit of actual physical measurement was not a ruler but our
own bodies.

Humans have related their bodies to the shape of the world in three distinct ways:

1. By creating systems of divine harmony that relate the perceived perfection of the human form to a perfect, unchanging cosmic order.

2. By measuring the world against the direct experience of the physical body; measurements like the inch, based on the length of the first joint in the thumb, were created in this way.

3. By developing rational and repeatable systems of measurement. The process began with the conversion of irregular, human-based units into standard units, and continued with the creation of classifications, like the metric system, that were ultimately detached from human experience. This rationalization of dimensions eventually led to standardized measurements for the human body, for use by designers.

The first and second systems are the oldest; they date back to the beginning of human history and competed with each other as the defining measures of the universe. The third system evolved out of the industrial manufacturing process, its need for coordinating parts and pieces, and the search for efficiency through repetition. It determines the shape of most of the design we encounter, since it is the basis of objects and environments. Yet standardization, often detached from actual human experience, has imposed a false and inaccurate uniformity that, in its perceived universality, is remarkably similar to the early systems of divine harmony.

The concept of divine harmony still has a remarkable hold over us, since it runs through centuries of canonical literature on the relationship between the human form and the shape of the universe. In the Western tradition, mathematical ratios superimposed on the human body were used to demonstrate a static cosmic order. Human dimensions revealed fixed ratios and proportions identical to those found in nature and, later, in the notes of the musical scale. These harmonies brought forth what we now refer to as the "universal man," an abstraction (though often not recognized as such) closer to a Platonic form than a flesh-and-blood human being (see illustration on page 56).

With the systems of divine harmony, the real and varied proportions of human forms were unimportant when considered against the perfect shapes that were thought to reflect a universal order. The universal man was drawn to conform to geometric proportions or ratios that were, in reality, implausible for the human body. The most famous example of the concept is the image of a man inscribed within a circle and square, as depicted in Leonardo da Vinci's celebrated fifteenth-century drawing based on a description found in Vitruvius' *De Architectura*. This image is now commonly referred to as Vitruvian Man (see illustration on page 58).[30]

Vitruvian Man is a perfect symbol of the orthodoxies of the

Chapter Two

universal man. The passage in question (it's worth noting that the copy of Vitruvius' book that survives from antiquity has no illustrations) contained two principal arguments: that the geometries of well-built buildings share fixed ratios with the human body, and, conversely, that the human body can be inscribed with perfect geometric shapes. Of the first proposition Vitruvius writes: "Without symmetry and proportion there can be no principles in the design of any temple; that is, if there is no precise relation between its members, as in the case of those of a well shaped man."[31] These proportions were considered numerically fixed, since nature had created them in the human body; for example, the ratio of the face (measured "from the point of the chin to the top of the forehead") was set at ten to one, the "foot goes six times into the height of the body, the cubit four times, the breast is also a quarter," and so forth.

It is unclear whether Vitruvius' list of proportions, which were apparently part of a widely accepted canon, were meant to reflect any real measurement of the human body or flowed from an established ideal only loosely tied to dimensions found in the body.[32] Indeed, as Joseph Rykwert writes: "No one has ever suggested that Vitruvius found this out by empirical measurement, though for all we know, he may have tried to check the traditional figures. In fact bodily members are the most obvious primary measuring tools, and their internal commensurability must have a part in the most ancient human experience."[33] But even if the origins of these ratios could be tied to earlier empirical measurements, the human body (a man's in particular) was secondary to the ratios themselves, once these had been discovered. Numbers counted more than flesh.

The second proposition in Vitruvius' text, and the one from which Leonardo's sketch was drawn, tied the symmetry of a temple to the symmetry found in the body as a whole:

> Similarly, in the members of a temple there ought to be the greatest harmony in the symmetrical relations of the different parts to the general magnitude of the whole. Then again, in the human body the central point is naturally the navel. For if a man be placed flat on his back, with his hands and feet extended, and a pair of compasses centered at his navel, the fingers and toes of his two hands and feet will touch the circumference of a circle described therefrom. And just as the human body yields a circular outline, so too a square figure may be found from it. For if we measure the distance from the soles of feet to the top of the head, and then apply that measure to the outstretched arms, the breadth will be found to be the same as the height, as in the case of plane surfaces which are perfectly square.[34]

For Vitruvius, man is the measure of all things, but only in the limited sense that the geometric ratios derived from the human body are part of an underlying divine order that governs the shape of the universe.

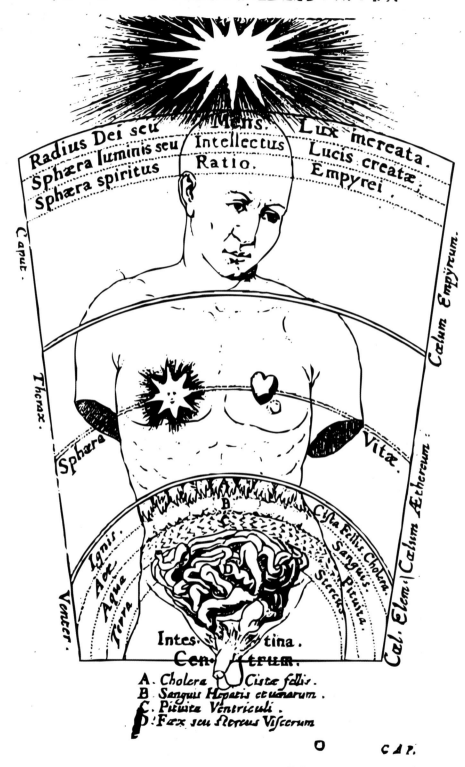

While understandable as a philosophical construct, Vitruvius' description inevitably distorts the human shape, since actual human variations would deform the perfect square and circle into an ellipse, rectangle, or non-pure geometry. In Leonardo's sophisticated sketch, there is no distortion of the human form; the drawing suggests that the system works just as Vitruvius' text describes. However, this is an illusion because the drawing, unmoored from any real human body, is merely conceptual.

This is the underlying irony of the Vitruvian formula: despite being profoundly anthropocentric, the system is detached from actual human bodies, even when direct measurements are called for, as Alberti did in his 1464 treatise *De Statua*. Alberti wrote that human measurements could be used to find the "highest beauty scattered, as if in calculated portions among many bodies."[35] As Rudolf Wittkower summarizes, taking those dimensions from "a number of bodies considered to be the most beautiful" would determine the ideal human form, eliminating the "imperfections in natural objects" even while "combining their most typical parts." For most orthodox humanists during the Renaissance, this ideal "seemed to reveal a deep and fundamental truth about man and the world."[36] This interpretation of the body was the source from which all art, architecture, and design could originate.

These beliefs held currency until the mid-eighteenth century, when rationalist thinking began to challenge the unquestioned faith in classical rules of proportion. In 1757, Edmund Burke, in a section of his *Philosophical Enquiry into the Origin of our Ideas of the Sublime and Beautiful* titled "Proportion not the Cause of Beauty in the Human Species," challenged the belief that proportion alone was the source of human beauty. Burke found the long-held proposition of a direct correlation between human proportions and built forms particularly troubling:

> I know that it has been said long since, and echoed backward and forward from one writer to another a thousand times, that the proportions of building have been taken from those of the human body. To make this forced analogy complete, they represent a man with his arms raised and extended at full length, and then describe a sort of square, as it is formed by passing lines along the extremities of this strange figure. But it appears very clearly to me, that the human figure never supplied the architect with any of his ideas. For, in the first place, men are very rarely seen in this strained posture; it is not natural to them; neither is it at all becoming. Secondly, the view of the human figure so disposed, does not naturally suggest the idea of a square, but rather of a cross; as that large space between the arms and the ground must be filled with something before it can make anybody think of a square.[37]

Burke's argument is interesting in two ways: first, it challenges the philosophy of universal harmony; and, second, it challenges the graphic representation of humans in simple geometric terms. Burke recognized that the human body, in all its complex-

This illustration from Robert Fludd's *Utrisque Cosmi* of 1619 shows the then prevalent humanist belief that man and his proportions were a direct reflection of the divine order of the universe. To illustrate that point, the human body is projected directly onto the cosmos; the proportions of the two are the same.

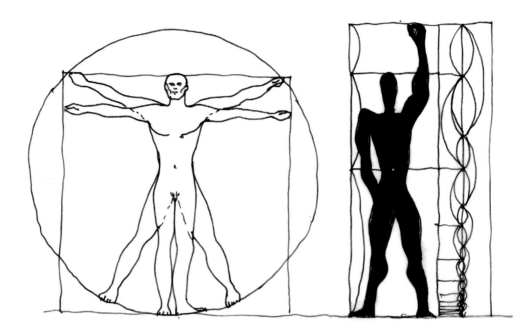

Comparison chart of anthropometric analyses of human dimensions. On the left is the most commonly known interpretation of human proportions in Vitruvius' *De Architectura* by Leonardo da Vinci in 1492. By placing the so-called Vitruvian Man's body in two perfect geometries, the circle and the square, a similar perfection is suggested for the human body. Second from left is Le Corbusier's 1948 system Le Modulor, which also tied the body to an idealized mathematical progression of measures not directly related to human dimensions. Second from right is a different attempt to provide a more rational basis for dimensions and to accommodate natural human variances. Adapted from Henry Dreyfuss' 1959 *The Measure of Man and Woman*, it gives human dimensions in varying percentile ranges. At the far right is an anthropometric dimensional chart depicting a wheelchair user, which extends the notion of human variances to include the needs of the physically challenged.

ity, does not, in fact, follow set rules of divine proportion. He continued: "No species is so strictly confined to any certain proportions, that there is not a considerable variation amongst the individuals; and as it has been shown of the human, so it may be shown of the brute kinds, that beauty is found indifferently in all the proportions which each kind can admit, without quitting its common form."[38] Freed from the dictates of divine proportion, the wide variation in human shapes could be seen, and perception of man's place in the world could be based on more than a series of abstract ratios and numbers. Nonetheless, proportional systems with different origins and explanations have remained with us. One example is Le Corbusier's post–World War II Modulor system, which claimed to be a "harmonious measure to the human scale universally applicable to architecture and mechanics."[39]

The system of functional dimensions taken directly from the human body existed simultaneously with the idea of the universal man. These dimensions were the dominant units of measurement before rigid standardization occurred. Man (and sometimes woman) was the direct physical means by which the world was measured. The names of the early units—for example, the foot in English, the French *pouce* (inch, from the word for thumb), and the Italian *braccio* (yard, the measurement of an arm)—all grow from a direct relation between the human body and the surrounding physical environment. Even when the nomenclature was shared the actual dimensions were not

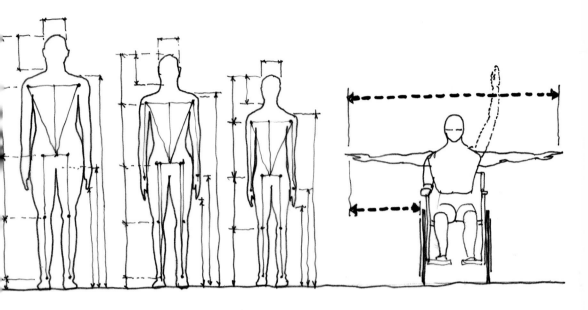

and tended to vary from locality to locality. One town's foot was not the same as that of the neighboring town (see illustration on page 62).

These anthropic measurements evolved to define the dimensions of our world, and they directly affect our comfort by allowing us to function and to build our environment. The names and units of the dimensions survive in modern standardized systems and continue to imply bodily interaction: foot still suggests both the standardized unit and the space a person's foot occupies on the ground.

What is important about the codification of these measurements is that it translated individual human experiences into terms that are easily understandable. It produced a vocabulary of dimensions that everyone can understand, even though they do not directly experience what is being measured.

Twentieth-century measurement systems show that designers have attempted to find more objective ways to escape the confines of the universal man. The most influential such work, at least in Europe, was Ernst Neufert's 1936 *Architects' Data*, a compendium of standardized measurements for architects and designers that covered the entire spectrum of the built environment (see illustration on page 63).[40] Henry Dreyfuss' American design firm also made a prominent attempt, in this case rationalizing human variations due to gender, age, and

Being

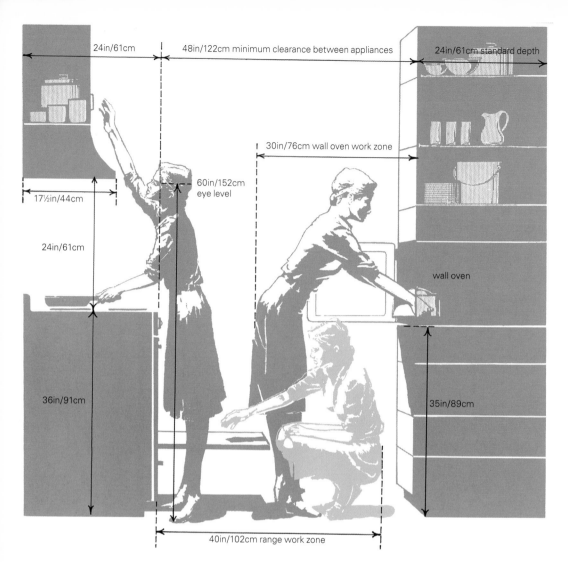

24in/61cm

48in/122cm minimum clearance between appliances

24in/61cm standard depth

30in/76cm wall oven work zone

60in/152cm
eye level

17½in/44cm

24in/61cm

wall oven

36in/91cm

35in/89cm

40in/102cm range work zone

These clearance measurements, applied to kitchen design, are derived from studies of human proportions and movement, such as reach. The planning of domestic kitchens has been found to be a factor influencing family relationships. Domestic engineering planning was appropriated by industry in the twentieth century without crediting the women designers who pioneered it.

disability. Dreyfuss' *The Measure of Man and Woman: Human Factors in Design*, first published in 1960, offers the diversity of human physical shape in graphical and statistical detail.[41] Indeed, in accounting for human variation as a design parameter the book might be said to shatter the mold of the universal man.[42]

But even the attempts to classify diversity threaten to be canonized as a new standard. Physical measures are, and will always be, incomplete. Our engagement with the built environment –in terms beyond the purely physical–has yet to be explored. Once established, experiential criteria should form the true measures of man and woman.

Design for Basic Human Needs (Measures of Man)

For design to produce solutions that truly address human concerns, the universal man must be redrawn and three distinct

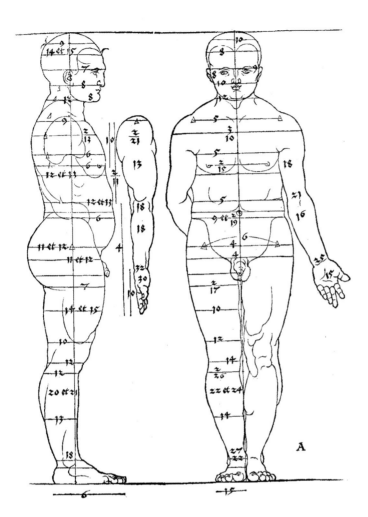

Illustration from Albrecht Dürer's *Four Books on Human Proportion* (*Vier Bücher von Menschlicher Proportion*), 1512–1523. The image reveals the dilemma between the orthodoxy of the ideal proportion and the natural variances of the human body. The numbers in Dürer's drawing correspond both to ratios cited by Vitruvius and to proportional measurements derived from measuring several hundred actual human beings.

categories of needs must be envisioned. The broadest category, which pertains to all of us, includes the innate physiological and psychological requirements that form our mutual, programmed inheritance. Social and ecological responsibilities are very much a part of these needs, which can be best described simply as human nature. This has remained unchanged since the dawn of time and has to be addressed by design.

Against this static backdrop there is another, more fluid, set of culturally specific needs, which can vary widely according to geography, over time, and through history. These fluctuate along with our changing (and often technologically driven) expectations of what the built environment can do for us.

Finally, the narrowest range of human needs consists of those that are specific to the individual, such as having a sense of belonging, trust, or pride. Clearly, each of us shares most of our needs with other people, but our individual perception serves as a unique lens through which we view the built environment. Fulfilling this last category of needs is the most difficult task for the designer to master.

Being

Diagrams of anthropometric terms. The earliest systems of measurement were derived directly from dimensions of the body, suggesting intimate contact with the exterior environment. For example, the tiniest units of length in the old English system could be held between the forefinger and the thumb; the next largest units corresponded to the measurement from the hand, which in turn could be multiplied into measurement units based on the lengths of the arm and foot, and in turn to units based on the length of a human stride.

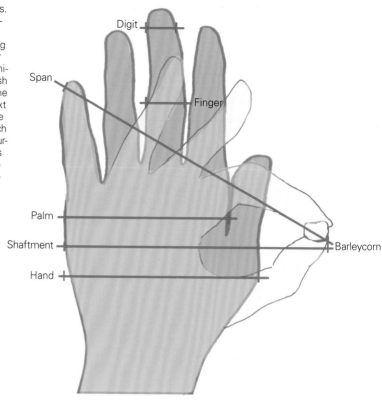

Basic Anthropomorphic Units

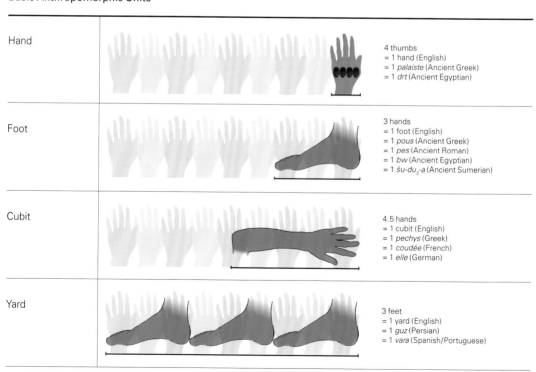

Hand	4 thumbs = 1 hand (English) = 1 *palaiste* (Ancient Greek) = 1 *drt* (Ancient Egyptian)
Foot	3 hands = 1 foot (English) = 1 *pous* (Ancient Greek) = 1 *pes* (Ancient Roman) = 1 *bw* (Ancient Egyptian) = 1 *šu-du$_3$-a* (Ancient Sumerian)
Cubit	4.5 hands = 1 cubit (English) = 1 *pechys* (Greek) = 1 *coudée* (French) = 1 *elle* (German)
Yard	3 feet = 1 yard (English) = 1 *guz* (Persian) = 1 *vara* (Spanish/Portuguese)

Chapter Two

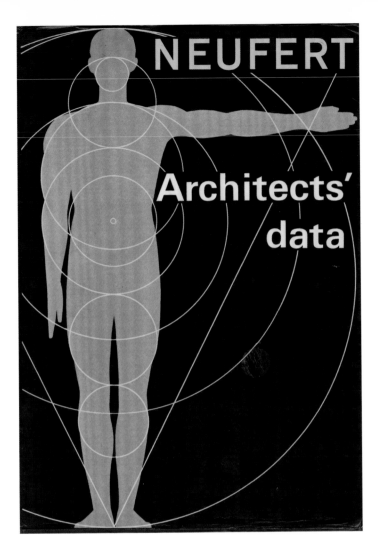

Cover of the English-language edition of Ernst Neufert's *Architects' data,* 1970. The book, which first appeared in Germany in 1936, is a compendium of standardized measurements for architects and designers and represents one of the earliest attempts to gather actual physical measures of human beings into a single comprehensive work.

These concentric layers of needs mean that the designer, always cognizant of our core requirements, must be fluent in the language of culture and sensitive to the unique demands of individuals. This presents great challenges, as these demands are often competing. The approach that is required goes well beyond awareness of average bodily measurements (as only the most sensitive anthropometric measures have done) toward a comprehensive understanding of the immaterial measures of human needs.

Accomplishing this requires establishing a basic vocabulary to describe and gauge our needs, since the existing design criteria do not sufficiently address them. What follows is an attempt to identify and describe, by means of example, a single design parameter for each level of need: the innate needs of safety and security, the culturally specific need for comfort, and, finally, the individual need for privacy.

Being

Innate Needs

The category of needs common to all humans can be represented through the instinct that we have already described in detail: the search for shelter. Our primal instinct for survival allowed the human species to survive, evolve, and flourish. A visceral response to real or perceived danger, the need for safety is never far from the animal psyche and was one of the prime reasons man created shelter. From a design point of view, providing safety means making an environment that protects us from harm. This search has been the subject of much debate, and the most sophisticated articulation appears in Grant Hildebrand's *Origins of Architectural Pleasure*.[43] The book posits that the "aesthetics of survival" are ingrained in humanity as a hard-wired psychological response.

Hildebrand argues that natural selection has given humans the means to detect natural threats and know exactly what causes harm—knowledge that is evident in the environments we favor. The pleasures we find in the built environment are an unintended consequence of our "innate predilections" for shelter and safety. While our search for shelter has always been deliberate, our actions and choices have not always been directly concerned with life and death.[44] Instead, these decisions have resulted in a genetically encoded network of assumptions about what we perceive as safe in the natural and built environment.

Hildebrand identifies the two principal elements of safety in the designed environment as refuge and prospect: "Refuge and prospect are opposites: refuge is small and dark; prospect is expansive and bright. It follows that they cannot coexist in the same space. They can occur contiguously, however, and must, because we need them both and we need them together. From the refuge we must be able to survey the prospect; from the prospect we must be able to retreat to the refuge."[45] Stated more simply, the human quest for survival is aided both physically and aesthetically by the nature of contrast in our physical environment. This includes areas of cover, intimate volumes within which we are in charge, and areas of openness, or massive spaces within which we relinquish control. While cover offers a sense of protection (especially from behind), the ability to see broad spans alleviates the fear of possible ambush—and both are essential. Related material and structural choices are equally important. A flimsy fabric covering (such as a tent) will elicit a very different emotion to a stone enclosure (such as a building). Understanding basic requirements, such as cover and open space, and how to begin to qualitatively respond to human needs should be part of the basic education necessary to practice design. When consciously in command of these principles, the designer has the tools to create the desired emotional response in all people.

As is so often the case, etymology provides some background to the meaning and origin of the relevant words—in this case, safety and security. Safety, derived from the Latin *salvus* (safe) translates as to *keep intact* or *keep whole*. The fundamental meaning of security, related to safety and originating in the Latin

Chapter Two

Sphere of Human Needs

ALL HUMAN BEINGS
innate psychological and physiological
needs that are common to all people

CULTURE-SPECIFIC
fluid needs, varying widely
by geography and over time

INDIVIDUAL
specific needs of
single human beings

Sphere and triangle of human needs. The factors that the sensitive designer must address reflect three layers of understanding of the human being, all of which must be considered at the same time for design to be successful.

Triangle of Human Needs

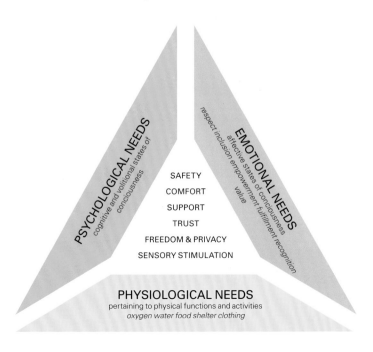

PSYCHOLOGICAL NEEDS
cognitive and volitional states of conciousness

EMOTIONAL NEEDS
affective states of conciousness
respect inclusion empowerment fulfillment recognition value

SAFETY

COMFORT

SUPPORT

TRUST

FREEDOM & PRIVACY

SENSORY STIMULATION

PHYSIOLOGICAL NEEDS
pertaining to physical functions and activities
oxygen water food shelter clothing

securus, is to be carefree; it can be interpreted as having peace of mind or a sense of confidence that allows someone to be free and unencumbered. A secure environment is more than just safe. It is not only devoid of any dangers; it allows people to relax, and perform their activities with confidence, free of worry. Moving beyond fulfilling basic functional needs into providing comfort and aesthetics requires a profound understanding of human nature and sound design knowledge.

Prospect and refuge, light and dark, small and large, are just some of the binary opposites required in designed environments to satisfy our need for safety and security.[46] And, of course, they also characterize primitive caves and huts. Once our need for safety is identified and analyzed, it can be translated into criteria for shaping new designs that foster a greater sense of security in people.

Discussions of safety are familiar from urban design and planning literature, the most famous example of which is Jane Jacobs' classic *The Death and Life of Great American Cities*, published in 1961. She defines the first role of city sidewalks—in her view, the most basic element of urban design—as ensuring safety, thanks to the many pairs of eyes on the street that offer constant, benign surveillance. She describes three necessary conditions for safety that are equally applicable to the design of exterior and interior spaces:

> First, there must be a clear demarcation between what is public space and what is private space. Public and private spaces cannot ooze into each other as they do typically in suburban settings or in projects.

> Second there must be eyes, eyes belong to those we might call the natural proprietors of the street. The buildings on a street equipped to handle strangers and to insure the safety of both residents and strangers must be oriented to the street. They cannot turn their backs or blank sides on it and leave it blind.

> And third, the sidewalk must have users on it fairly continuously, both to add to the number of effective eyes on the streets and to induce the people in buildings along the street to watch the sidewalks in sufficient numbers.[47]

Though Jacobs was writing specifically about urban encounters in public spaces, her ideas have had a wider currency. Another social theorist of the era, Oscar Newman, sought in his *Defensible Space: Crime Prevention through Urban Design* to outline the specific steps a designer can take to create safe public spaces. Jacobs' and Newman's key contribution was to see safety not just as a negative concern raised by hostile environments, but as an aspect of design that can contribute to the successful creation of a "collective habitat."[48] Indeed, Jacobs recognizes our need for safety as integral to design on a very basic level. And while Jacobs' and Newman's writings date from the 1960s and 1970s, their relevance to design is still

unmistakable; they have recently gained renewed attention in planning circles because they demonstrate that safety and security are of critical importance to the built environment.[49]

Culturally Specific Needs
Among the range of human needs that lie between those common to human nature and those specific to the individual is comfort. It is constant neither in time nor across cultures. Comfort exists in the gray zone between the universal and the individual experience of a particular environment.

Like all elements of design, *comfort* has both an internal meaning –as experienced by a person–and an external, readable measure. This is evident in the *Oxford English Dictionary* definition: the first meaning describes how a person feels ("A state of physical and material well-being, with freedom from pain and trouble, and satisfaction of bodily needs; the condition of being comfortable"); the second describes the physical factors that allow for the existence of this state ("The conditions which produce or promote such a state; the quality of being comfortable").[50] This dual notion of comfort establishes, at least broadly, that there is a connection between our internal gauge of being comfortable and the more directly measurable exterior factors that result in this sense of comfort. A good designer has to comprehend the first in order to create the second. Not surprisingly, the external requirements are easier to codify. However, the gap between mere survival and an existence that is pleasurable is the space

TWA Terminal, New York, Eero Saarinen and Associates, 1956–1962, photographed 1970. Prospect and refuge are concepts that break down the human need for safety and security into elements of physical design. Here, the meeting of the sloping elements of a building's roof creates a vista point that allows observers to look onto jet traffic on the runway from a protected viewpoint.

where comfort lies, so research into our internal gauge is needed.

Reyner Banham described this zone elegantly in his seminal 1969 book, *The Architecture of the Well-Tempered Environment:* "In order to flourish, rather than merely survive, mankind needs more ease and leisure than a barefisted and barebacked, single-handed struggle to exist could permit."[51] Operating at the two ends of the spectrum, literal comfort obtained through satisfactory physical conditions—controls for proper lighting, acoustics, and temperature; stimulating materials, colors, and textures; appropriate scale and proportions of space—combined with perceived comfort, such as feelings of being secure, upbeat, valuable, and important, can motivate people to perform at optimal levels.

Qualitative factors of comfort are often cited but rarely practiced. We may know that light is not simply a necessity but is also an emotional trigger, and that silent spaces evoke better human behavior, but too often we abandon this knowledge when the time comes to design. Consider arriving at one of the older terminals of New York's JFK airport (most of which will soon be gone), with its low ceilings and narrow, overcrowded, noisy corridors.[52] Now juxtapose that experience with the newer airport terminals in Denver or Beijing, which have wide, multistoried volumes with long-distance sightlines, a high level of illumination (both day and night), and less crowding. People invariably behave better in the Denver and Beijing airports than in those early JFK terminals, moving through them in a more rhythmic and civilized way. The reasons for this difference in behavior must be empirically documented and then incorporated into the design language so that we may improve all of our habitable environments.

The physical experience of comfort is represented by many variations of the word: *comforter,* the nineteenth-century noun for a quilted blanket, for example, or the more colloquial expression "being comfy." It is far easier to identify comfort by contrasting it with what is uncomfortable than it is to describe the intangible aspects of the experience. Emerson's lines on moderation offer this kind of conceptual distinction: "Everything good is on the highway. The middle region of our being is the temperate zone. We may climb into the thin and cold realm of pure geometry and lifeless science, or sink into that of sensation. Between these extremes is the equator of life, of thought, of spirit,—a narrow belt."[53] It is easy to define what makes a place uncomfortable: it is too hot, too cold, too bright, and so on. But it is far more difficult to ascertain the narrow belt of comfort, varying as it does from one person to another and over time.

We can begin to assemble a positive definition of comfort by starting with the basic idea of habitability. As early as the eighteenth century, Abbé Laugier stated that the purpose of the built environment was to provide livable space: "Buildings are made to be lived in and only inasmuch as they are convenient can they be habitable."[54] This already moves beyond the simple requirement of shelter toward convenience, a word that had a much broader meaning three centuries ago than it does today.[55] What

Architect Ludwig Mies van der Rohe, in his apartment in Chicago, not of his own design. Captured in a non-formal pose, Mies must hunch over to read the spines of books even on the top level of the built-in bookcase. What is more, the light level in the room is inadequate for reading the book spines, therefore requiring a flashlight for the titles to be seen. Designing for comfort is far more difficult than designing only for aesthetics.

constitutes habitability has naturally evolved a great deal through-out human history, as it is intrinsically connected to the great variables of wealth and technology. Apart from obvious functional requirements, habitability and thus comfort depends upon qua-lities that cannot be enumerated in checklist fashion. The result is a complex construct, only one contributing factor of which has to be off balance to make the whole experience uncomfortable.

When it comes to comfort, the requirements for furniture and equipment are easiest to articulate, since they are based on physical contact with the body. The study of ergonomics is a systematic evaluation of how humans utilize furniture that attempts to precisely predict degrees of discomfort, based on absolutely defined variables. But comfort cannot be derived from the sum of these analytical factors. Instead, it must come from an overall design sense that is not merely a matter of calculation but also of refinement and intuition. Designing interiors is gene-

Ergonomic chair designs, illustrated in Sigfried Giedion's *Mechanization Takes Command,* 1948. This US Patent drawing dating from 1885 is one of the earliest examples establishing an empirical relationship between furniture and body. This science, called ergonomics, involves the rational study of human-machine interaction, and has been especially influential in the design of equipment and environments for repeated use. However, ergonomics has been limited primarily to purely physical applications; the range of psychological and other internal needs has scarcely been reviewed or tested by design.

Opposite:
Nineteenth-century Dutch watercolor by Jacob Willemsz. de Vos (1774–1844), after a painting by Quiringh Gerritsz. van Brekelenkam, entitled *The Tailor's Workshop.* The attributes of interior domestic comfort familiar today were not formalized in the West until the mid-seventeenth century, when a newly prosperous middle class began to create a more universal idea of domestic ease. Nevertheless, the idea of comfort in part was merely a naming and formalization of sensations that humans have always felt.

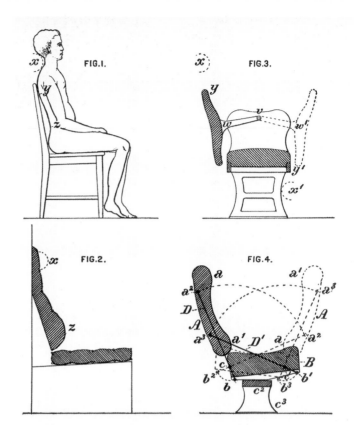

234 a, b, c, d. Posture Physiologically Considered: Car Seat, 1885. In the heyday of the ruling taste in Europe, American engineers took pains to curve the seat and back rest organically. The inventor begins by explaining the relation between seating and anatomy, and shows in diagrams the points at which support is needed.
a) Relation of the rear outline of the human body to an ordinary chair.
b) Ordinary American car seat.
c) English railway seat.
d) 'My invention is designed to afford suitable supports… Its upper portion acts as a head rest, and its lower as a support for the lumbar region of the back of the occupant, the seat being also rearwardly inclined, as is desirable for comfort.'

(U.S. Patent 324,825 25 August 1885)

rally misunderstood: it is confused with the simplistic act of pulling together components such as lighting, color, and furniture according to generic ergonomic criteria.

Our standards for comfort, part of the way we are made, predate the articulation or verbalization of the concept. Comfort is not an invention but the naming of certain sensations that had already been felt. Witold Rybcyznski has said: "People in the Middle Ages did not altogether lack comfort […] but what comfort there was never explicit. What our medieval ancestors did lack was the awareness of comfort as an objective *idea.*"[56] Similarly, once the factors that make up the concept of comfort are enumerated, it will be easier to elaborate on what design factors create the perception of what is comfortable.

Comfort, once identified, builds upon and reinforces itself, resulting in ever greater support for the human being. As architectural

Chapter Two

historian Sigfried Giedion wrote, the "notion of comfort means different things to different civilizations. Comfort can be achieved in many directions. It amounts to whatever holds necessary for his 'fortifying', his 'strengthening.'"[57] When experienced, comfort allows someone, almost subconsciously, to be at ease, to naturally be themselves. Regardless of the period, style, scale, or complexity of a design, this is one of the basic qualities that must be captured.

The rise of air conditioning in the United States over the past century is a good illustration of how our expectations for comfort can oscillate dramatically with regard to the environment. In the early 1890s, before its introduction, the interior temperature of buildings would have been far higher than Americans would expect today, and the levels of humidity—largely outside their control with those early systems—would have fluctuated with the weather. The proliferation of air conditioning gradually altered the expectation of what a comfortable ambient temperature should be and reduced it by at least some 10–15°F (5–8°C). Older buildings would have regulated a constant, yet much higher temperature.[58] Aside from domestic environments, where a greater degree of variance might be expected given the individual requirements of the inhabitants, such variations for personal preferences were not, until recently, considered desirable, or even possible, in spaces designed for multiple occupancies. A 1929 trade journal notice for the first air-conditioned office building in the United States declared proudly:

> The windowless skyscraper, already envisioned by others and made possible by air-conditioning plus artificial illumination, will surely become a reality … Let those who cry for "fresh" air through open windows from the out-of-doors be reminded that it doesn't exist in the congested city … So air-conditioning has come to make available every day the best in atmospheric comfort that nature offers so spasmodically.[59]

Such hermetically sealed structures forced a uniform thermal environment on all their occupants.

Today, notions of thermal comfort have begun to circle back toward valuing fresh air and operable windows, out of concerns for both energy efficiency and human comfort. The idea of unsealing windows that were previously sealed to ensure central control of internal temperature, as well as physical safety in highrises, is intended to return a modicum of control to the individual, since we now realize that not everyone has the same standards for thermal comfort. Reopening the interior to the outdoors has some psychological implications, as it offers a sense of freedom and a greater connection with the outside world. This reflects the contemporary cultural shift toward greater degrees of customization for all individuals, especially in the workplace. If nothing else, this reversal in our approach to climate control proves the transient, elusive, and ever evolving nature of our idea of comfort.

Individual Needs
The most basic needs are those that are specific to a particular human being. Privacy, a flexible concept that, like comfort, has varied widely over time is a testable gauge of exclusively individual reactions to the built environment. Most evidence suggests that it is not a deeply embedded human need but is, rather, determined by culture. Even if privacy is largely a cultural construct that varies according to time and place, it always exists in the relationship between the individual and the group or mass.

Chapter Two

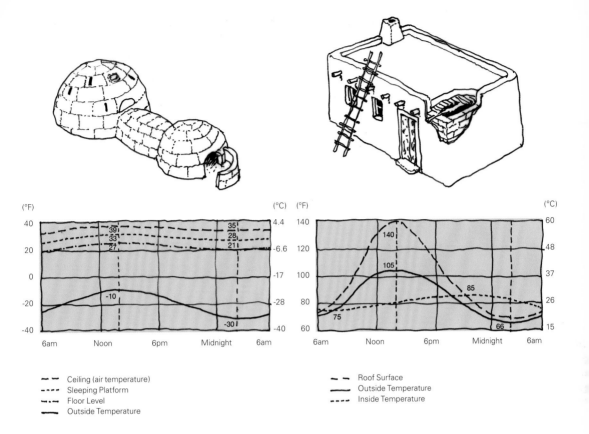

Ceiling (air temperature)
Sleeping Platform
Floor Level
Outside Temperature

Roof Surface
Outside Temperature
Inside Temperature

The etymology of *privacy* supports two meanings: a "state or condition of being alone, undisturbed, or free from public attention, as a matter of choice or right" and "freedom from interference or intrusion."[60] In the minds of many observers, the creation of a separate bedroom was the definitive moment that led to privacy being valued in the West, since the bedroom space officially created a zone where human actions could be screened; previously there had only been commonly distributed interior space.[61] However, this assumption is incomplete, since privacy cannot be read exclusively as a product of domestic interior space. Recall those earliest portable shelters—single-room barriers between interior and exterior space. The demarcation from outside to inside was the first step toward defining the human need for places of refuge and spaces where we are strengthened by our separation from the world. Privacy in interiors and design, then, is the ability to identify oneself as an individual within the context of the wider environment. It is as much an experiential measure as a spatial one.

Consider the now famous words of Walter Benjamin, who hints at the idea of privacy as an experience: "For the private individual the private environment represents the universe. In it he gathers remote places and the past."[62] Far more than comfort, the concept of privacy is reliant on a definition of the interior self.[63] This meaning, latent in Benjamin's assessment, also connects to our need for shelter and comfort, as Tomas

Diagrams charting indoor and outdoor temperatures for an igloo and an adobe house over a 24-hour period, based on James Marston Fitch's *American Building*, 1948. Even though comfort is based in innate human physiological reactions, standards of comfort vary according to culture and over time. Along with sound, one of the least fixed measures of comfort is the internal temperature of buildings: with the rise of air conditioning, we now expect building interiors to remain at a far lower constant temperature than ever before. This change is especially fascinating because buildings built before air conditioning successfully regulated temperature, even in extreme environments. Nevertheless, the stable internal temperature of these interiors was outside the "comfort zone" of temperature that we expect today.

Chapter Two

Maldonado writes in his essay "The Idea of Comfort": "The interior, Benjamin essentially says, is not only the universe, but also the care of the private individual. To inhabit means to leave impressions, and to acquire internally implies giving a certain relief to some perceptions." Only through the design of a private interior can we realize the full sense of ourselves as individuals.[64]

Seen this way, privacy is the divide between our interior self and our existence beyond the boundaries of our own mind and flesh. The individual's realization of his or her own self, the experience of privacy, can occur in any designed space, not just the home. Benjamin, it should be said, held the more conventional opinion that the deep privacy of the interior is possible only within domestic space: "For the private person, living space becomes, for the first time, antithetical to the place of work."[65] But we know that the successful fulfillment of privacy allows the individual to perform optimally in any setting, private or public, where he or she can sense their position in relation to the wider sea of humanity.

Privacy can be obtained by traveling into the recesses of the mind—a non-literal place of retreat—or to a physical environment designed specifically to aid quiet introspection, or a refuge. As with the qualitative criteria for safety and security, privacy is

Being

Rimini Convention Center, designed by GMP Studio, Rimini, Italy. Designed to showcase, house, and facilitate the movement of hundreds of people, this easily accessible and differently detailed void space provides a change of shape, form, materials, and experience. When standing in the middle and below the rotunda with its contemporary wood detailing, the quality of light and sound envelope the body in a starkly different manner to when moving through the wide (yet low-ceilinged) corridors or the extra tall major arteries which form the primary circulation axis. This kind of intentional change of experience is essential for sustained human attention and sensory satisfaction.

part of a balance of opposites: we can only understand it by experiencing its absence in any form.

Human nature exhibits consistent duality. For us to survive, the state of opposites – such as the private and the public – is a necessity. The element of contrast is rarely seen in terms of stabilizing counterparts, and within most foundational art and design education it is commonly and fundamentally discussed only in the context of visual balance; this needs to be expanded to include a broader range of experiences.

Design for Well-Being

The promotion of human well-being is the end goal of design. We realize well-being in design through careful consideration of qualitative criteria – a person's innate, cultural, and specific needs – which, when implemented, result in the optimal environment for the individual in question.

While the instinct for survival forces humans to find the means to live, attaining a state of well-being promotes efficiency, productivity, and satisfaction across society. This optimal condition elevates human behavior, inspiring people to do, and become, better. When people experience well-being they come together with more dignity and a sense of pride within their designed environment. But to foster this, design must promote intangible factors such as trust and respect. Successful design, therefore, does not rely only on artistic elements but also on factors that help to define the individual's place in the world at large.

Clearly, most design does not achieve this end. One reason for this may be the extent to which it is still preoccupied with formal or stylistic effects, on creating beauty with no consideration of how an environment supports the user. Beauty is integral to, but will not alone produce, human well-being. The Fluxus artist Robert Filiou stated the problem cryptically yet correctly: "Art is what makes life more interesting than art." Put another way, art is a part of life but is not sufficient to sustain us. Joy and satisfaction, those foundations of artistic pleasure, can be experienced only alongside the equally critical sensations of security and comfort – factors that design must address comprehensively.

Another gauge of total well-being could perhaps be explored through the ultimate measure of the user's sense of happiness, which also is a measure of successful design. Since we cannot aspire to be continuously happy, not only because this is impossible but also because happiness is experienced in contrast to our emotional valleys, the built world must mimic life's contrasts, whether it does this in terms of the inside versus the outside, darkness versus light, or loudness versus silence. We can only enjoy fugitive moments of happiness in an environment of sustained well-being, one characterized by elements that promote both psychological and physiological health.

Well-being is therefore not simply an internal measure, but is

reflected in our surroundings, and design must attempt to create it on two distinct levels: first, by creating a zone of comfort utilizing tangible criteria such as light, volume, proportion, color, and texture; second, by infusing design with a sense of inspiration, insight, and the impulse to strive to accomplish more and do better. Design that evokes or encourages a sense of passion, eagerness, or aspiration through what it satisfies or promotes, will simultaneously fulfill the human need for well-being. Achieving this is difficult because well-being is not a uniform goal or consistent experience, even for the same person. Instead, it is an ever fluid measure, contingent on changing circumstances. Design can respond by actively excluding elements that are harmful to health and actively including factors that are universally known to contribute to happiness. Finally— and most critically—designed space must allow for the kinds of experience that give individuals the opportunity to flourish on their own terms. Well-being is a criterion that should be integrated in the standard list of compulsory professional skills, which are currently limited to the fields of health, safety, and welfare.[66]

While it remains difficult to articulate well-being in precise design terms, there are ongoing attempts to measure its economic impact rationally (albeit, still too objectively)—the net dollar-value benefit of a well-designed office, for example, and the speed and quality of learning in an environment designed specifically for educational purposes. The most notable effort is the Gallup-Healthways Well-Being Index, conducted in the United States, which aims to combine broadly external developmental measures, like public health, with internal registers of psychological ease that are more difficult to measure. The Gallup-Healthways researchers use a psychological definition of "selective well-being," which is described as "all of the various type of evaluations, both positive and negative, that people make of their lives. It includes reflective cognitive evaluations, such as life satisfaction and work satisfaction, interest and engagement, and affective reactions to life events, such as joy and sadness."[67] The Well-Being Index is organized around conditions that can be read over time. For example, by using the "Cantril self-anchoring striving scale" it is possible to track the entire population's sense of whether they are "struggling" or "thriving." These methodologies indicate that we have developed an empirical means of discussing well-being with some success, but we do not have a similar vocabulary to deal with well-being in design.

What we can learn from such measures is that design must take into account both the immediate, palpable effects buildings and environments have on us at any given moment—experiences that we are immediately cognizant of—and long-term effects and memories. Even if we are not always aware of the feeling of well-being (either in the moment or in retrospect), we often sense its absence poignantly.

In *The Architecture of Happiness*, Alain de Botton describes how we may identify with beautiful objects: "What we seek, at the deepest level, is inwardly to resemble, rather than physically to

Chapter Two

Life Evaluation Trend

Monthly aggregates January 2008–March 2009
Source: Gallup-Healthways

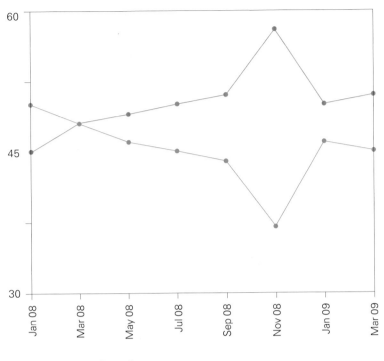

● Thriving   ● Struggling

The Gallup-Healthways Well-Being Index weighs a set of public health and psychological measures to establish a comprehensive, chronological index of well-being. This chart is one of several indices that have been developed recently to assess non-empirical factors affecting decisions, whether relating to marketing, sales, or economic policy. As shown in the chart, individual well-being dramatically decreased as the financial crisis peaked in November 2008. Developing similar scales for the measurement of how well-being is impacted and applied to design is a critical necessity.

possess, the objects and places that touch us through their beauty."[68] This self-identification brings us back to the definition of the interior in Diderot's *Encylopédie*, which suggests that design needs to express and embrace the self that is intelligible in psychological and physical terms. Design is the attempt to bridge the gap between who we are and who we aspire to be.

In the 1940s, architect and designer William Lescaze wrote about the divide between our expectations of the built environment and what we actually feel: "Can buildings contribute anything to our happiness? If they can, in what ways? Which of my friends want the same thing from their buildings as I do? If many of us want the same thing, why is it that none of our buildings seem to give it to us?"[69] To understand how buildings can foster well-being, we must literally and metaphorically first look within ourselves and then work our way outward.

Being

Chapter Three

Inside   81

The sciences are not like Minerva, who sprang fully armed from the brain of Jove; they are daughters of time, and take shape insensibly, first by the combination of methods learned from experience, and later by the discovery of principles deduced from that combination.

Brillat-Savarin
The Physiology of Taste[1]

If the interior is a second skin or an extension of human identity, then, to paraphrase Diderot, *the knowledge of the inside of a person is congruous to the knowledge of the inside of a space*. Thus, designing interiors is always simultaneously an addition to, and an intervention in, the human experience.

The designed environment must address human concerns in addition to understanding the artistic and physical properties of a space, since it is with the human being that design originates. Unfortunately, interiors practice today continues to deal almost exclusively with physical interventions, rather than the experiential engagement of the user. Catering to qualitative needs with the aim of promoting human well-being has never been adequately dealt with as a component of design, interior or otherwise.

There is also arguably no satisfactory understanding of the interior as a unified entity. Even though "interior design" is a popular activity and is accepted as an independent discipline, in practice it remains a compilation of disparate parts. A vacuum exists between the common perception of the tasks of interior design and the conceptual foundation the profession needs. We lack what might be deemed a *poetics of the interior*–the comprehensive knowledge of design that makes environments "sing" in harmony with their occupants.

It is imperative that today, before design becomes further distanced from its human roots, a comprehensive body of design knowledge is cultivated based on three basic tenets:

1. People ought to be the focus of all design. Therefore, design for human habitation requires a systemic understanding of the body, mind, and spirit. This demands the ability to couple an in-depth knowledge of physical, functional, and pragmatic criteria with a thorough command of perceptual and psycho-logical factors.

2. As the discipline most profoundly connected to human concerns, design for interiors must assume a broader role. Interiors address the intimate concerns that other areas of design can tackle only in disparate parts. The practice must, therefore, be defined more inclusively, with a clearer delineation of its relationship to the built environment and to associated professions.

3. Of all design practices, designing interiors requires an understanding of the shaping and sculpting of the void–the air and space delineated by the literal or non-literal surround. In this sense the art of the craft of interiors sits with the designer's ability to activate the negative space (or the leftover space within the built environment) and to cause affect and provide meaning as a holistic expression of the desired practical, qualitative, and aspirations criteria required both by the user/occupant and the environment.

Accepting these tenets is the first step toward developing an advanced empirical knowledge for the interiors discipline, one that attends to human interactions with the built environment in all their complexity.

The need has never been more urgent. The "designer," loosely defined, has secured a prominent place in the cultural dialogue as evidenced by the burgeoning interest in interiors in the popular press worldwide over the past decade or so. "Interior design" as a pastime has never captured more general interest –just consider the proliferation of lifestyle- and interiors-related media, home improvement shows and retail outlets. A growing appreciation for the value of design has fueled the advancement of the professions, but it has also led to dilett-antism in the field. Cable television shows and shelter maga-zines loudly proclaim that anyone can design, thus diminishing recognition for the designer's unique skills and abilities. As a result, the widespread impression of the role of the designer is that of surface stylist and form giver. There is also an unreal-istic perception of the mystique of a talented few "artists" who shape new trends by combining unusual shapes and mater-ials with a certain flair. While this interest in design serves to raise a general level of visual interest among the public, "design" in this most rudimentary sense falls far short of what is needed for the meaningful improvement of the human condition. Regarding interior design as an instrument of the "cool," "trendy," or stylish ignores its most important contribu-tion: the advancement of well-being. To determine how we arrived at this misconstruction–and to rectify the situation in order to move forward–we must examine the evidence of the recent past.

The Emergence of Prevailing Stereotypes

Interior design as we know it today evolved through two wide historical arcs. The first, the distant past, involves the deliberate modification of human circumstances that began in the cave. The second, much more recent and better documented develo-pment has to do with the emergence of the modern identity of the interior designer, a process that has taken place over the past two centuries.[2]

This second development is not an isolated one; the profession emerged at the same time as other specialized design discipli-nes, including industrial and graphic design. This period also saw the formalization of architecture as a profession that was almost wholly independent of the practical skills of the builder and the technical knowledge of the engineer. The shock of the Industrial Revolution–in particular, the mass production of goods by semiskilled laborers rather than accomplished crafts-men–forced the nascent design disciplines to assess their rela-tionships to the crafts they succeeded.

In fact, it was the desire to reestablish a measure of unity between manufactured goods and the craftwork of past eras that brought industrial design into being in the mid-nineteenth century. Both the Arts and Crafts movement in England at the turn of the twentieth century, and the Deutscher Werkbund in Germany a couple of decades later, sought to recapture for the production of industrial goods a know-how and sensitivity that had been lost to automation. More importantly, the profession that began to emerge aimed to create new knowledge that would make it possible to shape objects with care and quality without sacrificing the advantages of machine production.

While the interior and considerations about it, which have been present since man first evolved, predate all other design concerns, interior design does not have the sort of clear progression that can be traced in product design. Its very nature as a backdrop for all human activities, together with the lack of any defined theory of practice, make pinpointing its exact origins tricky. However, it is possible to uncover some information by looking at the crafts that have historically pertained to interiors.

Once an intuitive practice, the design of interior space evolved from a fragmented collection of skilled craft trades – the upholsterer, the furniture-maker, the carpenter, the mill worker, the plasterer, and the painter to name a few. Any one of them may have contributed individually to an interior space, but collectively these trades did not, and could not, provide the totality of experience that the discipline of interior design is called upon to do.

In contrast, a single craft profession – upholstery – generated the role of the interior decorator, as the application of textiles, originally used on walls, expanded to furniture, and eventually to the design of entire rooms:

> The fitting up of domestic textiles in large households was originally carried out by the *tapissier* and the *fourrier*. Their work included the supply of canopies, wall tapestries, table carpets and other soft furnishings for interior decoration. It was these posts that were subsumed by the upholsterer during the 17th century. As wealthy clients were beginning to require interiors that were consciously co-ordinated, it was the upholsterer who began to play a pivotal role in house furnishing supply. This role was eventually to develop into the profession of interior decorator. Upholsterers were becoming arbiters of taste, not only through access to important homes and the circles of the wealthy … but also through their skills in introducing new styles and tastes.[3]

In the early nineteenth century, the upholsterer evolved from furniture-maker to discerning selector of coordinated interior furnishings. By the end of the century, when the craft production of furniture had largely ceased, the upholsterer, who had now begun to be called an interior decorator, stood as an authority on domestic taste.

The interior decorator had emerged as an individual whose sensitivity helped shape the stylistic preferences of upper-class women. Many of the misconceptions about interior design that we face today spring from this development. It is the source

Charpente.

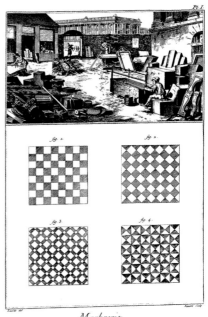

Marbrerie.
Compartiments simples de Carreaux de differentes formes.

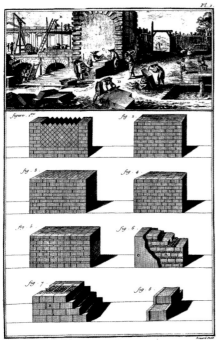

Architecture, Maçonnerie.

Couvreur.

of the idea that the history of interiors is merely a succession of stylistic reigns (sometimes quite literally–Louis XIV, XV, XVI); that interiors are a form of fashion, intrinsically transitional and temporary; that interior design deals primarily with furniture, curtains, drapes, and surfaces like wallpaper; that interior decoration is inherently soft (often quite literally, in using plush furniture and pillows); and that there is no intellectual component to interiors practice. The most pernicious misconception is that interior design is predominantly concerned with style and the latest trends, and has no philosophical basis. The assumption is that all the heroic qualities of the architect–personified by the fictional Howard Roark in Ayn Rand's *The Fountainhead*–are absent from the more intuitive decorator.[4] This conception, of course, distorts and dismisses the decorator's skill, albeit one that is limited to "finishing" touches at the final stage of the building process.

It is important that this description of *interior decorating* not be confused with the requirements of *interior design*. Given the general conflation of the two terms, and the lack of disciplinary clarity, simply negating the superficial stereotype of decorating will not grant interior design the weight it merits. Instead, interior design's complex nature must be clarified, with decorating playing a smaller yet essential role within the wider constellation of interiors practice.

To elaborate, an early twentieth-century article offered an intriguing answer to the question: "What is an interior decorator?": "[B]y the process of elimination, all of the preceding classifications being inadequate to his scope, the interior decorator should be considered an assembler."[5] Decoration, then, is not design– at least not design in its most comprehensive sense, understood as the practice of applying conceptual knowledge to spatial manipulation as the means for improving the human condition.

Another stereotype of interior design, so often and erroneously voiced, is that it is a profession uniquely suited to women, or one that seems to evoke feminine sensibilities. This stereotype is, in part, because so many of the famous early twentieth-century decorators–Elsie de Wolfe and Dorothy Draper are looming examples–were indeed women.[6] Understanding how this stereotype evolved is key to expanding the cultural perception of interior design.

Until the late nineteenth century it appears to have been primarily architects, builders, and craftsmen who designed interior spaces. They did so as an extension of their particular disciplines or trades, as the task was not delegated to any other, intermediary, designer. It was not until the 1880s that the figure of the professional (and almost exclusively residential) decorator appeared in America.[7] Even then, his or her exact status as a designer was unclear, since their professional responsibilities did not often extend beyond the tasteful assembly of furnishings and decorative elements produced elsewhere (though they were sometimes customized). Author William Seale described this evolution: "Even on the highest levels, the creative decision

Diderot's *Encylopédie* illustrates a plethora of the craft trades that go into the construction of buildings: carpentry, masonry, glass-making, furniture-making, metallurgy. Together, all these crafts were involved in the assembly of the built environments that we inhabit, both interior and exterior. Nevertheless, the practice of designing interiors cannot be said to have evolved directly from any of these crafts, since its primary aim is the treatment of human concerns through designed interventions. Physical craft is integral, but it is a means rather than an end.

Illustration from Elsie de Wolfe's
The House in Good Taste, 1913.
The book is the paragon of a sophisticated approach to residential decoration, and de Wolfe's instructions for
achieving formal effects in residential spaces are rigorous and complex.
Nevertheless, the decorator is still
called to rely on his or her taste, con-
verted into the measures of "simplicity, suitability, and proportion"–a
decorator's version of the familiar
Vitruvian trinity of utility, firmness,
and beauty.

of other times was replaced by a selectivity which applied not
only to costly new furniture but, ironically, to antiques as well,
giving rise to the 'period' room." Seale also observed: "A chief
influence here was that, generally speaking, the man was no
longer the builder of the house or the one who furnished it.
Household art, by the 1870s, was in the hands of women; the
architect's client was now female, and the wise owners of
furniture stores–and auctioneers–capitalized on that fact. To
the American room, women brought criteria that they applied
to the matters of personal dress. Now they were put to the
task of adorning rooms."[8] The decorator, in this 1880s genesis,
was a curator who shared the sensibilities of the women who
were his (or her) main clients. But that is not the exclusive
source of women's association with interior design. There is
also a very real history of practical design spearheaded by
women who did not work as decorators. Above and beyond the
growing interest in furnishing the home, the proper functioning
and efficiency of the household itself became a subject of
great attraction in the nineteenth century. As early as the
1840s, publications focusing on subjects such as domestic
economics and domestic science were published in the
United States. Interest in them was not limited to housekeeping but also addressed issues like the functional layout of
kitchen space, down to the exact placement of cabinets and
equipment (see illustrations on pages 90 and 91). This type of
planning and programming is now, of course, a critical part of

the process employed by the interior design profession. Women interior designers—even though they were not called such—can claim to have pioneered this detailed type of planning for buildings.[9]

The case can also be made that domestic-efficiency planning (which began as an exclusively feminine practice based on the study of repeated motions within the household) was the progenitor of the monumentally influential early twentieth-century programs to achieve industrial efficiency, best exemplified by the work of Frederick Winslow Taylor. Far from being dismissed as a superficial, feminine practice (as was the case with decoration), the domestic engineering profession was appropriated by industry with no acknowledgment of its feminine origins; a great irony indeed. The relegation of women to a marginal role was partially a result of their exclusion from other design arenas, as Robert Gutman writes in *Architectural Practice, A Critical View*:

> Beginning sometime at the end of the nineteenth century, women, in particular, who were discouraged from becoming architects or were excluded from architecture schools, began to design interior domestic spaces, often along with furniture. The concentration of women in the field during a century in which the principle of patriarchy dominated membership in the profession inevitably diminished the status of the interior designer. This condition began to change with the rise of industrial design as an identifiable specialty in the 1920s, and the slow blurring of the lines between the design of domestic space by the interior designers and the design of work space by the industrial designers.[10]

The question, then, is where to mark the beginning of interior design as a modern professional discipline. While the terms interior design and interior designer were used at the end of the nineteenth century, the appearance of interior design as a professional practice called by that name probably occurred sometime in the interwar era of the 1920s and 1930s; it seems to have happened almost parallel to industrial design being adopted as a service provided to corporate clients.

The complication in determining when interior design became a discipline is that the competing terms *interior decoration* and *interior design* were, and still are, used relatively interchangeably, even in a professional sense. Therefore they further confuse the division between interior decorators, interior designers, and architects. Sorting out the vocabulary should shed some light on the debate. In the English language, interior decoration seems to predate interior design; however, it appears that the two have since existed side by side with somewhat different meanings.

Interior decoration is most commonly used to denote the final stage of building, where plasterers, upholsterers, and other decorators—sometimes under the direction of an architect—complete the interior. At some point in the late nineteenth century *decoration* increasingly became the realm of a profes-

Plan of a house from Catherine Ward Beecher and Harriet Beecher Stowe, *American Woman's Home, or Principles of Domestic Science*, 1869.

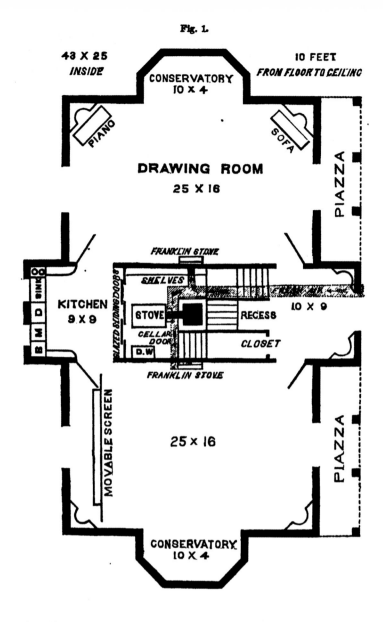

Fig. 1.

43 X 25 INSIDE

10 FEET FROM FLOOR TO CEILING

CONSERVATORY 10 X 4

PIANO

SOFA

PIAZZA

DRAWING ROOM
25 X 16

FRANKLIN STOVE

SHELVES

KITCHEN 9 X 9

STOVE

RECESS 10 X 9

CELLAR DOOR

CLOSET

D.W.

FRANKLIN STOVE

MOVABLE SCREEN

25 x 16

PIAZZA

CONSERVATORY 10 X 4

sional figure who was neither an architect, designer, or craftsman but, rather, like the upholsterer discussed earlier in this chapter, an arbiter of taste, who generally had no formal training. This shift in terminology occurred at nearly the same time (roughly from 1880 to 1930) that educational and professional organizations for architecture were established.

Interior design gained currency during the same period, and was in common usage by the 1930s. The term became popular because of the need to distinguish comprehensive interiors work from "mere" decoration.[11] Even though *interior design* appeared in newspapers and periodicals during the nineteenth century, most occurrences represented the conjunction of the two words and did not indicate a profession distinct from architecture.[12] A further complication is that many nineteenth-

CEILING

LID — MOULDING AND MEAT BOARD / DISH DRAINER / SINK

FLOUR BARREL DOOR — RYE — CORN MEAL — COARSE FLOUR — TOWELS — SCOURING

SUGAR — SUGAR — LARD

Perspective of a kitchen from *American Woman's Home*. The vastly influential books by the Beecher sisters (Harriet of *Uncle Tom's Cabin* fame) show the concern for the creation of functional interior space that corresponds to the practical needs of the occupants. Later called domestic engineering, these functional systems and methodologies were subsequently appropriated by other disciplines but remain at the core of design today.

century uses of the term signified architectural work inside a building, as opposed to work on the exterior, which may indicate that interior design was considered an element of architecture, separate from decoration.

It is worth emphasizing that the emergence of the decorator—at least, in the case of a highly sophisticated architect–decorator figure like Ogden Codman—was an attempt to establish an aesthetic unity between exterior architecture and the insides of buildings, to prevent "multiplication of incongruous effects." Codman's view, as he wrote in *The Decoration of Houses*, was that the upholsterer's role in dictating the decoration of nineteenth-century houses was due to a "deficiency." The lack of architectural training, he argued, led to a misunderstanding of general design principles and form, resulting in a "piling up of heterogeneous ornament."[13] In this context, the decorator was conceived to replace the dilettante upholsterer—though the accusation of dilettantism has now transferred to the decorator. And of course, making the distinction between the design knowledge and sophistication of the upholsterer and the decorator mirrors more contemporary attempts to differentiate *interior design* and *interior decoration*.

There was, in fact, a precedent for the semantic confusion over what to call design work inside a building: the potent debate over the role of interior planning in eighteenth-century France. Perhaps surprisingly—since there seems to be little serious writing on interior space even today—interiors were a major

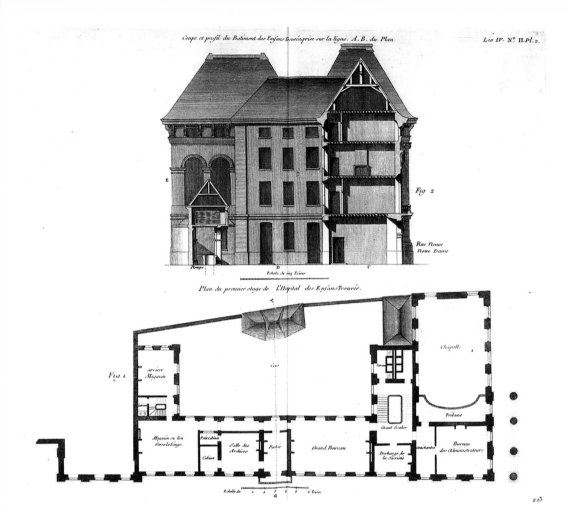

Coupe et profil du Batiment des Enfans Trouvés prise sur la ligne. A.B. du Plan

Lio IV. N.º II. Pl. 2.

Fig 2

Rue Neuve
Notre Dame

Plan du premier etage de L'Hopital des Enfans Trouvés.

Chapelle

Fig 1

arriere
Magasin

Cour

Tribune

Magasin ou l'on
serre le Linge

Petit Cabinet

Salle des
Archives

Parloir

Grand Bureau

Grand Escalier

Decharge de
la Sacristie

Bureau
des Administrateurs

Cabinet

Echelle de

6 Toises

225

Section and second-floor plan of the Hôpital des Enfants-Trouvés, built in 1727, by architect Germain Boffrand. The interior, both as an object of decoration and of interior spatial planning, became of great concern to eighteenth-century French architects. Here Boffrand, one of the major designers of Rococo interiors, shows a schematic plan and section devoid of decoration. Instead the focus of the design is interior planning (most notably distribution of rooms and comfort), then called convenience, which was one of the precursors to the formal identification of the interiors profession in the United States.

subject of the era's architectural theory. Certainly, in surveying the writings and works of Germain Boffrand, Robert de Cotte, and Jean-François Blondel, three influential French architects of the period, there is undoubtedly more space devoted to interiors than would be expected prior to the more highly developed twentieth-century concepts of architectural space.[14] To simplify greatly, interior decoration was viewed as the final stage in a building's completion, and should accordingly mirror its exterior decoration. The interior could vary from the exterior in that it had to address issues of *distribution* (roughly, space planning) and of *convenance* (which loosely translates as "convenience" –though it perhaps more accurately means an idiosyncratic gauge of comfort).[15] The existence of this sizable body of interiors discourse was tied directly to the nature of many elite eighteenth-century commissions in France, which involved reprogramming or redecorating existing spaces (especially in royal or aristocratic residences) rather than constructing new buildings.[16]

But even if interiors can be considered a prime focus of French eighteenth-century architectural thought, the ideas were not substantial enough to call this the moment that interior design was born. Rather, we probably have to attribute the discipline's origins to the conclusion that the interior space of a building has different functional and decorative requirements to its exterior. Though this might seem obvious in retrospect, this distinction did not emerge fully before the end of the nineteenth century and was critical to the twentieth century's interwar attempts to define interior design as its own practice, independent from both architecture and decoration.

This split between the exterior and the interior has continued into the present, where the design turf has been divided between the architect on one side and the decorator and interior designer on the other. One of the better early surveys of this rift is a 1914 article titled "Architect and Decorator" from *Good Furniture* magazine, which points to an inherent mutual suspicion between the architect and the decorator. The article states that, despite their animosity, the two professions are not necessarily isolated, especially since architecture has willingly surrendered so much of its most practical work to other specialists:

> Also, the two professions, as might have been expected, have developed considerably toward each other. The architect, sensing the invasion of his field, has bent much of his specializing of late toward interior decoration, and has turned over much of the detail of heating, lighting and the like to trade specialists in those lines, while decorators, coming more and more into contact with architecture, have developed large and efficient organizations to cope with its many problems, and even to directly serve the architect.[17]

Yet this collapsing of disciplinary boundaries did not result in a single practice. Since World War II, interior design has aligned itself more closely with architecture in order to distance itself from decoration's perceived lack of substantiality. The most

Works Progress Administration (WPA) posters from the 1930s. These posters, made for exhibitions of work by government designers, illustrate how a clear distinction between interior design and interior decoration has often never occurred at a popular level. This confusion continued even as interior design was offered as a professional service distinct from architecture and interior decoration, which started to occur in the United States during the 1930s.

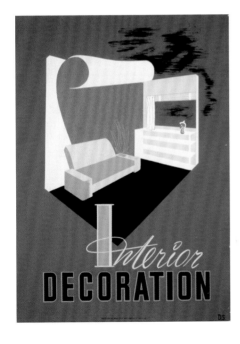

famous example of this was Florence Knoll and her Knoll Planning Unit. As described in a recent history of her practice, "Knoll was part of a broader American movement to dissociate the profession of interior design from the practice of the interior decorator, which had been associated with domestic environments and dilettantism."[18] By rejecting the job of decorative finishing, Knoll allied interiors practice with the functional and rational methods of modern architecture: "Decorating connoted a personal and idiosyncratic approach, by contrast to designing, which implied a systematic and efficient process."[19] The splintering of the National Society of Interior Designers from the American Institute of Decorators in 1957 not only reflected the separation of the two disciplines but also furthered the divide.[20]

But that step—and the culminating adoption of the name "interior architecture" over "interior design"—threatens to rob interior design of its unique characteristic, to divorce it from its prehistoric origins and its intrinsic connections to cognitive behavior and social science. Today's interior designer needs to be a comprehensive professional who can implement beneficial environments for human occupation. Such a designer must have expertise beyond the usual skills of an architect or a decorator.

To understand the professional role of the interior designer in the context of the wider, built environment, it makes sense to return to the concept of well-being discussed in chapter 2. The industrial era and the related building boom brought an increased focus on the dangers inherent in the changed physical environment, which spurred efforts to regulate health, safety, and welfare. Light, air, water, and sanitation, including sustainable practices, have become common concerns—and in some cases, areas of specialization—in professions that deal with the built environment. It is obvious that architects and engineers, whose job it is to design sound structures, play a critical role in the construction of safe and healthy spaces. However, providing for the mental and emotional health of the people within these spaces is the unique purview of the interiors practice. These considerations call for empirical investigations by specially trained and focused design professionals, but the body of knowledge and skills that would result from such research is key to the recognition of interior design as a distinct and essential profession.

The Psychology Analogy

The emergence of psychology as a legitimate science distinct from physiology, biology, and medicine offers a precedent for interiors as a unique design discipline based on a unique body of knowledge. In other words, interiors are to the built environment what psychology is to science, an analogy that can be demonstrated on three levels:

1. As a discipline
Interior design, like psychology, complements an established area of scholarship (for instance, the various sciences and disciplines that explore the built environment) but ultimately compri-

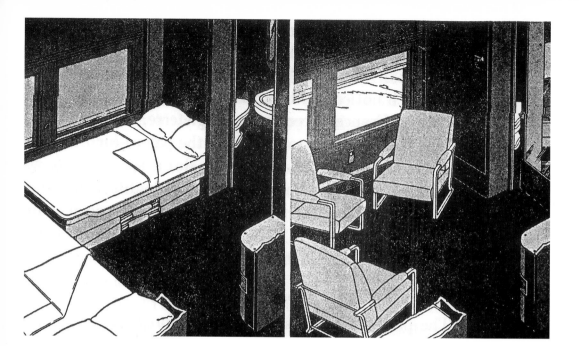

The notion of "interior" or "inside" is not restricted to the commonly understood room. Atria, town squares, and piazzas are large public spaces that require careful "interior" and design considerations as the illustrations on these pages demonstrate.

Above:
Master room of a Pullman railroad car, 1939.

Right:
Interior of a Boeing 377, Walter Dorwin Teague, 1949. Many interiors, including those of a railroad car or an airplane, involve the creation of a space for human occupation where the exterior form has already been determined and cannot be altered by designed interior. Although the work of industrial designers, these two images illustrate the familiar residential quality of these interiors which are (perhaps incongruently) housed within high-speed transportation systems.

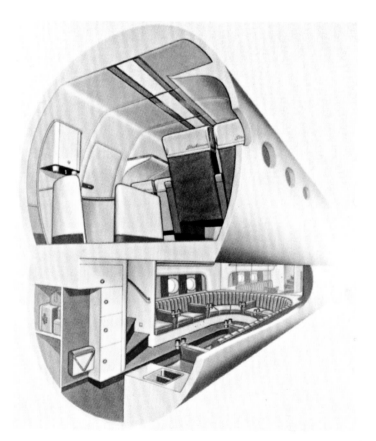

ses an independent area of practice. Psychology deals with mental and behavioral health, and goes beyond biology and physical medicine in accounting for their effect on the body; interior design addresses the qualities of human experience (security, comfort, and well-being) in the built environment as no other design discipline can.[21]

2. As a science

Psychology offers a rigorous, empirical methodology to explain the mysteries of cognition. It is critical for designers to develop similar and equally empirical protocols pertaining to the interior. Psychology created a science of the mind; interior design must create a science of human experience in the built environment. In both cases, scientific methodology allows for the understanding of mental processes where none was previously thought possible.

3. As an understanding of the human being

Finally, both psychology and interior design have created a means of understanding the human being outside the parochial boundaries of established disciplines. Just as psychology now informs our perception of human behavior, a science of interior space will influence our view of all human interactions in the built environment.

Though psychology is the study of the mind (its first use in English meant "knowledge of the soul"[22]), its modern connotation encompasses the relationship between the mind and the body, defined in the *Oxford English Dictionary* as follows:

> The scientific study of the nature, functioning, and development of the human mind, including the faculties of reason,

Above left:
Ford Foundation Building, New York, Kevin Roche and John Dinkeloo, architects, Warren Platner, interior designer, Dan Kiley, landscape architect, 1967. The Ford Foundation building, a masterwork of collaboration, focuses on a multilevel landscape atrium, a void that takes up 50 percent of the building's volume. This giant "main room" is covered by a skylight and the massive volume is proportioned to the human scale by the use of terraced landscaping and trees and foliage, helping to divide the space into a number of subrooms and spaces. These smaller "rooms" allow for a variety of zones of privacy.

Above:
Rimini Convention Center, designed by GMP Studio, 2001, Rimini, Italy. The interior court provides a welcome change with the use of texture (through materials including water) and movement (rippling of water in the reflecting pool). Here the contrasting experience of the covered yet open at the side walkway, and the walled yet open to the sky center court exemplifies spatial variation. These design elements help to enhance an intentional and varied experience.

Inside

Chapter Three

Paley Park, New York, Robert Zion, landscape architect, Zion and Breen, in association with Albert Preston Moore, 1966. An urban "living room" without a roof, Paley Park provides intentional sound stimulation through the cascade of the waterfall which helps to baffle the noise of the nearby busy street while also providing visual stimulation. The trees and foliage help to screen the space from the harshness of the adjoining urban fabric and the hustle and bustle of midtown Manhattan.

Inside

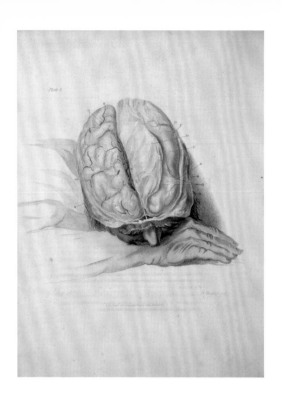 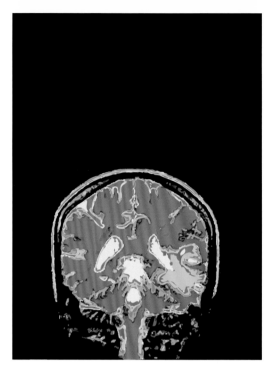

emotion, perception, communication, etc.; the branch of science that deals with the (human or animal) *mind as an entity and in its relationship to the body and to the environmental or social context*, based on observation of the behaviour of individuals or groups of individuals in particular (ordinary or experimentally controlled) circumstances.[23]

Psychology's foundational breakthrough was to establish that the internal workings of the mind could be investigated with the same depth and rigor that physiology had already established for purely physical bodily processes. The mind, for centuries thought explicable only in terms of philosophy, became a valid ground for critical investigation, subject to its own discoverable laws.[24] This assumption and the subsequent findings were revolutionary, and today it is not easy to appreciate the significance of this breakthrough in the context of the mid-nineteenth century. Since the turn of that century, physiology and biology had evolved into respected sciences that offered rational explanations for the life processes of animals and humans, but psychology would lag behind by at least half a century.

Thomas Huxley's 1879 description of psychology shows that the concept was so fresh it still had to be explained to a skeptical audience and defended as a legitimate endeavor:

Psychology is a part of the science of life or biology, which differs from the other branches of that science, merely in so far as it deals with the psychical, instead of the physical, phenomena of life.

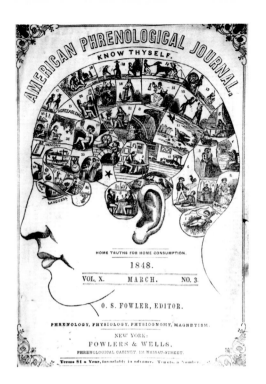

As there is an anatomy of the body, so there is an anatomy of the mind; the psychologist dissects mental phenomena into elementary states of consciousness, as the anatomist resolves limbs into tissues, and tissues into cells. The one traces the development of complex organs from simple rudiments: the other follows the building up of complex conceptions out of simpler constituents of thought. As the physiologist inquires into the way in which the so-called "functions" of the body are performed, so the psychologist studies the so-called "faculties" of the mind.[25]

Huxley's explication is based on the subdiscipline most relevant to interiors: experimental psychology, which was formulated simultaneously in the late nineteenth century by William James (1842–1910) in the United States and Wilhelm Wundt (1832–1920) in Germany. Experimental psychology argued that there were direct, external measures that could be used to test and quantify internal mental processes. This premise dissolved two millennia of dogma about human perception of the world, previously held to be knowable only in philosophical or physical terms (as in the theory of the humors, according to which bodily fluids affected a person's temperament).[26]

Experimental psychology unlocked what had always existed within humans, but which no one had been able to probe. Likewise, the discipline of interior design must take steps to better understand the intangible qualities of interior space and the effect the built environment can have on people. But as long as designers believe that they do not have—and cannot create—the means of measuring human experiences, this will not happen.

Facsimile of Linnaeus, *Systema Naturae*: CAROLI LINNÆI — REGNUM ANIMALE. (I. QUADRUPEDIA. II. AVES. III. AMPHIBIA. IV. PISCES. V. INSECTA. VI. VERMES.)

IV. PISCES.

Corpus apodum, pinnis veris instructum, nudum, vel squamosum.

PLAGIURI. *Cauda horizontalis.*	Trichechus.	Dentes in utraque maxilla. Dorsum impenne.	Manatus f. Vacca mar.
	Catodon.	Dentes in inferiore maxilla. Dorsum impenne.	Cot. Fistula in rostro *Art.* Cete *Cluf.*
	Monodon.	Dens in superiore max. 1. Dorsum impenne.	Monoceros. *Unicornu.*
	Balæna.	Dentes in sup. max. cornei. Dorsum sæpius impenne.	B. Groenland. B. Finfisch. B. Maxill. inf. latiore. *Art.*
	Delphinus.	Dentes in utraque maxilla. Dorsum pinnatum.	Orcha. Delphinus. Phocæna.
CHONDROPTERYGII. *Pinnæ cartilagineæ.*	Raja.	Foramina branch. utrinq. 5. Corpus depressum.	Raja clav. asp. læv. &c. Squatino-Raja. Altavela. Pastinaca mar. Aquila. Torpedo. Bos Vet.
	Squalus.	Foram. branch. utrinq. 5. Corpus oblongum.	Lamia. Galeus. Catulus. Vulpes mar. Zygæna. Squatina. Centrine. Pristis.
	Acipenser.	Foram. branch. utrinq. 1. Os edentul. tubulatum.	Sturio. Huso. Ichthyocolla.
	Petromyzon.	Foram. branch. utrinq. 7. Corpus bipenne.	Enneophthalmus. Lampetra. Mustela.
BRANCHIOSTEGI. *Pinnæ ossic. carentes. Branch. off. & membran.*	Lophius.	Caput magnitudine corporis. Appendices horizontaliter latera piscis ambiunt.	Rana piscatrix. Guacucuja.
	Cyclopterus.	Pinnæ ventrales in unicam circularem concretæ.	Lumpus. Lepus mar.
	Ostracion.	Pinnæ ventrales nullæ. Cutis dura, sæpe aculeata.	Orbis div. sp. Pisc. triangul. Atinga. Hystrix. Ostracion. Lagocephalus.
	Balistes.	Dentes contigui maximi. Aculei aliquot robusti in dorso.	Guaperua. Histrix. Capriscus. Caper.

V. INSECTA.

Corpus crusta ossea cutis loco tectum. *Caput* antennis instructum.

COLEOPTERA. *Alæ elytris duobus tectæ.*	Blatta.	§. FACIE EXTERNA FACILE DISTING. Elytra concreta. Alæ nullæ. Antennæ truncatæ.	Scarab. tardipes. Blatta fœtida.
	Dytiscus.	Pedes postici remorum forma & usu. Ant. setaceæ. Sterni apex bifurcus.	Hydrocantharus. Scarab. aquaticus.
	Meloë.	Elytra mollia, flexilia, corpore breviora. Ant. moniliformes. Ex articulis oleum fundens.	Scarab. majalis. Scarab. unctuosus.
	Forficula.	Elytra brevissima, rigida. Cauda bifurca.	Staphylinus. Auricularia.
	Notopeda.	Positum in dorso exsilit. Ant. capillaceæ.	Scarab. elasticus.
	Mordella.	Cauda aculeo rigido simplici armata. Ant. setaceæ, breves.	Negatur ab *Aristotele.*
	Curculio.	Rostrum productum, teres, simplex. Ant. clavatæ in medio Rostri positæ.	Curculio.
	Baceros.	Cornu 1. simplex, rigidum, fixum. Ant. capitatæ, foliaceæ.	Rhinoceros. Scarab. monoceros.
	Lucanus.	Cornua 2. ramosa, rigida, mobilia. Ant. capitatæ, foliaceæ.	Cervus volans.
	Scarabæus.	§. ANTENNÆ TRUNCATÆ. Ant. clavatæ foliaceæ. Cornua nulla.	Scarab. pilularis. Melolontha. Dermestes.
	Dermestes.	Ant. clavatæ horizontaliter perfoliatæ. Clypeus planiusculus, emarginatus.	Cantharus fasciatus.
	Cassida.	Ant. clavato-subulatæ. Clypeus planus, antice rotundatus.	Scarab. clypeatus.
	Chrysomela.	Ant. simplices, clypeo longiores. Corpus subrotundum.	Cantharellus.
	Coccionella.	Ant. simplices, brevissimæ. Corpus hemisphæricum.	Cochinella vulg.
	Gyrinus.	Ant. simplices, corpus breve. Pedibus posticis saliens.	Pulex aquaticus. Pulex plantarum.

Addressing the dichotomy between exterior form and interior space has long been held to be critical to design, but the discussion has been conducted more in conceptual or subjective terms than rational ones. The former approach was hinted at by Gaston Bachelard, who in his 1948 book *La Terre et les rêveries du repos* describes the psychological difference between interior and exterior space as follows: "At base, the closed-in and the extroverted life are both psychic necessities. But so as not to become abstract formulas, it is necessary that they be psychological realities with a setting, a decor."[27] By the late nineteenth century Huxley was calling for connections to be made between the sensations we experience and the physical instruments that create them:

> But there is more than a parallel, there is a close and intimate connection between psychology and physiology. No one doubts that, at any rate some mental states are dependent for their existence on the performance of the functions of particular bodily organs. There is no seeing without eyes, and no hearing without ears. If the origin of the contents of the mind is truly a philosophical problem, then the philosopher who attempts to deal with that problem, without acquainting himself with the physiology of sensation, has no more intelligent conception of his business than the physiologist, who thinks he can

Top:
Durkan Patterned Carpet installation, Hospitality Design Expo 2004, Las Vegas, Shashi Caan Collective. Replicating techniques used in the manufacturing of printed carpet, this conceptual three-dimensional interpretation involved individual pattern layers printed onto sheer fabric. These separate layers of color and pattern were realized in a sequence of volumes, allowing them to become overlapped and spatially collapsed while remaining dynamically and volumetrically experienced and explored. Although an abstraction of a two-dimensional carpet, the stimulation of the sense of discovery was shared by the public and experts alike.

Bottom:
DuPont Corian Surfaces installation, NEOCON 2002, Shashi Caan Collective. The design brief called for fresh interpretations of this brittle and malleable material and for exploring new forms and uses. Deploying perception and phenomenal illusion, this image, at first glance, appears to be a mirrored image of the vase. Closer inspection reveals two identical vases, carefully positioned and viewed through a cutout (with color shift). However, in order to understand this, the individual is required to enter the installation for a closer viewing. The installation was designed as a series of manipulations of spaces and objects, with visual effects that made it possible to see into other adjacent spaces and for objects to appear as if they were floating on plinths.

Opposite:
Amber Fort and Palace, Jaipur, India, sixteenth to eighteenth centuries. This historic example demonstrates sophisticated wisdom and knowledge deployed by sensitive designers. This interstitial hall, open on one side to an interior courtyard garden, incorporates a water channel. A gently gurgling cascade of water is captured at the bottom of the channel and used to water the rose bushes in the garden. Windows on either end of the feature ventilate the space. The water would have been fragranced with rose essence which would also have been distributed by the cross breeze, thereby delighting several of the human senses.

discuss locomotion, without an acquaintance with the principles of mechanics; or respiration, without some tincture of chemistry.[28]

Similarly, it is the role of the interior designer to uncover the exact means by which designed spaces affect the faculties of human behavior and emotion. With this purpose in mind, Huxley's definition of psychology's unique relationship to physiology might be reformulated to express the interior's place in relation to the built environment:

Interior design is a part of the science of the built environment, which differs from the other branches of that science merely in so far as it deals with the qualitative, in addition to the physical, transformation of space intended to enhance human experience.

Inside

Ideally, interior design would generate desirable cognitive responses, just as the engineer resolves structural and mechanical systems within a physical shell. The architect plans the physical building brick by brick, while the interior designer seeks to combine experience, feeling, and perception in material form. As the architect and engineer explore the means by which a building will stand, so must the interior designer explore the means by which to create the optimally supportive environment, spaces in which human beings can thrive.

Empirical Knowledge

> I wished, by treating Psychology like a natural science, to help her to become one. William James, "A Plea for Psychology as a 'Natural Science'"[29]

Experimental psychology posited that emotion and aesthetics were part of the same sensory apparatuses, and thus the experience of beauty and other artistic feelings could be quantified through psychology. In his seminal 1890 book *Principles of Psychology,* William James wrote:

> [W]e must immediately insist that aesthetic emotion, pure and simple, the pleasure given us by certain lines and masses, and combinations of colors and sounds, is an absolutely sensational experience, an optical or auricular feeling that is primary, and not due to the repercussion backwards of other sensations elsewhere consecutively aroused. To this simple primary and immediate pleasure in certain pure sensations and harmonious combinations of them, there may, it is true, be added secondary pleasures; and in the practical enjoyment of works of art by the masses of mankind these secondary pleasures play a great part. The more classic one's taste is, however, the less relatively important are the secondary pleasures felt to be, in comparison with those of the primary sensation as it comes in. Classicism and romanticism have their battles over this point. Complex suggestiveness, the awakening of vistas of memory and association, and the stirring of our flesh with picturesque mystery and gloom, make a work of art romantic. The classic taste brands these effects as coarse and tawdry, and prefers the naked beauty of the optical and auditory sensations, unadorned with frippery or foliage. To the romantic mind, on the contrary, the immediate beauty of these sensations seems dry and thin. I am of course not discussing which view is right, but only showing that the discrimination between the primary feeling of beauty, as a pure incoming sensible quality, and the secondary emotions which are grafted thereupon, is one that must be made.[30]

James' line of reasoning manifests itself today in the copious research being done on the interplay between perception and the arts, as well as in the popularity of neuroscience as a catch-all tool for explaining human behavior. But these investigations have, for the most part, kept the process of scientific discovery

Chapter Three

separate from that of artistic creation.[31] An analysis of how we experience the world has to come before we can design the world to be experienced in the ways we want.

Design can function simultaneously as a creative endeavor and as a science, but first we need to clarify just what sort of science interior design should be. The popular understanding of the subject—as it is taught in schools through the so-called scientific method—is the product of nineteenth-century logical positivism, a philosophy which held that "genuine scientific theories, such as Newtonian astronomy, are hypothetico-deductive, with theoretical entities occupying the initial hypotheses and natural laws the ultimate deductions or theorems."[32] The goal of this kind of scientific exploration is to prove or disprove all parts of the original hypothesis. With sufficient repetition, the hypothesis can be strengthened into a defensible theory of natural processes that ideally, though not exclusively, will result in a simple mathematical formula.

However, many of the "hard" sciences (biology, for one) do not operate within this rigid framework. Rather than attempting to formulate an overarching scientific theory based on immutable laws, the objective is to assemble a more nuanced view through the accretion of empirical observations. This framework of inquiry directly affects how theoretical constructs are formulated. Many theories, like Darwin's on evolution, simply are not, by nature of their diversity, reducible to mathematical or statistical models but rely on the interpretation of a preponderance of empirical evidence.

This is how psychology functions as a science, and it is the mode of research that can inform interior design, which still relies too much on intuition, even in codified professional guidelines. Rational investigations into human behavior within built environments should begin to create the shared knowledge with which individual designers can make more thoughtful decisions.[33]

Making an analogy between interior design and psychology is relevant in so far as it allows for a shift in focus toward the intangible (experiential) substance of interiors. This does not mean that psychology provides a blueprint for interior design. That is impossible, and not even germane. The purpose of the analogy is to offer a precedent for establishing a protocol and body of knowledge for understanding the requirements for human well-being.

For interior design to incorporate an empirical and rigorous means of research and ultimately behave as a living science, a workable investigation methodology must be devised. Although certain innate factors influence the human experience of interior space, the individual experience is highly subjective and mutable according to time and place. Research aimed at uncovering absolute laws of design thus would be problematic (recall the shortcomings of the universal man as a measure of the human body, as described in chapter 2). Instead, the aim must be to establish overall parameters within which the skilled designer can fill in necessary elements based on an understanding of likely outcomes grounded in theoretical fact. No grand theory is needed. Design principles must stem from data acquired in numerous smaller experiments and tests in the field.

Many investigations have reflected the assumption that a new interiors knowledge will be largely derived from the vast cognitive research already conducted in other fields, which may be limited in scope or not applicable within design of the built environment. Instead, "live labs," where the practitioner can observe and understand behaviors in the context of the built environment in its totality, are what is essential for interior design knowledge. The lack of this kind of research is one of the fundamental hindrances to the meaningful evolution of the interior design profession.

Since little of the necessary empirical data for interiors practice has been gathered or articulated, the question is how to begin this new mode of inquiry in this specific context. That depends upon expectations of what a science of interior design should accomplish. The most basic definition of science may offer some guidance. Science is:

> ... any system of knowledge that is concerned with the physical world and its phenomena and that entails unbiased observations and systematic experimentation. In general, a science involves a pursuit of knowledge covering general truths or the operations of fundamental laws.[34]

The definition notes that scientific knowledge has to be based on "unbiased" and "systematic" observations. It is by no means an overstatement to say that systematic experimentation is almost entirely missing in interiors practice; while any designer may consider his or her project experimental, this is not accomplished within the necessary systematic and unbiased protocols for creating empirical understanding. The "physical world" in the definition could easily be the habitable environment, and "its phenomena" might refer to how its spaces are perceived by human beings. It follows that as long as interior design seeks to uncover "general truths" through "unbiased observations and systematic" experimentation, it can be classified as a science, even while retaining its artistic component. In other words, information that is proven to enhance the quality of human lives can be applied by the skillful interior designer in fresh and innovative ways. Of course, if all design had to follow fully quantifiable and repeatable laws, there would be no art nor creativity and the process would be reduced to "painting by numbers." The attempt to establish an empirical foundation for the discipline does not change the fact that interior design is ultimately a creative act that requires individual agency. Thus, it will always be up to the designer to interpret disciplinary data.

While professional groups and educators have tried to define a core knowledge for interior design over the past 50 years, those attempts have yet fully to result in the kind of comprehensive project-specific, human-behavior-related research that would inform a common practice.[35] In order to be regarded as a serious intellectual pursuit, the field still needs a design science with a focused research methodology. The generally held "truths" of interior design (that tall ceilings promote their occupants to think loftily, for example, or that sunny yellow environments make people happier) must be proven so that they can justifiably become part of the disciplinary canon. Finding the means for systematically exploring the emotive, perceptual, sensory, and phenomenological qualities of space and the behaviors they elicit, would empower designers to respond with greater sensitivity to the needs of people, and also consciously effect conceptual and creative solutions that move society and culture forward.

Efforts have been made legislatively to create licensing standards for the interiors profession, similar to those of other disciplines. However, these attempts have focused on a circumscribed, practical idea of the interior, not on the qualitative knowledge the field needs. Plus, one of the shortcomings of such licensing efforts is that they attempt to clarify the role of interior design from an architectural point of view—in terms of health, safety, and welfare—and thus continue to portray interiors as an extension of architectural practice rather than confirming its independent origins and central reason for being. Considering that the interior existed long before architecture, to restrict it to this relatively narrow professional definition is to deny it the scope to provide for the whole spectrum of human needs.

Over the years many have sought to use design as a positive force. In the 1950s the architect Richard J. Neutra positioned the designer as an "artist of empathy" in his book *Survival Through Design* and in papers.[36] He argued that design was necessary for survival because technological advances have overwhelmed the capacities of human beings to adapt through biological evolution. The place of the designer is, therefore, to create an environment that supports human physiology and psychology, which remain fundamentally unchanged in spite of the wave of technological advances: "We shall have to survive by design and not by natural adaptation because there is no time for adaptation in our technological rush and advance."[37] The role of the enlightened designer, Neutra believed, was to provide an ameliorative zone in an artificial environment that was antithetical to human occupation. As Neutra described the problem in *Survival Through Design:*

> It has become imperative that in designing our physical environment we should consciously raise the fundamental question of survival, in the broadest sense of the term. Any design that impairs or imposes excessive strain on the natural human equipment should be eliminated, or modified in accordance with the requirements of our nervous, and more gradually, our total physiological functioning.[38]

The goal, then, was that design be imagined not in physical terms, separate from the human occupant, but rather as being intimately linked to his or her prosperity.

Chapter Three

Spatial Color, a collaborative team experiment conceived and orchestrated by Shashi Caan and The Collective. This experiment was conceived as an examination of the popular preconceptions of the effects of red, blue, and yellow, within a real life setting. For example, that red inspires people to eat more; blue is calming; yellow evokes happiness … and aggression, etc. Three rooms of equal dimension were identically outfitted with a bar, 12 stools, and four computers on pedestals. Each room was bathed in red, yellow, or blue light during an actual reception. The results, compiled both from surveys and on-site observation, were intriguing. The majority of participants *reported* that while in the red room, they felt thirsty and hungry (supporting the commonly held myth), which was not the primary comment in the yellow room. However, when analyzing the data for food and beverage consumption, people actually consumed twice as much in the yellow room. The Emotional Association Survey seemed to confirm the initial assumption that blue was calming and caused time to lengthen. The blue room was by far the most sedate, with remarkably little body movement and with people lingering much longer than in the other rooms. This blue environment was considered to promote asocial behavior as opposed to being calming.

Opposite:
Nokia Flagship Store, 57th Street, New York, by Eight Inc. Made possible with developments in light, color, and technological sequencing of movement and change at a large architectural scale, this three-story space was designed to have dramatic immersive color changes for an unusual and fresh retail experience. Flat-screen monitors display suggestive marketing messaging. On the upper level, the designers deployed the sounds and humidity of a tropical rainforest to provide a complete and transformative experience.

Inside

Neutra coined the phrase "biological realism" to refer to the facts of human evolution that technological progress could not wipe away. "Beneath all surface artificialities of progress, nature in its most minute manifestations and essential needs can never be discounted, after all. It is responsible for our very existence and has been our formative setting and mold for hundreds of thousands of years."[39]

Neutra's biological realism is important because it recognizes human needs as central to the design process. While his focus was largely on the application of clinical psychology to design, his approach presages many of the ecological developments that first became popular in the field in the late 1960s. In the case of two more recent environmental practices—permaculture and biomimicry—the designer seeks to learn from nature in order to arrive at solutions that are sustainable for both man and the environment.[40]

Designing Habitable Space

We have already established that the territory of interior design is broader than providing health, safety, and welfare—in fact, it cannot be limited simply to indoor spaces. The definition of the *interior* should be expanded to include any space with full or partial enclosure that caters to human needs and promotes well-being. True design for human habitation occurs only when the designer first conceives of space in terms of the experience of occupation. Our understanding of interior design, then, needs to include any three-dimensional envelope, whether it is a temporary spatial installation, a band shell, an "urban room" with the sky for its ceiling, such as Paley Park in midtown Manhattan, in New York (see page 98), or a more conventional project, like an airport, hospital, or multistory office environment.

A designer who approaches space in terms of human habitation has the ability to conceive, organize, plan, and create volumes of varying scales to suit the needs and aspirations of future occupants. The only constant for all spaces is a necessary attention to functional comfort based on the human scaling of its elements. Positioning a coffee table at the perfect arm's distance and height, for example, allows a person to place a glass there without straining. Fundamental details such as air quality, light levels, thermal and acoustical properties, and intuitive organization for optimal order and function need a similar level of consideration.[41] But beyond these functional requirements are the factors that cater to psychological needs, stimulating the mind and senses, and uplifting the human spirit. If a space fails at either of these levels it should no longer be regarded as a work of design.

The successful designer of habitable space has one clear ambition—to improve the human condition—and is never to be driven singularly by ego, image, or style. He or she designs thoughtfully and sensitively so that space can be understood intuitively, with minimal, if any, external intervention. It is almost to be

Chapter Three

expected that graphic way-finding aids for basic navigation, for example, would become superfluous.

Unfortunately, it is not only the design knowledge that is lacking. The tools for design representation are also still locked in the familiar language of architecture–invented some two centuries ago–and must evolve. For the mature practice of interior design, perspective drawings (rendered pictures of the interior), small-scale models (miniaturized 3-D mock-ups), and sometimes even full-scale mock-ups, used as visualization presentation tools are no longer adequate for fully representing the interior experience. This calls for a more appropriate means of communication. Luckily, today there are rapidly developing technologies, such as immersive mock-ups, that can simulate a built environment at full scale. This simulation will inform the designer during his or her decision-making process and the occupant will know what to expect from a fully finished environment.[42]

The design process requires agile, creative minds engaged in a collaborative effort. Carrying an idea through to a physical solution involves the following nine distinct phases:

1. Research to address specific issues
Gathering information about the specific–programmatic and conceptual–challenge at hand using global and local resources.

2. Analysis and deduction of needs
Applying the research according to the demands of the project in order to establish general criteria for creating an optimal environment.

3. Developing a project-specific quantitative and qualitative program
Structuring the project needs based on analysis of the research and client/user aspirations.

4. Conceptualization and planning
Using the devised program (not just the brief as provided by the client/end user or design consumer) to begin to form a creative/ functional holistic design solution. This also includes site/ context consideration and smart layout and planning.

5. Design development
Evolving and advancing the project in terms of its physicality. This includes developing all elements such as systems, lighting, materiality, ambience, detailing, furniture, and accessories.

6. Construction documentation
Translating the design into the language of contractors, craftspeople, and the trade, so that the end product can be implemented. Note: Knowledge of the industry conventions included in engineering and architectural drawings is essential for this phase.

7. Construction observation
Ensuring that contractors and craftspeople are building the
design as it was planned.

8. Occupancy
People inhabit the designed space and it begins to function.

9. Post-occupancy observation and research
Surveying and documenting whether, and how successfully,
human needs have been met.

This process and the understanding of design that is necessary
to complete it are far removed from the narrow art of decorating.
The skill of assembly is only one part of the interior designer's
arsenal for transforming void space into an optimal environment
for human occupation.

The crises presented by global demographics, including population expansion and longevity, force us to imagine a future in
which the habitable environment assumes new forms and new
responsibilities. The urban megastructure, which is depicted
as either an ideal or a dystopian environment, symbolizes the
new metropolis and possibly also aspects of rural life inside a
single, expansive volume; it is now not far from the realm of
possibility and the concept is coming ever closer to being realized.
When the designer of habitable environments is called to take
on the enormous responsibility this will involve, he or she will
need considerable creative talent, disciplinary knowledge, and
design skills. They must be broadly attuned to shifts across technology, culture, and the environment, as well as being sensitive
to needs as individual as the child-rearing demands placed on
a single mother. A designer narrates stories by translating them
spatially. Spaces come to life when the logic behind each of
their constituent parts is evident but the sum of those parts
yields something much bigger, sometimes referred to as *gestalt*.
Design has the greatest impact when the end result improves
the life of not just one person but is beneficial to many, if not
all, people. We have all—even if only rarely—experienced designed spaces that engage with the human spirit and seem to
come to life; similar words are consistently used to describe
them ("calming" or "inviting," for example).

Finally, it is important to reiterate and recognize that developing
the kind of knowledge described above is not only beneficial;
it is also critical, in all fields and disciplines of design. If the
interior constitutes not only indoor space but also the designed
plane upon which all human interactions take place, establishing a scientific basis to supplement the creative pursuit of
interior design will lead to improved encounters between
people. Armed with empirical knowledge of the human condition and clarity of purpose (distinct from that of the architect,
craftsperson, and decorator) the designer of the habitable
environment is poised to make a substantial contribution to
mankind's well-being.

Animation stills from "Subterranean Retail," a student project at Parsons The New School For Design, New York, 2005. This immersive interiors installation presented a view for a changed and more appropriate representation for interiors. The installation utilized a technological backdrop for the showcasing of a well-researched and designed architectural experience with a comprehensive understanding of the interior projects as designed by the students. The change in exhibiting methodology was the end product of a totally changed process surrounding the arrival, determination, and development of the design brief along with the conceptualization and development of each project. Students were required to make a business proposal, determine the best location and site (within a given context), research, design, and develop the project. Final presentations comprised a two-minute animated walk-through of the project, each of which showed the resolved state of volumes, lighting, materials/color, construction methodology, and details. Students used sound as an integral component of their project development. The change in representation methodology resulted in a change in the quality of questioning and exploration processes for the project. End results demonstrated a greater inventiveness and deeper understanding of the comprehensive nature of the shaping of human-occupied environments and their consequences.

Inside

Mohawk Showroom, New York, designed by the Shashi Caan Collective, 2006. The cylindrical reception room uses the metaphor of entry into the innermost section of a roll of woven carpet, one of the products showcased in this environment. The architectural form and the use of materials are evocative of psychological comfort akin to the womb or an inner sanctuary, appropriate in the context of products that form the bases of an architectural materials palette. This, the first impression of the showroom, sets the emotional tone for discovery and experience in the rest of the premises.

Opposite:
View of the public zone and plan of the Mohawk Showroom. Designed to exhibit flooring materials, this multifunctional showroom can be transformed to make individual bays designated for specific brands or opened up for gatherings and events. The spatial openness and designed personality promoted an attitudinal flexibility and camaraderie among the staff, who were often representing competing brands. The use of actual carpet backing material for translucent curtains is both metaphorical and practical, since these help to screen the flood of southern sunlight from the windows—which were intentionally left uncovered to capture optimal light and heat for environmental efficiency. The plan illustrates the "unfurling" of the metaphoric carpet roll, which helps to spatially connect all the brands and organize the space into designated public and private zones. The simplicity of the planning aims to promote clarity of operations, functions, and behavior.

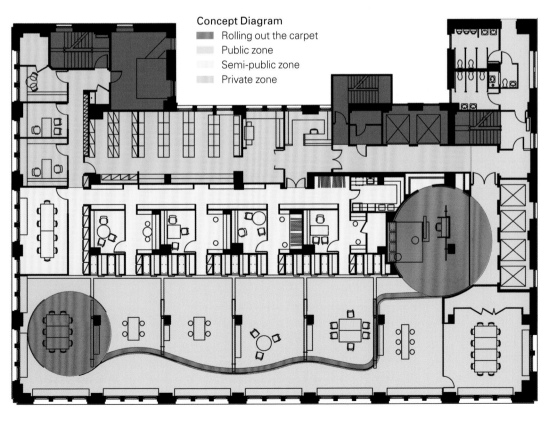

Concept Diagram
- Rolling out the carpet
- Public zone
- Semi-public zone
- Private zone

Chapter Four

Design   119

Not the fruit of experience, but experience itself, is the end. A counted number of pulses only is given to us of a variegated, dramatic life. How may we see in them all that is to be seen in the finest senses? How shall we pass most swiftly from point to point, and be present always at the focus where the greatest number of vital forces unite in their purest energy? To burn always with this hard, gemlike flame, to maintain this ecstasy, is success in life.

Walter Pater
The Renaissance[1]

Evolution of the crushing tool	Periods in time	Extension of human ability to crush/reshape objects manually
Realization of extent of unaided human ability		Stone
Discovery of tool-making process		Basic metalwork
Development of tool-making processes and adaptation of tools in society		Advanced metalwork
		Tool resembles modern hand-held hammer
		Tilt hammer
Refinement of tools due to technological and material evolution		Steam hammer
		Electric press
		Laser technology

The evolution of design, viewed from the perspective of one tool—the hammer. Design for the most fundamental of human needs—for example shelter (including clothing as protective second skins) or as enhanced extensions of human capacity, such as the chair to support the intermediate posture—and tools are often innate and intuitive expressions of human outreach and creativity. Certain modern items, such as the hammer, bear a direct resemblance to their origins and inherently express their original purpose and function. Interestingly, while they may have become refined, designed items that satisfy our most basic needs have not changed dramatically through the ages.

Design is everywhere and all-encompassing; it is a universal language. It originated with man's quest for survival, from which interactions with the environment were born, first to meet basic needs and later to expand upon them. It was pervasive long before we recognized the act of *designing* or gave the process its name. Design has always existed in the form of an intention, a deliberate action, or an intervention into an existing circumstance for the sole purpose of improving the human condition. It is integral to life and is therefore, for every person, a fundamental conscious manifestation of the process of living.

As a result, it runs the gamut from subsistence to aesthetics. This comprehensive view is contrary to the widespread conception that design is primarily concerned with stylish and beautiful solutions to specific problems and desires. The higher cultural awareness of beauty, while vital, remains incomplete without substance and meaning.

In the modern sense, the definition of design has to be expanded. Design, regardless of specialization, shares a core knowledge that is fundamental to all of the fields that make use of the term. Whether applied to buildings, products, or communications, *design* speaks of the creative process by which art, science, and logic are brought together to solve problems and create unique solutions.

All of the objects, environments, and processes that we encounter today, save those of biological origin, have been created by us. However, the ever expanding nature of design has not been matched by a parallel expansion of the knowledge that underpins the various professions anchored in the discipline's utility. Instead, our general understanding has been limited by a rather narrow delineation of the role design plays in creating supportive environments and influencing interaction between people. As such, while the built environment remains of paramount importance, the optimal contributions of design remain wanting. With specific reference to the interior, once we recognize interior space in its broadest sense—to include the psychological and social as well as the physical zones that surround us—we must develop comprehensive knowledge that covers all aspects of the design of interiors, from the expertise necessary to design a rotationally molded and physically supportive chair, for example, to the emotionally uplifting, life-enforcing environments necessary for healthcare.

Interior design's twentieth-century professional identity, which in its foundational underpinnings informs all fields of design—at least in the Western world—evolved out of the mid-nineteenth-century crisis in the decorative and building arts. The realization that mass production had greatly changed the work of the creative individual in shaping an object led to a massive debate about the role of the designer; and the rationalization and industrialization of the manufacturing and building process had a direct impact on the efficiency of design in all its forms. To simplify greatly—and skip over a large amount of history—the side of the debate represented in England by John Ruskin, William Morris, and the Arts and Crafts movement held that signs of handicraft were the defining criteria for a designed object. Though this argument retains some popularity today, another view ultimately prevailed. As Edgar Kauffman wrote, it is the "reforming, eloquent handicrafters" that history remembers, yet those who have ultimately been more influential are the "pioneering designers for industry who welcomed the machine and believed medieval methods could not satisfy the wants nor express the character of their civilization."[2] The idea of the designer, whether industrial, graphic, interior, or from any other discipline, as someone who conceives the form but is not intimately involved in its physical creation has become the accepted philosophy and established the professional role for the contemporary designer.

The acceptance in the interwar years of "designer" as describing a professional was in large part based on the recognition that many of the most widely used objects, from utensils all the way up to heavy machinery, were created by what we would today describe as industrial designers.[3] During that period many designers and members of related organizations promoted design and affordability as signs of cultural and material progress, as vehicles for raising the standard of living for the masses. Design was seen as an instrument of democratization.

At the same time, the invention of "styling" became a factor in the discipline's rise to prominence, especially in industrial design. Function remained the province of the engineer. Stylistic flourishes began to hide the workings that lay just beneath the surface of an object. For example, a Ford Model T was not viewed as the work of a designer, but a streamlined General Motors car was later seen as a product that had been designed.[4] The Ford production process was based on the ability to create identical, mass-produced automobiles that changed little from year to year. Such production efficiencies rendered the cost low enough for the majority of working families to afford a car. The Model T varied little from 1908 to 1927, either technologically or in appearance. As Henry Ford famously said: "Any customer can have a car painted any color that he wants so long as it is black." In contrast, in the 1920s and 1930s General Motors president Alfred P. Sloan and stylist Harley Earl realized that providing new body styles every year would increase enthusiasm, sales, and customer identification with the company's vehicles. On a functional level, GM cars still evolved slowly. With the division between aesthetics and function widespread by the 1930s, style alone became perceived as the principal element of design.

Such stylistic superficiality in the appearance of any type of design subsequently spread to the means by which design was communicated. For instance, in an essay on architectural criticism, James Marston Fitch attacked the role photography had assumed in architectural thought. In his opinion, in assessments of architecture buildings were being judged from photographic images and not through actual experience. He argued that such criticism created a "double isolation," or a "filter through which only visually accessible data are transmitted, introducing a profound visual bias into all esthetic judgments." A similar complaint could just as easily be directed at all design disciplines for delivering surface effects primarily suited to the pages of books and magazines rather than creating objects and places suitable for use and habitation.[5]

It is important to correct the perception that, at its core, any design can be reduced to styling and instead cultivate a widespread awareness that human needs drive what is designed. Aesthetics, while very important, remain secondary to outcomes that go beyond surface appearances and can be understood viscerally. The designer's role is to solve societal problems by creating spatial, sensory, and visual solutions that, while beautiful, are fundamentally concerned with improving a person's quality of life as broadly as possible. Therefore, in addition to reflecting the formal language of design, the solutions have to address our innate desires. Practicing in this way requires the designer to have greater knowledge of his or her specific area of expertise, within the context of a profound understanding of the complexity of human needs.

Toward a New Design

By placing the genesis of design *in the discovery and use of the cave,* the way toward establishing a more comprehensive and inclusive approach to its distinct disciplines can be justified. As already acknowledged, whether graphics, objects, or buildings, the design process has always shared common attributes, which remains the case today. With technological advancement and a broadening of design-related services, the conventional boundaries between the disciplines are forced to dissolve and the fields blur. However, designing an object still requires skills and knowledge – regardless of the object's scale and function – that are distinctly different from those required to design a void.

Recently, the greater acceptance of the design process has manifested a phenomenon called "design thinking." In the past three decades this has migrated from a relatively esoteric subdiscipline of computing to a management service offered by consultants to high-profile clients. The popularity of the concept as both a design methodology and a comprehensive service necessitates closer inspection.

Design thinking as it has been introduced in business-school environments refers to the cultivated ability to integrate rigorous analysis with creative ideas. The careful observation of people, markets, and behaviors is undertaken to envision the kinds of outcome that analytical thinking alone cannot offer.[6] This expanded application allows the generic design process to serve as a method for problem solving (particularly at a strategic level). Design thinking has now taken a place alongside other models of organizational theory and systems analysis. Here, the designer's role lies closer to management consulting than to the more traditional job of design making. Indeed, any physical design work is mostly left to specialists since design-thinking services tend to be offered by non-traditionally trained designers. This development is not surprising, given the increasing popularity of, and desire to use, the marketable label of "design."

Alongside design thinking, another reason why the definition of design has expanded comes from the specialized disciplines themselves, which are attempting to extend the boundaries of their practices. This trend was originally initiated by industrial designers in the interwar years when the services they provided to their long-standing corporate clients evolved from product stylization to include packaging and marketing materials (branding) and, eventually, commercial interiors. A case in point: In the early 1950s, after working with Lever Brothers for many years, Raymond Loewy was retained to design the interiors of the company's new office building on Park Avenue, designed by Skidmore, Owings & Merrill. More recently, graphic designers have expanded their outreach by identifying themselves as communications designers. Today, all the design disciplines claim to have the skill to design anything from a logo to a uniform to architecture. In theory this may be the case, but in practice designers' expert knowledge has been diluted. Though we may interpret such developments as proof of design's omnipresence, they have not provided any clarity about what it is and what designers actually do. If anything, the popularity of design thinking has made design less accessible to the general public.[7]

A number of leading American business schools have introduced curricula geared toward integrating design thinking into corporate operations. One of the most sophisticated documents of design as a management strategy was formulated in 2003 by the Danish Design Center (DDC) in the form of a ladder or hierarchy that is reminiscent of psychologist Abraham H. Maslow's pyramid of needs from 1943.[8] The ladder, based on a survey of business practices conducted by the DDC along with a research firm and a university, reads from the bottom up:

> Step No. 1 Design is an inconspicuous part of, for instance, product development performed by members of staff who are not design professionals. Design solutions are based on the perception of functionality and aesthetics shared by the people involved. The points of view of end-users play very little or no part at all.

> Step No. 2 Design as styling: Design is perceived as a final aesthetic finish of a product. In some cases, professional designers may perform the task, but generally other professions are involved.

> Step No. 3 Design as process: Design is not a finite part of a process but a work method adopted very early in product development. The design solution is adapted to the task and focused on the end-user and requires a multidisciplinary approach, e.g. involving process technicians, material technologists, marketing and organizational people.

> Step No. 4 Design as innovation: The designer collaborates with the owner/management in adopting an innovative approach to all—or substantial parts—of the business foundation. The design process combined with the company vision and future role in the value chain are important elements.[9]

Companies may organize themselves around a design-thinking methodology, but to this day the general public barely understands design's relevance beyond level two of the ladder: styling. This confirms the need for a better understanding of design.

Design

Just as companies see the benefits of design thinking,[10] governmental agencies around the world are identifying design as a vehicle for economic development that can bring about innovation and clean industries: many cities have established design centers for the purpose of marketing everything from buildings to furniture to consumer products. But while the DDC ladder recognizes the importance of design in an economic sense, it fails to recognize qualitative issues and forms—a step that should be added to the ladder.

The focus on design thinking does draw attention to what has always been a critical design skill: the ability to visualize and imagine an end result well before its physical realization. In the words of Rudolf Arnheim: "Creative designing always involves the solution to a problem, the carrying out of a task, and therefore, the image unfolding in the mind always refers to a goal image. The final objective manifests itself at some degree of abstraction."[11] Traditionally, the design process involves a two- or three-dimensional representation (a graphic abstraction) of an actual realized physical outcome. When transferred to design thinking this process, which in its artistic sense involves many investigative sketches, can be applied to generate alternative scenarios that are purely exploratory and anticipate various end results. These "sketches" then serve as the basis for further action. While design in a conceptual context is mostly about process, it has rather different implications in a physical one, where the focus is on the manifestation of the totality (the intended narrative, experiential aspects, and overall form combined). With this framework, the designer must always be aware of how his or her work affects the user's well-being and enhances their capacity and capabilities. Existing design knowledge largely fails to integrate human experience in the creative process. Design aims primarily at visual results and, accordingly, designers are most often taught to develop artistic and formal skills. This may be due to the ethos of design education, which is still defined by its eighteenth- and nineteenth-century Beaux-Arts and early twentieth-century Bauhausian origins. In both instances design education considered artistic and conceptual abstraction, which tended to be removed from the real-world concerns of function.

Design education must not only strengthen fine art and compositional skills but must also expand to include the factors that affect cognition and improve the welfare of people. Rethinking it in this way will lead to a new understanding of the disciplines and their importance in human evolution. There are four criteria that should comprise this expanded body of knowledge:

i. Acknowledging design's complex nature
Design is a complex discipline. Its purpose is to be both artistic and functional and, while not specifically stated earlier, designers must be abreast of the latest social, technological and scientific advances if they are to be responsibly creative. As already stated, design also has an inherent commonality with specialized disciplines (such as interior, industrial, and communications design) in that they share a core process and fundamental skills

Main Reading Room, New York Public Library, New York, Carrere & Hastings Architects, c. 1905. This series of images shows the construction of one of New York's most celebrated public interior spaces. Though the intention of the photography was to document construction progress, as is typical even today, it also can parley the process of thinking and how the designer must envision the completion of a space from an empty shell to its final shape when devoid of object necessities or people. Of course, this does not require that a volume be existent. The good designer will imagine the whole devoid of any given fragment or regardless of the vast difference of the original to its final form. The well-trained designer must be able to envision this completed *gestalt* state from the very beginning of a design.

requirements without the depth of specialized knowledge to allow practitioners to expertly design in one another's domain.

ii. The development of experiential knowledge
An experiential literacy must be added to the visual literacy that has been the traditional focus of design education and practice.

iii. Establishing a protocol for phenomenological investigation
Scientific and rigorous research methods need to be blended with designers' more intuitive explorations to produce a formal structure for the documentation and comparative analysis of behaviors and phenomena.

iv. The identification of qualitative design factors
The final criterion is in many ways the outcome of the first three. Once the means to investigate human behavior and reactions to designed and built environments have been established, a quantification of qualitative factors can be developed to serve as a foundation for all design.[12]

Acknowledging Design's Complex Nature

Design is fraught with an inherent contradiction. It contains elements of art, yet its ultimate purpose is nonartistic. Often described as an applied art, it intends to create usable objects and environments that serve human needs. The designer must have formal skills close to those of an artist, but his or her sensibilities are not primarily directed toward personal commentary. Instead, designers apply their potent artistic sensitivity to ends that are functional.

At its vernacular roots, design (before it was called design) was not conceived as an artistic expression. The forms of the very first tools and rudimentary shelters were driven by how effectively they performed. They were born out of need—functionality was of primary importance and any awareness of how an object looked and felt was probably subconscious. This innate ability to adapt something to perform a particular function helped the human species to survive and furthered the development of mankind.

The word *design* as used in the English language can be traced back as far as two centuries. This does not mean design suddenly came into being when the term was coined; rather, the word was applied to something that had already been created. The meaning of design has changed since the term was first used: over the past century and a half it has undergone a fundamental shift, from describing a specific act of creative planning to encompassing numerous broader concepts. As we have seen, design emerged as a discipline, distinct from the fine arts and earlier craft traditions, during this period. However, the old meanings of the word have not completely disappeared. The "preliminary sketch for a picture or other work of art; the plan of a building or any part of it" is still called a design, and the term also applies to "the artistic idea as executed," that is, the final product.[13]

Chapter Four

The critical semantic shift that occurred when *design* began to be applied to mass-produced objects in the mid-nineteenth century[14] is important because it explains how the word was gradually used to describe technical and functional processes that had few or no artistic connotations. This shift is related to the other rationalized reforms that influenced design in the early twentieth century, notably studies and ideas about efficiency as formulated by Frederick Winslow Taylor in his theory of scientific management (Taylorism), Henry Ford (Fordism), and domestic engineering.[15]

Now also used to refer to a field or practice, the meaning of design is still ambiguous. There is arguably no comprehensive dictionary definition of the word. The most basic definitions, and still the most serviceable, are two 60-year-old classifications in Edgar Kaufmann's *What is Modern Design?* He characterizes design as "conceiving and giving form to objects used in everyday life," while, in his words, "Modern design is the planning and making of objects suited to our way of life, our abilities, and our ideals."[16]

Though Kaufmann specifically mentions objects and seems oriented toward style, his two definitions represent a slight change in meaning, toward design as a practice that involves making physical objects that are suited to the task of shaping lives. While this may seem frustratingly vague, it suggests the twenty-first-century idea that design can refer to all areas of practice. Meanwhile, designers and theorists continue to debate what the practice should be and search for an appropriate definition.

While the definition and discipline of design expanded and was greatly influenced by theories and methods of fabrication and functionality, visual quality and the teaching of visual literacy remained primary concerns. For instance, Rowena Reed Kostellow, who developed an important curriculum as one of the founders of the industrial design department at Pratt Institute,[17] not only focused on the functionality of an object but also brought a high level of rigor to her teaching of visual literacy, with formal and well-structured exercises that helped to cultivate this skill; her teaching was thus germane to, and serves as part of, the foundation of all design disciplines. Kostellow, echoing to some extent Kaufmann's definition, provided some guidance for integrating aesthetics with broader design concerns:

> Not enough time and attention are given to the designer's first responsibility to find and develop the visual solutions for living in our environment. Of course, a product is no good to anyone unless the function is properly worked out. The object should express what it is very directly, but it is possible for a design to express what it is and also be a beautiful object in its own right.[18]

While Kostellow refers to the designer's responsibility—without differentiating the discipline—she does not directly address the role of function in directing form, a given for teaching industrial

Overleaf:
Volumetric studies by students of Rowena Reed Kostellow. The integral first layer of design knowledge is the creation of the skills of visual literacy. One of the most compelling models is Reed's method, as taught for decades at Pratt Institute in New York. Reed had students create repeated three-dimensional exercises, so that they would be able to envision three-dimensional space mentally through the constant manipulation of these forms. As with any other learnt art, practice (in this case of looking, seeing, and assessing) makes for a better inherent literacy and knowledge. The ability to visually compare and contrast is an important component for learning visual literacy.

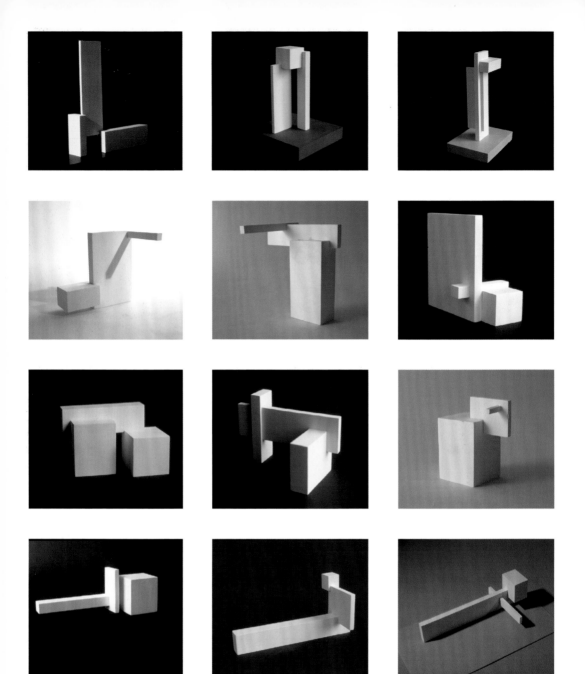

Chapter Four

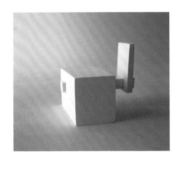 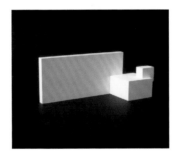 

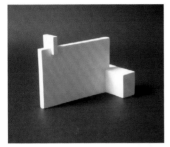  

Design

design, but focuses instead on "visual solutions." However, she did teach students to sketch both objects and spaces, a type of training that provides the designer with the necessary skills for creating compositional, sculptural, or spatial art.[19] While the ability to practice visual conceptualization is critical to three-dimensional thinking, as evidenced in Kostellow's exercises, this skill alone is not enough to create meaningful objects or spaces. However, it gives designers visual literacy, to be applied to the functional and qualitative content that ultimately makes a design usable and which is more difficult to survey and quantify.

John Chris Jones acknowledges the complex nature of design in his 1992 *Design Methods*, which often serves as a basic textbook:

> [D]esigning should not be confused with art, with science, or with mathematics. It is a hybrid activity which depends, for its successful execution, upon a proper blending of all three and is most unlikely to succeed if it is exclusively identified with any one. The main point of difference is that of timing. Both artists and scientists operate on the physical world as it exists in the present (whether it is real or symbolic), while mathematicians operate on abstract relationships that are independent of historical time. Designers, on the other hand, are forever bound to treat as real that which exists only in an imagined future and have to specify ways in which the foreseen thing can be made to exist.[20]

This is the crux of the matter: the task of design is not limited to the creation of a few incidental or stand-alone objects. It is a comprehensive means of shaping the future of the entire built environment and every human interaction that takes place within it.

Design, which is inherently concerned with progress, must maintain step with the technological and scientific influences that shape the world. In an era when the duplication of man itself is scientifically possible, the designer is charged with helping us to understand the impacts of these and other advances, and finding appropriate and imaginative responses that support individuals and society at large.

In 1967 James Marston Fitch, a prominent educator and journalist who wrote about architecture and design, had argued that the designer of the built environment was more similar "to the artist than to the scientist" since, like the former, the designer "aspires to the creation of formal order."[21] The creation of a building or any designed space was, for Fitch, a rigorous and structured exercise that sought "to resolve the contradictions between form and content in such a way as to extract from it a work of high esthetic value."[22] In this model, a building must begin with an artistic goal but can be considered successfully complete only if its function is fully resolved. Fitch elaborated: though design for the built environment must "be susceptible of manipulation for purely formal ends, the content of [the designer's] work is wholly different: social process and live human beings, each with ineluctably non-aesthetic requirements."[23]

The tension between functional and aesthetic considerations has been captured in recent debates in the nascent field of design studies, which is attempting to give design history the same level of comprehensive scholarship that architecture and art history have long had. In 1995, in *Discovering Design*, the philosopher Albert Borgmann complained of a separation between design for artistic and pragmatic ends: "Aesthetic design inevitably is confined to smoothing the interfaces and stylizing the surfaces of technological devices."[24] Or, as the design scholar Richard Buchanan wrote in the same book: "The element of forethought in making is what subsequently came to be known as design although no distinct discipline of design emerged in the ancient world, perhaps because forethought and making were most often combined in the same person, the master builder or craftsman."[25] Both these points of view are pervasive in the ongoing debate about design. However, the reality is that design is simultaneously a general and deeply specialized activity. It is at once practical and esoteric. We must embrace the current popularity of design thinking to extend our understanding of design in both its practical and abstracted aspects, but without losing general skills through concentration on disciplinary expertise or losing disciplinary expertise through concentration on general skills.

In the 1940s, the architect and designer William Lescaze expressed his objections to the whims of fashion dictating the tenets of design rather eloquently when he commented on the relationship between architecture and interior decoration:

> Architecture is *not* a package to be 'styled.' … Architecture is *not* fashion. Hair now up, now down; waist lines now high, now low. Scorn last year's styles, tout the ones of the moment. Interior decoration should not rightfully be a matter of fashion, either, though it has unfortunately become so. As recent eclectic architecture failed to manifest any particular conviction, as it flitted from one 'style' to another, people were led to divorce more and more completely the exterior from the interior. They came to feel that one belonged to architecture, the other to interior decoration.[26]

Though Lescaze decries the distance between architecture and interior decoration, he raises the need for a comprehensive knowledge and expertise in the individual disciplines that come under the general umbrella of design. This is not to say design should be fragmented into subdisciplines; rather, it must be embraced as an elastic art with a scientific and empirical process that can be applied from the macro to the micro scale. This point is central to the principles of this book.

Lescaze, who is speaking from a professional world, not an educational or intellectual perspective, recognizes that where there should be a foundational commonality between disciplines there is a split. His mid-century argument underscores the need

Airport hallways, from top: Chicago O'Hare, Beijing International, and London Heathrow Terminal 5. An appropriate shaping of human behavior requires sharp observation and analysis by the designer. A consideration of one's own actions and reactions is telling and often indicative of common behaviors. Comparing the catalysts for behavioral extremes can be enlightening and provide important knowledge and understanding.

These three images intrinsically describe human behavior. The narrower, lower-ceilinged corridors at Chicago O'Hare (typical of many airports around the world) can foster frustrated passengers, raised tempers, and bad manners. A smaller space with hard materials will become loud and shrill quickly. Poor lighting can add to a sense of confusion and disorientation. The new Beijing airport provides the opposite experience. Here many arriving passengers can move through the wide, tall, brightly lit (augmented with natural light) corridors and still have the ability to see past large groups to where one might need to head. People are generally calmer, composed, and happier as they make their way to immigration and security. London Heathrow Terminal 5 is a hybrid airport terminal, which addresses well the movement and passage of the masses while providing retail activity and open vistas for an optimal experience.

to recognize our primal design needs and integrate them in the current body of knowledge and skill sets.

Holistic designs can be realized only if the designer thinks in terms of both how to work from without (attending to aesthetic elements) and from within (addressing individual functional and experiential needs). As Fitch insightfully says, the occupant of a space is necessarily central to its design: "Whatever formal characteristics a work of architecture may share with other categories of art, there remains this fundamental difference: architecture has no spectators, only participants."[27] Design in any form is meant to be used; therefore its power is exponentially greater when it touches and inspires the soul, a task far more demanding than looking good. Fitch's quote reveals another important point: that the boundaries between creator and audience dissolve into what may be called a shared experience. The successful comprehensive design will be informed equally by the specific proclivities of the user and the designer's mastery of universal human requirements.

The Development of Experiential Knowledge

So how do we get from design as it is practiced today to a discipline that is able to create design in which well-being is intrinsic? In focusing on our habitable environment, for example, we know that before we can produce fully balanced spaces we need to better understand what drives human behavior and the effects interiors have on people. A thorough comprehension of the physical, emotional, and psychological impacts of our built environment has to become a foundational requirement for every designer. Building upon the purely formal skills that design education already provides, the interiors expert must master the ability to experience and interpret the world analytically, and express those observations in built form. Shifting the practice toward a balance between artistic and scientific methods will depend upon a deeper appreciation of the social and cognitive sciences.

Design education has long cultivated hand–eye and mind–eye coordination, as reflected, for example, in the teaching and educational philosophy of Rowena Reed Kostellow. Like so many others, then and now, she emphasized the importance of rigorously repeated exploratory sketches. In her words:

> We introduce the student to an ordered sequence of purely visual experiences by which an artist may develop his [sic] understanding and his recognition of the abstract elements in any design situation. Our goal is the training of a designer so familiar with the principles of abstraction that he automatically thinks of a visual problem in terms of organized relationships and then feels free to study other aspects of the problem or to confer with specialists in related fields. He is a designer who can visually cross boundaries and suggest new forms for new materials and techniques.[28]

Kostellow's method, developed for a particular discipline—industrial design—is similar to what takes place in art education. The industrial designer J. Gordon Lippincott—who created, among other things, the much celebrated Campbell's soup can—wrote in 1945 that industrial design education must combine art, engineering, economics, and the humanities. It may have been thought that the designer of industrial and commercial objects needed a diverse and comprehensive knowledge, but artistic skills remained the baseline requirement, and educational methodology was almost exclusively centered on art. For example, Lippincott continues:

> Art. He *[sic]* must understand and have an appreciation for the basic elements of visual design: color, proportion, form, unity with variety, etc. He must have a cultured background in the arts of past eras, an appreciation of the history of art. He must have creative ideas. He must be able to draw and express these creative ideas on paper and in clay. Of all basic qualities, the industrial designer must have art—without this, he is not a designer.[29]

Lippincott's statement reflects the post-World War II perspective on industrial design education, which had only been formalized in the United States in the 1930s. But despite the emphasis on art, the artistic component of design education was not viewed as being entirely interchangeable with that of fine art education. Unlike fine art, design is not an open-ended artistic pursuit—*l'art pour l'art*—which is one of the reasons why early design schools used the term "applied art" when referring to industrial design. If we were to update Lippincott's description, we would have to add that today's designer needs to have research skills, a strong global awareness of social and cultural issues, and a general knowledge of the latest technological, material, and scientific advances.

To understand the tension between art and function it is important to remember how art and design education evolved. Historically, the two major pedagogical trends in design education have been the art and, to a lesser extent, architectural curricula from the Ecole des Beaux-Arts (which existed in Paris from the late eighteenth century until 1968) and Germany's Bauhaus (1919–1933). While both schools have become almost synonymous with certain stylistic eras of art and architecture, their more salient influence has been educational—and has far outlasted the particular stylistic periods with which they are identified.

As with most design schools, the Beaux-Arts and Bauhaus teaching methods had a strong visual bias, exploring form and detail through two- and three-dimensional exercises.[30] Drawing two-dimensional orthogonal projects of buildings and objects using different graphic media was common to both. Training hand—eye coordination and observation by drawing three-dimensional representations, whether of plaster-cast or life models, was core training. In the case of the Bauhaus its connection to industry led to more three-dimensional explorations and material studies. While its training may have been far closer to applied art than fine art, it was, nonetheless, based on a similar premise.

Despite modern interpretation, the Ecole des Beaux-Arts presumably did not promote the design of buildings in a particular style per se, but—like any art school—sought to influence the student's interaction with the visual environment by using traditional representational methods and media. While fine art methods, such as drawing and painting in watercolor, were used to render schematic images (plan, section, elevation), the outcome of such training was arguably no less effective an analytical tool than later modernist teaching methods. After all, converting three-dimensional objects into two-dimensional drawings (and subsequently visualizing three-dimensional objects from those two-dimensional representations) required a visual literacy, not unlike that called for by the more abstract methods employed by the Bauhaus, which focused on particular effects and visual abstractions that resembled modernist art rather than the figurative representations that had been customary earlier (see illustrations on pages 140 and 141).

The influential American educator A.D.F. Hamlin's 1908 essay "The Influence of the Ecole des Beaux-Arts on our Architectural Education" sums up the strategy in detail:

> This is the function of the "plan type" and the "parti type" of so many of the familiar problems given out. The fundamental importance of the plan is always insisted upon; composition is exalted above detail; the presentation or "rendering" is according to well-developed principles and traditions. The student is made to study and restudy his design in all its aspects, to draw and redraw, constantly revising the design—plan, section and elevation being carried along more or less together through all these revisions.[31]

The Beaux-Arts exercises can be broadly placed into two categories: drawings from three-dimensional objects, whether from life or plaster casts, and drawings of buildings.[32] The most frequent objects of study were plaster casts of classical architectural elements or sculpture.[33] The second category, the repeated drawing of buildings (often in extremely beautiful watercolor renderings that suggested three-dimensional detail) placed emphasis on the ability to create precise renditions using the customary views of plan, section, and elevation (see illustrations on page 138).

Unlike the Ecole des Beaux-Arts, whose name suggests emphasis on the fine arts, the foundation course at the Bauhaus, which symbolized the school's purpose, sought to provide "thorough craft, technical, and formal training for artistically talented individuals with the aim of collaboration in building."[34] Walter Gropius, the founder of the Bauhaus, was at the time reflecting the ideas of the Werkbund, an association of manufacturers and designers who sought to bring beauty to industrial objects.[35] According to the 1925 curriculum, teaching at the school was split between "practical instruction" in materials (wood, metal, color, fabrics, printing) and "form instruction," which was divided into three

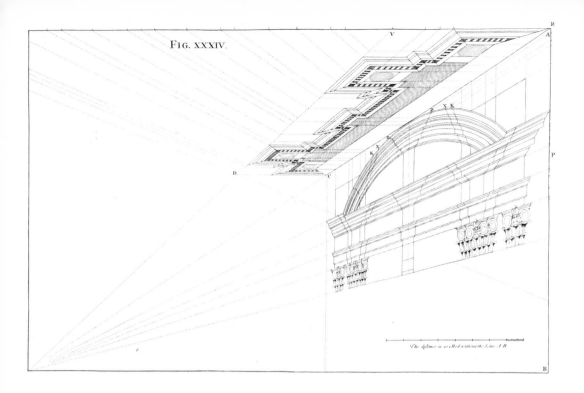

FIG. XXXIV.

The distance is 12 Mod. without the Line A B

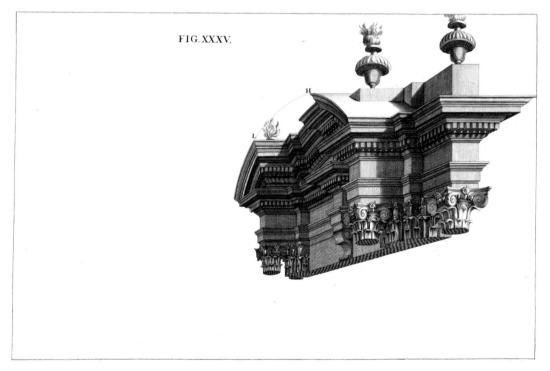

FIG. XXXV.

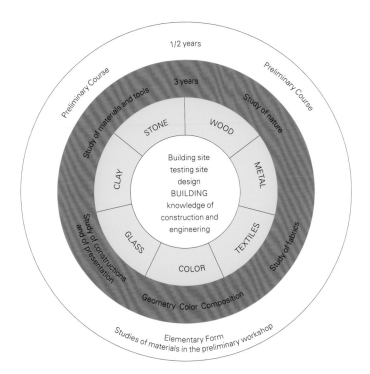

Diagram illustrating the course structure of the Bauhaus, as formulated by Hannes Meyer in 1928 when he assumed the directorship of the school. The design curriculum was founded on creating a basic artistic foundational knowledge, including Josef Albers' material exercise, Wassily Kandinsky's courses on abstract form and color, and Paul Klee's general and planimetric design. During its various incarnations, the Bauhaus teaching methodology sought to instill both knowledge of physical manipulation of materials and the abstract thinking skills to be able to conceive of doing so.

Opposite:
Exercises in perspective as seen in Andrea Pozzo, *Rules and Examples Perspective Proper for Painters and Architects, etc,* London, 1707. These plates, redrawn from an earlier Italian edition of a perspective manual by Baroque painter and architect Andrea Pozzo, showed designers and draftsmen how to create perspective drawings "Wholly free from the Confusion of Occult Lines." Design has always involved the ability to envision the final physical manifestation of design, but these exercises show that the refinement of the skill of mental projection is critical to building the design faculties that can be translated into realization in the physical world.

areas: representation, the illustration of ideas, and the delineation of interpreted visual explorations using drawing or sculptural means; perception, consisting of the "science of materials" and "study of nature"; and design, containing the subjects "study of space" and "study of color."[36] The course taught respect for craft together with abstract formal knowledge, in contrast to the more academically oriented course of study at the Beaux-Arts.

It is important to note that color, taught by artists such as Josef Albers and Johannes Itten, was studied as an integral component of "design" and explored particular visual effects (see illustrations on pages 140 and 141). One such is "simultaneous contrast," the effect of enhanced vibrancy and a non-literal sense of "light"(visually experienced when primary colors that are opposites on the color wheel, like red and green, are juxtaposed to cause their inherent fight for equal attention; see illustrations on page 148 and 149). Even though materials and their characteristics were heavily emphasized, the "practical instruction" at the Bauhaus was intended not to teach a craft but, rather, to impart a common knowledge that would be an integral part of the skills for any design discipline.

The school aimed to reintegrate craft into design teaching. In the eyes of Gropius, the craft tradition of the building trades represented a connection to the final design that had been lost to specialized practices and mechanized fabrication. The name Bauhaus (Building House) was an attempt to give design practice a broader identity, since it avoided the term *Baukunst,* the German word for architecture: a compound of *building (Bau)* and *art (Kunst).* The idea was to treat the building not only as

Design

Josef Albers-inspired color studies. The phenomenological investigation of color—that is, of testing how humans experience color—earlier explored by Johann Wolfgang von Goethe in his 1810 book *Theory of Colors,* and developed in a systematic fashion by Josef Albers and Johannes Itten in the twentieth century—are enlightening and essential for visual literacy. Albers and Itten created visual analogues to highlight the differences of such qualities as depth, weight, mass, and surface appearance—evident in the illustrations below. It looks as if the blue squares and rectangles are all different, when in fact they are identical in size and color. A further conceptual leap—especially from 2-D to 3-D—is needed for the rigorous exploration of this phenomenon from the twentieth to the twenty-first century.

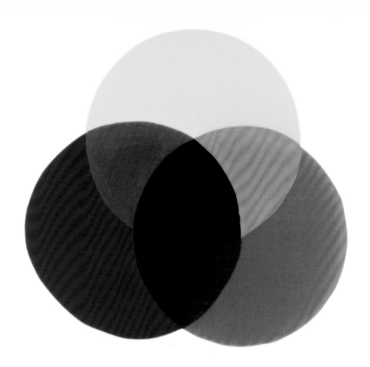

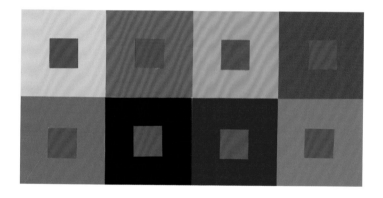

Explorations of phenomenal transparency in the second and third dimensions, studies by Shashi Caan with students over a period of two decades. In these compositional exercises, opaque color is used to create the appearance of translucency, which is then taken into the third dimension for both literal and phenomenological layering and experimentation. Much further experimentation and exploration is needed for both the artful and masterful use of color in the built environment and its impact on human behavior.

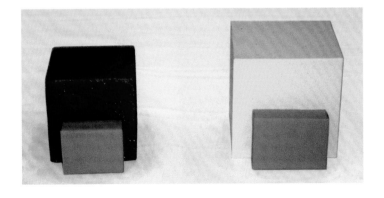

Homage to the Square: Yellow
Climate, Josef Albers, 1962.
Courtesy of the private collection
of Mr. Brent R. Harris. The artwork
was made following Albers' retire-
ment from Yale University Art
School, where he taught color as
an integral component of design,
and before the 1963 publication of
Interaction of Color.

an aesthetic object in its own right but also as an assemblage
of the various crafts into a single new trade. Gropius' 1919
Bauhaus manifesto spoke of the need to restore this lost unity
of the building arts: "The complete building is the ultimate aim
of the visual arts. Their highest function was once the decoration
of buildings."[37]

Gropius, an architect, claimed that designers could successfully
manipulate any subject at any scale, since their skills were interchangeable at any level. In his 1947 essay "Is there a Science
of Design?" he wrote: "The process of designing a great building or a simple chair differs only in degree, not in principle."[38]
Although this sounds feasible in theory, it doesn't hold true for
twenty-first-century practice. Bauhaus teaching integrated
theory and abstract ideas, and also focused on the materials
and methods for manifesting those ideas. Almost a hundred
years later, we are far removed from this way of designing,

and the divide between thinking about design and the hands-on making of it is bigger than it ever was. This has been augmented by the change in the designer's representational tools, which are now primarily technological (and computer aided) with decreased emphasis on traditional hand–eye skills. So while today's designers still have to be able to manipulate scale, subject matter, and function as well as the related materialities, their interaction with tools, and the practicalities of fabricating or building have been completely altered. This is gradually being remedied by reintroducing fabrication in teaching, using sophisticated cutting tools. Whether this restores knowledge of materials and three-dimensional perception, or whether it leads to an even greater abstraction remains to be seen.

Another way to view this is that the Bauhaus education provided the strong beginnings of a core of design knowledge that may be compared with the fundamentals of language–like alphabet, vocabulary, and grammar–which allow us to communicate and thus express our thoughts and ideas. But just as mastery of these fundamentals does not necessarily make us poets or novelists, designers must have basic skills but also need higher levels of expertise, creativity, and specialization to design everything and anything. In other words, every specialist is a medical doctor but not every doctor is a medical specialist.

An important factor to consider is that while most of the design specialties deal with sculpting a physical object, the shaping of mass differs greatly from the shaping of a void or activating a space. In each case, developing the necessary proficiency and talent requires the cultivation of very different sensitivities, which are not often possessed by one person. While designing either mass or void draws on the same design fundamentals and expertise, developed through rigorous exercises, individual talent and passion determine the quality of the end result. This could almost be analogous to the act of cooking: we know that a domestic cook is not always a good chef and a good chef is rarely also a good baker.

Gropius' universal concept of design advocates a core knowledge common to all disciplines. This works as a building block upon which to base specialization. Whatever the design specialty, it is not simply a matter of applying the same principles at varying scales: a chair and a building require different expertise and sensitivities that a single approach defies. Because specialized knowledge is necessary, the design process needs to become ever more collaborative. Sharing the language and visual literacy that are fundamental to design, specialist designers must perform their work together and in concert with a wider sphere of experts.

The educational program of the new Bauhaus in Chicago, which was founded in 1937 and attempted to establish an American version of the school as it had existed in Germany, provides one of the most compelling insights into the debate over how the fundamentals of design and visual literacy should be taught. Laszlo Moholy-Nagy, the director of the school, said the "basic idea" of the instruction was that "everybody is talented–once

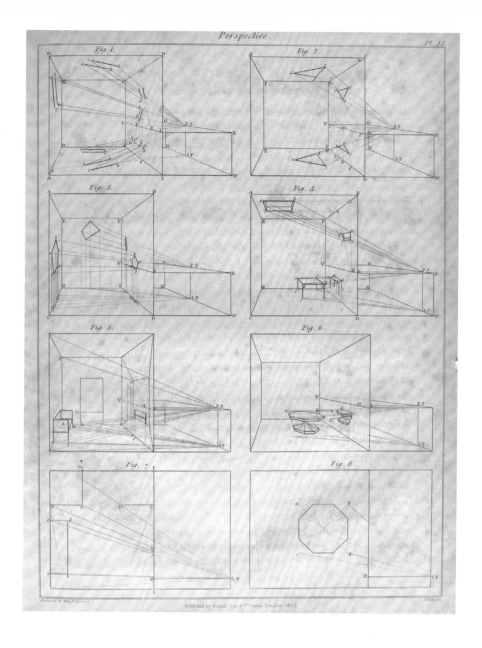

the elementary course has brought all his powers into activity, every student will be able to do creative work."[39] He described the goals of the program in this way:

> Bauhaus education gives first the fundamentals of design, a comprehensive knowledge of all fields connected with the future tasks of a designer. Independent workers with new ideas can only grow in an atmosphere of intellectual and artistic freedom.[40]

Moholy-Nagy's argument, which reinforces the Bauhaus teachings, also suggests that design education merely exposes innate skills that, once uncovered, will benefit society at large:

As members of human society, they must first learn to think in terms of materials and tools and functions. They must learn to see themselves as designers and craftsmen who will make a living by furnishing the community with new useful ideas.

He added:

The Bauhaus-trained architect [sic] will know that only closest collaboration in every aspect guarantees a unified building, co-ordinating appliances, furniture, color scheme and design, a finished product that guarantees welfare and satisfaction.[41]

The approaches of the Ecole des Beaux-Arts and the Bauhaus may have been very different, but they had the same goal: to establish a process for visual research and investigation. However, both schools focused almost exclusively on visual literacy and artistic discovery. Although their methods remain critical to the teaching of design, they did not instill any direct understanding of the human experience of objects or spaces.

While examples of programs that partially integrate the teaching of formal design skills with experiential principles can be found at some design schools, the most compelling model is in a completely different arena, at Reggio Emilia preschools. The Reggio Emilia method was developed in Italy in the aftermath of World War II, and is designed to encourage children to learn through discovery and sensory experience. The approach relies on a wide variety of representational tools – including, but not limited to, words, movement, drawing, painting, building, sculpture, shadow play, collage, dramatic play, and music – to develop a child's thought processes and render them visible through his or her many "natural" languages.

Reggio Emilia schools use the classroom not just as a backdrop for discovery but also as a space that is integral to learning. The program's website reads: "The environment is conceived and lived as an educational interlocutor [to give] structured spaces with stimuli for play, discovery, and research."[42] The classroom is organized as an atelier (subdivided into smaller ateliers) with an emphasis on creating learning experiences that last longer than a single day.

Teachers do not lecture in front of a class but instead guide children by asking questions and responding to queries. Rather than simply providing the answers, they gently guide their pupils to discover them independently, as revealed through their own experiences. During this process, children explore many facets of a problem in a physically secure and intellectually supportive context. There are no wrong answers or choices, as they are part of the process of discovery. The experiences are invariably complex and often deal with an individual child's relationship with the world. This, of course, includes carefully planned and intentioned human encounters as well as the random and unexpected interactions that life and nature provide. By learning

Page of diagrams from Peter and Michael Angelo Nicholson, *The Practical Cabinet-maker, Upholsterer, and Complete Decorator,* London, 1826. Architect and mathematician Peter Nicholson and his oldest son prepared this manual, which included extensive exercises in constructing perspectives. The teaching of three-dimensional visual literacy in design has a long history. Sophisticated exercises, as evident in this engraving, allowed designers to imagine a furnished room in three dimensions.

The Reggio Emilia preschool teaching philosophy is loosely demonstrated in these images, where, while at play, children are made to become aware of everyday and worldly interactions. Children become conscious of shadow and hence light, the passage of time, the movement of the earth and its materiality. Commonplace settings are used as backdrops for heightened awareness of the myriad of interactions between the seemingly ordinary happenstances that contain the mystery and magic of our physical world and experiences.

through play, children experience, rather than regurgitate, information. As a result, they not only have a better understanding of subjects such as communications, sciences, mathematics, and the arts, but they also develop a strong awareness of their ability to solve complex problems through inquiry and adventure. What's more, personal exploration and collaboration seem to unlock the children's inner creative potential.[43]

Reggio Emilia's progressive pedagogy serves to shed light on how design could be taught to include the experiential through a natural process of collaboration–an essential way of working for this century. Unlike the well-structured and established pedagogies of the Ecole des Beaux-Arts or the Bauhaus, the Reggio Emilia methods are as much about the interaction between people and things, including teacher and child, the collaboration between pupils, and growing through experience –the seemingly unstructured, yet intentional, goal for the final outcome.

Rather than quoting the published literature, Reggio Emilia's experiential process is best described as witnessed during a workshop which outside observers were allowed to attend. The methods used to allow children to discover and learn the properties of light are a good example of the schools' instruction.[44] Unlike conventional science teaching, where a lesson on light may not occur until much later in a child's education and would be accompanied by charts and numbers, the Reggio Emilia exercises are structured to first expose children to the phenomenon of light.

Through gentle guidance the pupils, working together, gradually unveiled the properties of the light spectrum, especially its two invisible ends: ultraviolet and infrared light. They observed and manipulated the light source's color, temperature, and shadow, as well as investigating reflection, refraction mirroring, density, and speed. The experiments utilized tubs of water, metals, plastics, wood, photosensitive paints, and physical volumes in which children walked and crawled. The insights garnered were especially creative and clever for pupils under the age of six. At the end of the session, the children, all age five, had firsthand knowledge that prepared them to understand light as a scientific abstraction at a later stage of their education.

Two facts about the Reggio Emilia approach are worth emphasizing. First, the kindergarten holds experiential learning as critical to understanding the world, and the systems it has developed for observational studies are worth thinking about for design pedagogy.[45] Second, while these exercises are intended for children between the ages of 18 months and five years, the experiential knowledge imparted is arguably just as advanced as that gained by the typical first-year design student. The Reggio Emilia method presupposes that this foundation will inform all future learning, experiential or not.

Experiential learning lends itself to a classroom structure different from the traditional design studio[46]—inherited from Beaux-Arts education—which may not be most conducive for a twenty-first-century design education. A more appropriate model may include a research laboratory with formal and informal interactive learning zones where work can be undertaken over a longer time span than is typically allotted to studio instruction, a model that many design schools in name have accepted.[47] Phenomenological studies require a variety of interactive and flexible setups for group engagement, and careful observation and monitoring. In the Reggio Emilia example, for instance, it is not possible to explore light without simultaneously learning about materials, volume, space, proportions, texture, color, etc. By embracing nature's complexity, rather than rote learning and memorizing select information that may some day come together, children master a deeper understanding of the physical world. This would be invaluable for designers of the built environment. An example is that of designers who, when redesigning hospitals, did not rely on institutional or professional statistical data to tell them about the patient's journey through the hospital—a frightening experience for most people. Instead, they checked into

the hospital and experienced the process as one undergone by a typical patient. Selected aspects of what they discovered began to shape and influence the design in a meaningful way.[48]

Establishing a Protocol for Phenomenological Investigations

Experiential learning must not be interpreted as the private pursuit of knowledge by a single person or any one designer: such individual experience does not offer universal lessons. Rather, experiential learning calls for the collective gathering of data that can be employed to design objects and spaces for all people but remains flexible enough to be customized for each individual. Thus far, only disparate studies of visual phenomena have been carried out by artists and designers. Developing the necessary depth of understanding requires a more rigorous investigation of *perception*.

Phenomenology is the "study of structures of consciousness as experienced from the first-person point of view" through an experience "directed toward an object by virtue of its content or meaning (which represents the object) together with appropriate enabling conditions."[49] Two centuries of investigation into the formal effects of color provide one example of the kind of phenomenological research that is further needed in design. From Johann Wolfgang von Goethe to Johannes Itten to Josef Albers to the present, color has been the subject of rigorous

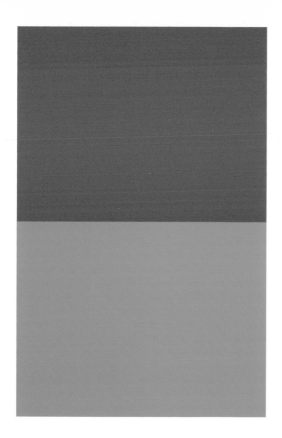

and systematic exploration. Goethe's 1772 essay about the effects of color, "The Experiment as Mediator between Subject and Object," recognizes that because the conditions of an experiment fluctuate, the relationship between the viewer and the object that is being viewed necessarily fluctuates as well.[50] In his 1810 book *Theory of Colors*, Goethe goes on to describe the experience of color: "color is an elementary phenomenon in nature adapted to the sense of vision; a phenomenon which, like all others, exhibits itself by separation and contrast, by conmixture and union, by augmentation and neutralization, by communication and dissolution: under these general terms its nature may be best comprehended."[51] Thus, in his research Goethe attempted to arrive at a general understanding of the varieties of color perception rather than a single overarching explanation.

Physicists Neil Ribe and Friedrich Steinle explain his experiments as follows: "Goethe systematically varied the experimental conditions—the shape, size, color, and orientation of the images viewed; the refracting angle of the prism; and the distance of the prism from the Figure—to determine how they influenced what he saw."[52] This method of exploratory scientific investigation is less favored today, especially in comparison to the physical investigations begun by Newton that have formed the backbone of our understanding of the physics of light considered as a distinct phenomenon from human perception. Goethe's method, however, is no less valid as a means of scientific investigation. Ribe and Steinle have argued its relevance and viability:

[E]xploratory experimentation has been relatively neglected by historians and philosophers of science. Its defining characteristic is the systematic and extensive variation of experimental conditions to discover which of them influence or are necessary to the phenomena under study. … Exploratory experimentation typically comes to the fore in situations in which no well-formed conceptual framework for the phenomena being investigated is yet available; instead, experiments and concepts co-develop, reinforcing or weakening each other in concert.[53]

While Goethe's explanation of the physical properties of color may not be fully defensible today, it does remain valid as a phenomenological analysis of the way color is experienced by human beings. Scientific exploration of perceptual phenomena does not claim to explain underlying operational mechanisms, such as the photons and waves that compose light or the neurons in our brain, and the laws underlying such science are less relevant to design. Stated differently, the exploration of experience itself is as valid a scientific underpinning for design as is the study of physics.

Over the next two centuries Goethe's work stimulated a whole range of new systematic color investigations, ranging from, for example, Schopenhauer's *Vision and Color,* which appeared in 1816, shortly after Goethe's *Theory of Colors,* or the perceptual issues of influences of colors on each other, as in the twentieth-century work of Josef Albers and some of his students.[54]

More recently, numerous artists have created three-dimensional installations that explore human perception in different ways. The viewer is no longer a passive spectator of these artworks, but enters them as an active participant. Artists like James Turrell, Olafur Eliasson, and Richard Serra are celebrated for having tested the boundaries of perception in such participatory installations, and, more than designers, have been able to investigate specific phenomena. They have explored perceptual experiences with a singularity, precision, and rigor that would not be possible in practical environments but are very useful in pointing out how similar exploration might benefit designers and design students, and their work.

Their work is not just about color but also about the sense of enclosure and the experience of space. Serra, for example, often constructs forms from rugged, weathered steel, which elicit a visceral, perhaps atavistic, reaction. Serra's most infamous work is his 1981 *Tilted Arc* sculpture, commissioned specifically for New York City's Federal Plaza in lower Manhattan (see pages 152 and 153). A 12 foot (3.65 meter) high, 1¼ inch (3 centimeter) thick rusted steel wall bisected the public space, forcing pedestrians to consider how they would navigate the plaza in relation to a wall that appeared, from some angles, to be in danger of imminent collapse. This sculptural manipulation was, according to Serra's own description, intended to force those who encountered it to become aware of their perception of the physical surroundings:

Chapter Four

Design

Chapter Four

Richard Serra, *Tilted Arc*, Federal Plaza, New York, erected 1981, removed 1989. Serra's sculpture disconcerted many who experienced it, since it was deliberately designed to appear in danger of immediate collapse. Due to the public's general discomfort and subsequent outcry (which led to extended litigation), the sculpture was removed, and it remains a potent example of how design can powerfully affect human perception.

An experimental installation demonstrating the phenomenon of afterimage as experienced in the built environment. The room in the foreground is physically painted in primary yellow. The room in the background is actually white, but due to the vision's saturation with the yellow, the afterimage of the complementary color purple (produced by the brain as a balancing response) is experienced as a physical reality.

The viewer becomes aware of himself and of his movement through the plaza. As he moves, the sculpture changes. Contraction and expansion of the sculpture result from the viewer's movement. Step by step the perception not only of the sculpture but of the entire environment changes.[55]

Ironically, the immediate controversy over *Tilted Arc,* which resulted in it being dismantled after years of litigation, reflected Serra's success in achieving exactly what he wanted the sculpture to do: make people aware of their movements in a way they would not normally be—painfully aware, as it turned out.[56] Serra's sculpture, the addition of a single wall to a physical environment that intensified people's perception of the space to the point of discomfort, highlights the impact of design decisions and how important it is to fully understand them through appropriate phenomenological investigations.

Turrell's work focuses on the experience of light and color within the natural and built worlds. He often explores interior space by manipulating the element of light, either through total enclosures, where he provides only artificial light, or with "skyspaces," rooms topped by a round or square opening in the ceiling. Both of these kinds of environment serve as elegant examples of how to create a focused experience in three dimensions.[57] His *Tending, (Blue)* installation at the Nasher Sculpture Center, in Dallas, for instance, is effectively a room open to the sky: the walls of the space and their enclosure frame the viewer's perception of the sky, allowing them to experience the changing light and colors as a dynamic painting. In Turrell's own words: "We teach the color wheel, but we really should speak about the light frequencies of each eye, and then the context of vision in which they reach the eye, because that's how we perceive."[58] Removing the roof and limiting our view of the sky through a single opening radically changes our relationship with the most familiar element of shelter. The sky functions as both the roof of the building and a window onto the heavens, evoking the static ceiling paintings of skies from earlier centuries (minus the cherubs).

Eliasson's methods are perhaps more systematic than Serra's or Turrell's and, in some sense, similar to tests that Goethe devised. For example, his *Room for one colour* bathes an otherwise bare space in an intense yellow light. At the far end of the room there is an entry to a smaller room that is lit by natural light (windows run along one side but are not visible from the yellow room) and represents a normal condition. As the yellow light saturates one's vision, the mind strives for balance by producing yellow's complementary hue –purple–which becomes strongly visible in the antechamber. The yellow is literal and real, and the purple merely the phenomenological counterpart –its afterimage. But both hues are clearly experienced side by side. A description in the catalog for a recent Eliasson retrospective provides a succinct account of the effect on the viewer:

> At the same time that we are experiencing the color yellow, we are also neurologically compensating for the

Before (left) and after (right) photos of two lobbies in the corporate office building of a financial services client, Shashi Caan, 1995. Phenomenological investigation into experience can be applied in design terms. The actual physical interventions to the before-and-after states of the two hallways are minimal but result in a massive experiential impact. The top two photos illustrate the dramatic change in the spatial and qualitative perception of the same lobby after it was modified with the use of tonal variation (of the same hue) and sound (through the introduction of marble borders). In the bottom images the design intervention was even smaller. Only the light bulbs were changed from a cool to a warm color light. But as a result, the two lobbies appear to be differently proportioned and with very different experiential qualities.

lack of other colors in the room. As a result, when we look through the space to the next gallery, it seems in the glow of retinal excitement to be bathed in deep purple (yellow's opposite and afterimage)— though the walls are actually white.[59]

This process is predicated on a method similar to Goethe's: "Eliasson thus makes the spectator's visual processing part of the aesthetic equation, opening the space of his work to the generative workings of human vision and in turn interweaving body and room, 'external' events and 'internal' sensations."[60] The project offers a visceral and three-dimensional experience of the afterimage effect commonly studied in color-theory classes, mostly in two-dimensional applications. Just as art renders perception visible, design should pursue phenomenological explorations in order to be able to manipulate both the internal and external sensations that comprise human experience.

Installation by Joseph Hilton McConnico, Hermes Museum, Seoul, South Korea, 2006. This clever and conceptual space is wonderfully balanced with its inspiration of intrigue and call for exploration. A small, narrow space, the room appears to be heightened and widened with the use of mirrored walls and a backlit ceiling. The exhibition displays are evocative of ever extending tree trunks, which are solid from one viewpoint and showcase small display windows from the opposite side. The viewer is invited to move closer to view the treasures exhibited in the enclosures.

Design

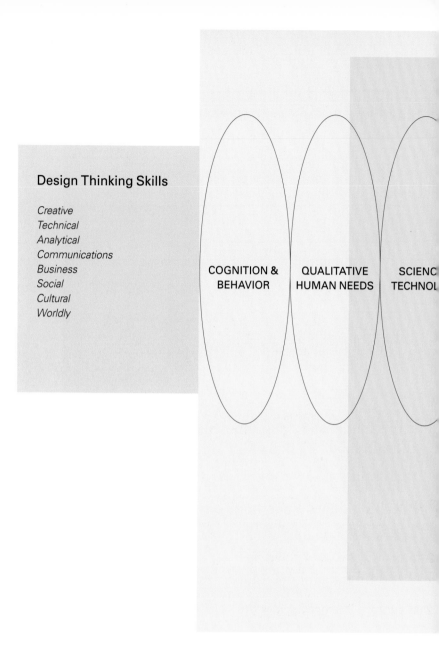

Design Thinking Skills

Creative
Technical
Analytical
Communications
Business
Social
Cultural
Worldly

COGNITION &
BEHAVIOR

QUALITATIVE
HUMAN NEEDS

SCIENC
TECHNOL

With massive advances in technology and shifts in cultural, social, political, and economic conditions, the twenty-first-century designer requires a far more integrated and diversified knowledge than ever before. For a designer who shapes the built environment for people, it is important to have a broad overview of all design-related and general global impacts. But it is also very important to cultivate a depth of expertise which can be put to specialist use.

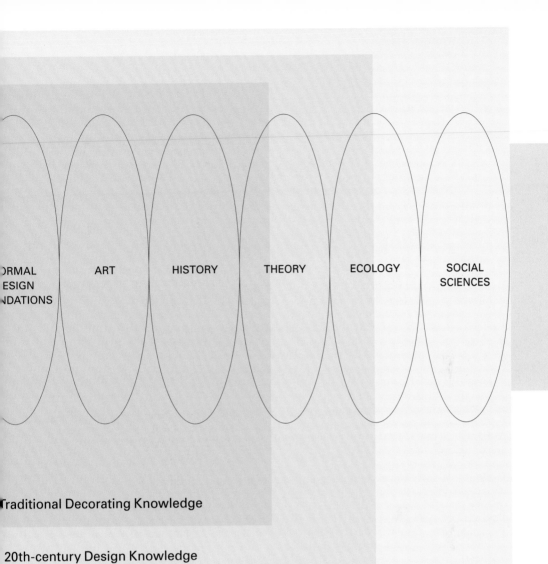

ORMAL
ESIGN
NDATIONS   ART   HISTORY   THEORY   ECOLOGY   SOCIAL SCIENCES

Traditional Decorating Knowledge

20th-century Design Knowledge

21st-century Design Knowledge

The Identification of Qualitative Design Factors

While the previous examples have mostly focused on color in three-dimensional applications, developing a broader body of experiential knowledge of our built environment is essential for the more meaningful and distinct contribution that is the purview of design. The accumulation of this knowledge will help to transition design into an ever-vital discipline that is capable of creating enrichment, and experiences that invite the occupant to be a participant, and not merely a spectator. It is not the purpose of this book to try to capture the entire scope of the new and additional knowledge that is needed, or to provide a summary of already existing research; rather, its objective is to draw attention to the necessity to cultivate fresh and non-typical integrations in conjunction with other disciplines—integrations that need to be developed and explored. Some obvious areas for collaboration are the social and cognitive sciences, liberal and anthropological studies, and the technologies.

The means of creating trust

We no longer face or fear the same threats as our primitive ancestors. While there is still a risk of physical harm by man, beast, or the elements, this is not a primary concern within the developed world. Generally speaking, then, the human search for safety has taken another form: the need to trust. In order to feel secure, people want to know that they are valued members of their community, whether this means being indispensable at work, being an important contributor within a collaborating team, or taking care of family members.

Design must still help to inspire trust in places, objects, and systems. It plays a role in offering people psychological confidence and is the most successful when it enables our full and democratic participation in society. This requires intentionally designing for ease of access and mobility and for all people regardless of gender, age, economic status, nationality, ability, or education. By creating a climate of equality, it allows community members to be better versions of themselves. Though this task doesn't fall entirely within the designer's realm and should not be confused with the much maligned term "social engineering," each individual must be made to feel valuable, important, and be placed in a position to contribute in meaningful ways.[61] Design can play its part by providing an environment that allows for appropriate physical democracy and equality, one that helps foster the necessary culture of transparency and open communication. Allowing trust to develop within our shared settings and surroundings will intrinsically help to satisfy our newfound awareness of global interconnectedness and our inherent desire for collaboration, while mediating our sense of self-preservation.

Comfort and strength

Comfort is another expression of our basic requirement for safety and security. Once a primarily physical need, today it is largely a psychological one and must be satisfied by design.

Left:
Detail of the Hall of Mirrors, Amber Fort, near Jaipur, India, sixteenth to eighteenth centuries. The sophisticated sensory effects that can be achieved in designed interior space are evident in this famous room, which allowed a single lit candle to light the entire room through reflection. The effect creates a shimmering, constantly changing ceiling that transforms the static room into a diaphanous, shifting canopy. Intended for romance and delight, the architectural detailing is mentally stimulating.

Center and bottom:
Beinecke Rare Books and Manuscript Library, Yale University, New Haven, Connecticut, Gordon Bunshaft/Skidmore, Owings & Merrill, 1963. Both an iconic building and interior, the Beinecke library utilizes opacity and transparency for both functionality and evocative qualities. In sunny conditions, the inside of the library appears to glow and conceptually reinforces the promise of deep wisdom waiting to be unlocked within the pages of the books it contains.

Design

Comfort, derived from the Latin verb *confortare* (literally, to give strength) is elusive because it is so all-encompassing, involving all of the senses in varying degrees: the physiological experiences of temperature, humidity, light, sound, and smell contribute to our sense of comfort, as do more intangible psychological factors, such as scale, proportion, hue, texture, and pattern. Comfort is both a physical condition and an ease of being that is rendered palpable. Far from being easily attained, this ease occurs when our self-image is reflected in, and supported by, the environment.

The opposite impulse: the chiaroscuro of life
The world as we experience it is one of fleeting, contrasting sensations: a glint of sun that is too bright for our eyes, followed at once by the calm of a shadow; the sharp, cold wind of fall juxtaposed with the secure warmth of wool against the skin; the loud clamor of traffic before we step into the peace and quiet of an urban church. These contrasts, enhanced by good design, keep us in a necessary and invigorated state of sensory stimulation. The designer must translate the richness of nature's opposites and reintroduce them into the often monotone environments we build for ourselves. We are happiest and most well-balanced when we are mentally stimulated rather than stuck in a monotonous existence, be it visual or intellectual –a reality that the spaces we design should reflect.[62] The well-trained designer, like the artist who exploits light and shadow, can inspire a sense of peace and harmony as well as anticipation and a sense of discovery by manipulating what is public and private, quiet and loud, small and large, opaque and transparent. Just as we need rest and recuperation for greater vitality and energy, we crave the stimulation of contrast in our built world in order to experience the true invigoration of being alive.

The requisites for sensory stimulation: elevation through design
The scientific fact that humans are healthier when their senses are stimulated is rarely fully articulated in design. When consciously crafted for touch, smell, sound, taste, and, of course, sight, designed objects and environments provide a fullness of experience. So far, design knows a great deal about vision, and design education has been built almost exclusively around what is seen: there are many excellent examples of how visual experiences evoke strong visceral responses. However, this knowledge must be augmented with an equal depth of understanding of the other senses.

When doing desk work, it is commonplace to find ourselves looking up to take in the world surrounding us while we contemplate a problem. After focusing intensely on the task at hand, we are temporarily mentally diverted by the reflection of light from a passing vehicle or the rustling of leaves in trees. On returning to the papers on the desk only moments later, our mind has cleared and we can study the problem with renewed energy and greater clarity. Designers need to consider these subtle occurrences and employ the design equivalents of nature's bounty. This is not to suggest that they must literally incorporate nature indoors (although there are successful examples that use running water and trees): a mix of pattern, color, and texture combined with a change in the scale, shape, and size of design elements can create the desired stimulation.

In addition to developing a greater knowledge of the senses, the field of design should undertake the study of movement. Motion, literal or perceived, can be used to achieve mental calmness or activity. While motion producing calm may seem contradictory, consider the psychological effects of gently flowing water. Although light on surface patterns (the rough grain of wood on a door or furniture surface, a printed or woven textile, hammered steel, the layering of brickwork) may not actually move, it seems to flow. Patterns that mesmerize people in the same way as dancing flames or the surface ripples of running water can be identified and intentionally utilized as sensory stimulants. When our focus is captured by movements like these, the deeper mind is left free to concentrate on the task at hand. Movement and motion as design elements are present in any successfully supportive environment.

The shape of experience
The meaning of the word *experience*, which comes from the Latin word *experientia* (to test or try) has expanded to a current usage that encompasses a *totality of cognition; to include all that is perceived, understood, and remembered.* An experience is inherently active. In order to know something we must participate, and the presence and movement of the human body in relationship to the surroundings that frame it is therefore an important design consideration. To craft the desired experience, the designer must be able to choreograph a narrative sequence. "What and how do I feel?," "Does this experience make a difference?," and, if so, "What kind of a difference does it make?" These are some of the questions that need to be asked, and answered, by design and using design language.[63] Such qualitative, sensory knowledge is necessary to inform conceptual and pragmatic design decisions that interweave functional and structural requirements with the designed spatial arrangement, organization, accessibility, visibility, and the intended overall experience. Design has the greatest experiential impact when crafted for the journey, its discovery, and the arrival.

Aside from fulfilling purely functional requirements, designers should be able to arrange a space and its objects in a meaningful composition. Incorporating choices that return intellectual control of the experience to the user encourages more exploration, which in turn allows new and unenvisioned or unanticipated experiences to be created.

Gestalt: creation of the whole
Good design inherently embodies the concept of *gestalt*: a successful integration of constituent parts that produces a single, unified experience. This experience is a matter of perception

"Structures," Shashi Caan Textile Collections, 2004. Pattern, texture, and color combined can weave a rich tapestry of sensory delight. However, when movement is carefully evolved and traced through pattern to become slow enough to activate a sense of discovery yet fast enough to hold mental stimulation, the human brain comprehends and can simultaneously be free to "wonder" and calmly address other issues. These patterns demonstrate the controlled differences of shape and scale for a mental and sensory stimulation.

and happens when all elements—from the biggest gesture to the smallest detail or flourish—fuse into a whole that the individual parts did not foretell. This unification cannot be summed up in purely aesthetic terms. To achieve *gestalt* in design requires connecting the formal and phenomenological (the intentionally embedded) with an unexpected change of meaning. This change of meaning must then be illustrated in all the constituent parts and through the essential qualitative criteria (the choreographed narrative of an intended experience) that are only partially expressed or witnessed in art. The *gestalt* experience, then, fuses all elements of design. It represents a holistic completion of the whole.

The total work of design
The *gestalt* experience is not the final measure for comprehen-

sive design. Unlike artists who continue to conceive, articulate, develop, and construct their singular creative intentions, the complexities of the twenty-first century's highly segmented manufacturing and construction practices prohibit sole authorship in design. Because we increasingly rely on shared intellectual knowledge rather than specialized craft skills, we must cultivate trust and respect between the disciplines. This new approach can best be summarized by the German word *Gesamtkunstwerk,* or the total work of design.[64]

Richard Wagner, with whom the word is often associated, wrote in his 1849 treatise, *The Art-work of the Future,* the "Art-work of the Future is an associate work, and only an associate demand can call it forth."[65] He suggested that the total work of art can be attained only through collaborative effort but allows for a primacy. The comprehensive design envisioned is almost seamless, and although constructed parts are the work of different individuals it presents an experiential totality.

To understand the largely unexplored territory of how we perceive design and our interiors, we need to adopt new principles and protocols that will guide us with criteria for further research. Then, through sensitivity and an informed articulation of purpose, design can meet our innate needs as they are manifested in modern life: the desire for trust, comfort, and dignity. As long as the world around us remains largely beyond our immediate control, we will need design. We needed design in the cave (although we did not know it then) and we need it now—and always will.

Epilogue

Out from Within   167

An epoch not only dreams the one to follow but, in dreaming, precipitates its awakening.

Walter Benjamin
Paris, Capital of the Nineteenth Century[1]

We shape design, and thereafter it shapes us.[2] The world we experience today has a limited resemblance to the natural world that existed before humans transformed it to their advantage. Instead, we are born, live, and die in environments whose every element has been designed by someone unknown to us. The basic tools and places on which we stake our survival have, to a large degree, already been determined by the distant hand of others. The human landscape, always perceived from within the frame of interior space, is an accumulation of premeditated situations and experiences. This can be seen more clearly through the long lens of history, looking to the events of our distant past with which this book began. From this vista, broad patterns emerge, and the evolution of design can be divided into four eras, the last of which belongs to the future: the Intuitive Era, the Craft Era, the Design Era, and what may be best titled the Holistic Era.

The moment we entered the cave, we began to adopt design as the universal language of creative realization; we can call this process the Intuitive Era. As society evolved, specific trades developed with skilled individuals who catered to the material needs of their community; this was the Craft Era. During the Design Era, this outcome-based creative act was adapted for industrialization and became recognized as *design,* separating design and making. Today, however, we recognize a disconnection between this era and the Intuitive Era from which it sprang. We must progress—and rapidly—from the soon to be obsolete Design Era, which is focused on style and detached from human concerns, by once again reconnecting our modern design problems with their earlier origins. Design now calls for big-picture thinking and strategies carried out by highly trained individuals to honor and detail the same basic needs and problems that faced our ancestors. Let's call this future design epoch the Holistic Era.

The Intuitive Era began in prehistoric times, when humans shaped their shelters and tools with no formal concept of design. However, this instinctual creation of objects and environments was an act of design, even if it has not been recognized as such. There was no separation between the designer, the craftsperson, and the end user. Design was practiced by all people collaboratively, in a mutual understanding of the stakes of survival. Mankind depended on design for its progress, but only so much functionality and beauty were possible without specialization.

Thus began the second era of design, the Craft Era, in which individuals acquired discrete areas of knowledge and design skills, resulting in more narrowly defined trades.[3] In these trades, the craftsperson was able to create a far more accomplished and refined product than the users themselves could have made. In the Craft Era, design knowledge was highly codified, even though it was largely transmitted orally. The skills of master craftsmen were imparted through an extended learning period, the apprenticeship, which allowed very complicated design knowledge to be passed down over generations. During this era, users were separated from the creation of a work of design, but the other two parts, form giving and the fabrication of objects, were accomplished by a single individual.

The third era, in which we continue to live today, dates roughly to the early nineteenth century and the beginning of the Industrial Revolution. Mass production, which transferred the making of objects from human hands to machines, coupled with the increased complexity of the built world, forced the separation of design from craft. The result was the complete breakdown of what had long been a unified understanding of human needs and appropriate solutions for them. The designer, the craftsperson, and the user were now entirely separate. This breakdown was recognized very early in the process of industrialization, with design reform movements attempting, for the most part in vain, to reunify design and craft, in ethos if not in practice.[4] As a result of this split, the core issues of survival and well-being, once thought about and acted upon by the same person, have been scattered, threatening to obscure human components of design. The very structures of progress fall apart if design's human center cannot hold.

The physical, philosophical, and psychological separation between designer, maker, and user is the dilemma we face today. Even though we cannot reverse the specialization that has taken place or prevent it happening further, we can restore the human as the focus of all design and, by doing so, provide a new umbrella of knowledge under which to proceed in the future. This will define the era of Holistic Design. The primal motives for design spring from within each of us and cannot be suppressed, even if they have been disregarded.

The way we interact with the world has never before undergone such rapid change. The revolution of the Internet and digital communication has upended many long-standing conditions of human relations, and the world we inhabit is no longer only a physical environment, but also a landscape that we occupy virtually. What was already false—the perception that the physical limits of our body define our personal space—has been clearly exposed as a fiction, since we now live in a global village that extends beyond the tangible boundaries of our neighborhoods and cities.[5]

Marshall McLuhan coined the phrase "global village" in his remarkably prescient 1960s work on the transformative role of information technology and how it collapses the geographic and spatial barriers that separate city from city, region from region, and culture from culture. He made comparisons to the earlier role of urbanization:

> If the work of the city is the remaking or translating of man into a more suitable form than his nomadic ancestors achieved, then might not our current translation of our entire lives into the spiritual form of information seem to make of the entire globe, and of the human family, a single consciousness?[6]

McLuhan suggests that the very nature of human interaction has been so radically altered that our second skin has become permeable and today has, perhaps, even dissolved completely as we move into the digital realm.

These technological upheavals are occurring just as science is beginning to probe more and more the deepest recesses of human understanding. For the first time, humanity is searching for internal answers in the microscopic and even in the abstract. Through advances in cognitive science, we are on the cusp of being able to know the exact bases for thought; meanwhile, we can now unlock the very genetic fabric of life. We understand the internal makeup of the human being as never before.

Yesterday's future may not have come to pass exactly as initially imagined–there are, after all, no regular flights to the moon. But many of the technologies that were fanciful only a short time ago have become commonplace: the videophone, genetic engineering, and robotics, to name only a few. Because designers will be the primary interpreters of how we deal with these new technologies, both as objects and as integrated environments, they must evolve from form givers in ivory towers to become sensitive individuals who are fully cognizant of the changing shape of the world.

While the environments we will inhabit in the future are often imagined with beaming optimism, there is also a darker side that presents us with enormous challenges. There is the unfortunate reality: one-third of the global urban population still lives in slums–that's a staggering 15 percent of the total world population.[7] The explosion of slums is directly tied to increased urbanization, which to a large degree, was precipitated by the Industrial Revolution. The urban population of the world's less developed countries is projected to double by 2050, while both the urban and total populations of the world's most developed countries will have risen only very gradually, due to declining birth rates.[8] Design will thus not only have to accommodate the process of design itself but also cope with an exponential growth, the global impact of population longevity, and the social imbalances of the future, all of which will bring new and diverse challenges and expose new needs.

Driven in part by need and the very makeup of human nature, our built world has increased in size, capability, and sophistication over the course of history. In parallel, our systems of living have become more integrated and interdependent. When we could no longer afford horizontal expansion, our buildings went up vertically. While monuments have existed since ancient times, such as the Egyptian pyramids, most were uninhabited and purpose-built for rituals or commemoration. In contrast, the development of industry and the related nineteenth-century population boom resulted in the earliest skyscrapers, which emerged out of necessity in the land-strapped areas of booming metropolises such as New York, Chicago, and London toward the end of the nineteenth century. Initially their height was hampered by the lack of development of suitable structural

Burj Khalifa, Dubai, the world's tallest building at the time of publication. Designed by Adrian Smith and Skidmore, Owings & Merrill, 2009. At 2,717 feet (828 meters) tall, with 162 floors of mixed-use amenities, the building is home to (among other support functions) a hotel, residences, offices, and retail spaces. High-rises containing an assortment of mixed-use amenities are normal in contemporary urban settings and we know them as stand-alone buildings providing a higher density use of real estate. High-rise towers are predicted to be superseded by megastructures containing a myriad of functions such as farming, housing, universities and office complexes under one roof.

technology, and concerns about fire safety.[9] These early social and technological hurdles were overcome, and today's largest and most sophisticated buildings have evolved from their single-use ancestors into high-density, multifunctional superstructures that compete for the title of the tallest building on earth.

Socialization and community building, fostered by living in villages and neighborhoods, will in the future occur within interior shells that are unprecedented and massive in scale and occupancy. This is already evidenced today in the contemporary shopping mall complex, which has become the modern equivalent of the town square or piazza, providing a meeting place, often for both urban and suburban dwelling.

Given the demographic predictions, it makes sense to examine how hyperdense environments might be constructed. The

1960s vision of megastructures is once again relevant, and such buildings are shown more and more frequently in art galleries and design schools, since they pose a single solution to the problem of housing many people and help to solve a myriad environmental ills. Constant Nieuwenhuys' New Babylon (see photograph on page 174), Cedric Price's Fun Palace, and the work of Buckminster Fuller are among the most famous projects that imagined the end of tectonic architectural monuments and the distinct individual building of today whose exterior appearance to a large degree establishes its architectural presence.[10] They proposed structural solutions, predominantly creating enclosure with the ability for infinite expansion and growth, while providing generic interior space. All necessary infrastructure for the support of people would occur inside, yet there was rarely adequate detailed consideration of the design of the interior. In such megastructures, urban space will consist only of interiors and will increase by millions the fundamental human issues still to be addressed since the earliest shelter.

Shimizu TRY 2004 Mega-City, a still-utopian pyramid mega-structure proposed to house 750,000 people in Tokyo Bay, Japan, is imagined as a gigantic sculpture—it is 12 times higher than the Great Pyramid at Giza—and would not typically be viewed from the outside (see illustrations on page 175). When inhabited, megastructures would for the most part be experienced as a sequence of interiors within interiors, fundamentally altering our experience of the built environment as we know it. Similarly the Ultima Tower concept, by Dr. Eugene Tsui, proposes an enormous vertical enclosure, 2 miles (3.2 kilometers) high by 2 miles (3.2 kilometers) wide (at its base), in the San

The Abasto de Buenos Aires was, from 1893 to 1984, the central whole-sale fruit and vegetable market in the Argentine capital. Since 1999, it has served as a shopping mall. Shopping centers such as these have become modern meeting places around the globe. Often replacing the town square, contemporary shopping malls contain a multitude of amenities, including entertainment, pampering, eating, and shopping. These are the places where the young meet, parents and the elderly socialize, and all provisions and chores can be easily accomplished. Abasto even contains a ferris wheel (located in the arched window at the far end of the image on the right) for the entertainment of young children.

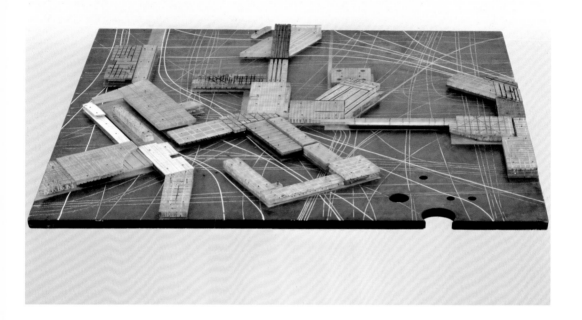

Constant Nieuwenhuys, New Babylon project, 1963. This visionary project was one of the first attempts to articulate and design a gigantic structure that would house whole populations under one roof. Nieuwenhuys proposed gathering under one roof (with the aid of moveable elements) shared residential clusters and nomadic camps of a planetary scale. The structures were conceived as being ever expandable and growing across the landscape, over national boundaries and across the oceans. Though Nieuwenhuys' vision was utopian rather than practical, it nevertheless represents the attempt to imagine a future in which urban space would become entirely interior space, and where occupants' identities would become synonymous with the space that they transported with them.

Francisco Bay area in the United States (see illustration on pages 178 and 179). This trumpet bell-shaped tension structure lifts the natural and usable environment upward in a series of stacked landscapes, with neighborhoods replacing traditional floor plates. It is more of an ecosystem than an architectural habitat, and inside its vast enclosure the designer would be challenged to create a new universe within a man-made world. We might do well to consider such future habitats, which should probably be described more accurately as metastructures—not one large whole, but structures within structures, communities with thousands upon thousands of disparate cultural and individual needs, unified only by a single, shared roof or structural framework and boundary in space. The issue, then, is not about designing at a larger scale; rather, it is about designing smaller and at the human scale, within colossal environments.

So how will we make people comfortable in surroundings and settings where people don't have to contend with the unpredictability of nature? How does an environment that entirely excludes the outside world create design equivalents for the variety of sensory stimulation we need and expect from nature? Can we place a neighborhood under a single roof, as a completely internal entity, and still call it a neighborhood? How do we support someone on an individual level when they are merely

Epilogue

The Shimizu TRY 2004 Mega-City Pyramid is a proposed project for the construction of a massive pyramid over Tokyo Bay. If built, this structure would be more than 6,500 feet (2,000 meters) high–12 times higher than the Great Pyramid at Giza. The pyramid would house some 750,000 people. Accommodating a multitude of community amenities such as hospital/wellness facilities, schools/colleges, entertainment, office, and residential, this structure would contain a unique ecosystem and transportation systems. This self-contained, under one roof, neighborhood would help aid Tokyo's increasing lack of space, by accommodating $\frac{1}{47}$ of greater Tokyo's population. It is so large that it cannot be built with currently available technology or materials, due to their weight. Its design relies on the future availability of super-strong lightweight materials based on carbon nanotubes.

one among thousands in an internal megalopolis? How do we individuals retain a sense of dignity, ownership, and pride in structures where individual and communal spaces are stacked horizontally and vertically? How will we cope with compounded questions of privacy, security, and safety that are well beyond the experience of our current urban environs and densities? Do we lose sight of individual needs altogether when they are subsumed within a single gigantic mass?

Given the likely possibility of megastructures in our future, it is also worth considering how such a scenario shapes our definition of design and the interior, when the contrast between inside and outside as we know it has been completely altered. Where the fulfillment of refuge, exploration, and delight, and considerations of the private and public space are profound aspects of the external world and may be so removed from the

Percentage of Population Living in Urban Areas

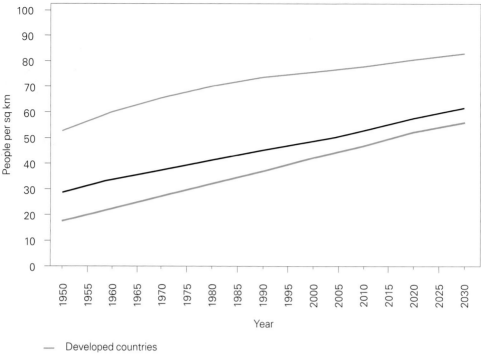

— Developed countries
▬ World
— Developing countries

The number of people living per square kilometer, also known as population density, has increased at an almost constant rate since 1950, as demonstrated in this bar graph. In addition, the percentage of the population living in urban areas has also steadily increased. This rate of increase is similar in both developing and developed nations. This raises questions about healthy support and the provision of resources for large populations within the built environment.

Data source for population density: U.S. Census Bureau, Population Division: http://www.census.gov/ipc/www/.

Data source for percentage of population in urban areas: United Nations, World Population Prospects 2004.

innermost realms of society that it ceases to have any place in the lives of the inhabitants. Under those circumstances, designers would assume the extraordinary responsibility of creating self-contained environments upon which the entire survival of our species depends.

If in the future we have primarily interior space, its role in shaping society and culture expands in significance and importance, as will the role of its designer. This is one hypothesis that can provide impetus for rethinking design fundamentals. The generalist designer must be able to meet the unforeseen demands of tomorrow and, thus, must be better prepared, and better educated and trained with a broader knowledge base including research, experiential experimentation, and an understanding of phenomenology. The specialist designer is required to develop a much deeper knowledge and expertise relevant to his or her chosen expertise (product, industrial, fashion design, etc.). Just as earlier theories emphasized the need for building as a complete experience, looking to the future, life's activities are not to be seen as segregated or compartmentalized, but are to be understood as pervasive networks and systems. This requires an interdisciplinary and interdependent approach that combines both the generic and the specialized. Design education must embrace the interconnectedness of art and science, incorporate social and foundational knowledge and recognize the essential role of collaboration and teamwork.

Epilogue

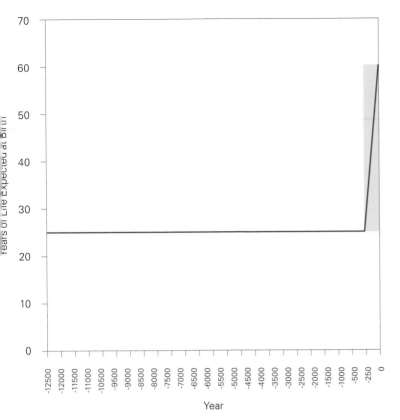

Global Life Expectancy
12,500 years ago–present

The life expectancy of humans was, for many thousands of years, somewhere in the region of 20 to 30 years of age. However, since around 1820 and the age of industrialization, life expectancy around the world has dramatically increased and continues to rise, as demonstrated in the enlarged detail. In 2010 global life expectancy was almost 69 years of age. It is predicted that the world population will triple by the end of the twenty-first century, a development that will necessitate dramatic changes to the way we live.

Data source: Indur M. Goklany, "The Improving State of our World," Washington, DC: Cato Institute, 2007, page 36. Life expectancy is believed to have been 20–30 years prior to 1820. Age 25 is selected as an average.

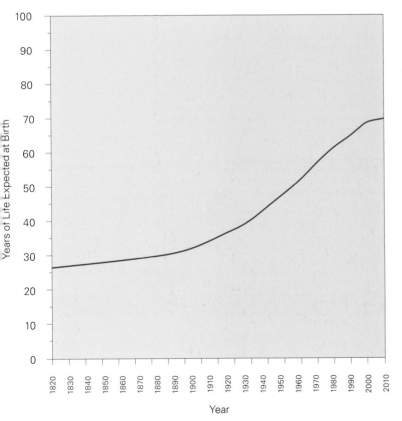

Increase in Life Expectancy
1820–2010

Grey shading indicates area of detail illustrated in the expanded graph above

Incomparable exponential shift in the conceptualization of future megastructures

Feet	Meters
11000	3352
10000	3048
9000	2743
8000	2438
7000	2133
6000	1828
5000	1524
4000	1219
3000	914
2000	609
1000	304

The two-mile-high "Ultima" Tower
Eugene Tsui

Eye-In-The-Sky Tower
Oakland, CA, 2010

| | Feet | | 10600 | | 2600 |
| | Meters | | 3230 | | 792 |

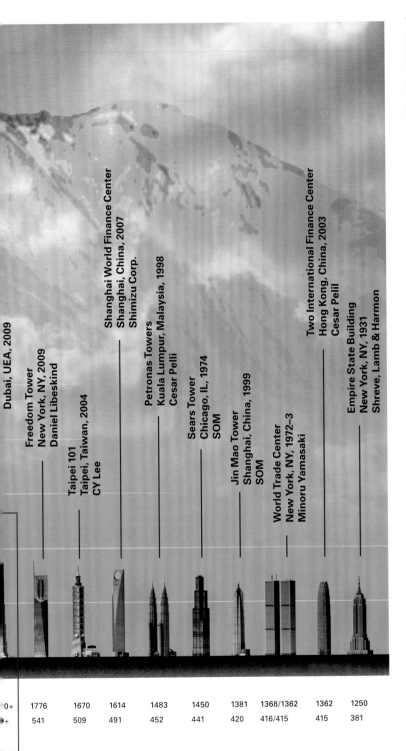

The Ultima Tower, a proposed development of tiered natural environments within a single megastructure, by Dr. Eugene Tsui. Envisioned for the city of San Francisco, this tower will stand more than two miles high (more than three times in height and exponentially greater in width than the Burj Khalifa, which is framed in the illustration). The trumpet-shaped tension structure is arguably the most stable and aerodynamic shape ever conceived for a tall building designed to withstand natural calamities. It is not built in terms of floors but rather in terms of an entire small city, which is landscaped and contains districts with "skies" that are 100 to 150 feet (30 to 50 meters) high. The Tower will contain ecologically balanced conditions and support sustainable lakes, streams, rivers, hills, and ravines with soil and landscape on which residential, office, commercial, retail, and entertainment buildings can be erected. Within built environments such as these we will be able to keep sheep, vacation in resorts, and visit grandmother in her supportive and assisted-living elderly residence complex.

Dubai, UEA, 2009

Freedom Tower
New York, NY, 2009
Daniel Libeskind

Taipei 101
Taipei, Taiwan, 2004
CY Lee

Shanghai World Finance Center
Shanghai, China, 2007
Shimizu Corp.

Petronas Towers
Kuala Lumpur, Malaysia, 1998
Cesar Pelli

Sears Tower
Chicago, IL, 1974
SOM

Jin Mao Tower
Shanghai, China, 1999
SOM

World Trade Center
New York, NY, 1972–3
Minoru Yamasaki

Two International Finance Center
Hong Kong, China, 2003
Cesar Pelil

Empire State Building
New York, NY, 1931
Shreve, Lamb & Harmon

| 0+ | 1776 | 1670 | 1614 | 1483 | 1450 | 1381 | 1368/1362 | 1362 | 1250 |
| + | 541 | 509 | 491 | 452 | 441 | 420 | 416/415 | 415 | 381 |

st building in the world 2010

Foundational design is required to be taught as its own expertise in the context of university-level learning. Research and methodologies of the sciences and humanities will complement, and contribute to, a new fundamental knowledge for design. The concept of abductive logic, which can be seen as the basis for creative reasoning in design, brings a valuable new dimension to the inductive and deductive logic of the sciences.[11] The fine arts and design will find opportunities for higher research and expression (and thus academic legitimization) and art and design's centrality to life will be more fruitfully recognized.[12] The visual literacy and experiential approaches of the fine artist will be utilized by designers at a larger scale, to stimulate and support people within immersive environments. Developing a new and expanded dialogue across wider and sometimes seemingly divergent disciplines will stimulate a greater creativity and provide a fresh and much needed intellectual impetus. This will reposition design in what is called the knowledge economy of the twenty-first century, with its complex disciplinary, spatiotemporal, conceptual, sociopolitical, cultural, and material contexts.

The promise of the century ahead comes with inherent challenges of social and environmental sustainability that are not new to our age. Although the scope of our use and abuse of the earth has greatly expanded, this is largely the result of the technological and industrial revolutions that have so greatly increased standards of living in the developed world.[13] Here, once again, the sensitive designer has a role to play. Responsibility for sustainability should cover not only the preservation of the physical world, but also how we sustain ourselves in concert with the environment. It must become an integral and inherent basis for all design exploration. If design's primary goal is to foster well-being, the question of how we further human survival without irrevocably harming the natural world cannot be ignored.

Design can still learn from earlier humans who left a lighter footprint on the planet. The tenuousness of subsistence before the rise of industrial agriculture illustrates the delicate balance between human survival and ecology. In around 1275, the Anasazi people constructed dwellings in hollowed-out sandstone caves in the cliffs of the American Southwest so that the maximum amount of arable land was available to them in the fertile valleys below. Many of the sites were abandoned in the thirteenth and fourteenth centuries when the ecology of the valleys changed, probably due to water shortages that made survival impossible, even for small bands of humans.[14] On a small scale, the Anasazi appear to have achieved, if only for a matter of decades, the problem of maintaining a balance between population and resources—fundamentally the same problem that we need to resolve on a very large scale. While the elemental stakes of survival are no longer as evident in our modern world, they have not changed. Rather, they have become layered in more sophisticated surroundings; this makes, and has made, survival no less precarious. Supplies of food and water—our most basic necessities—may become inadequate.[15] Scarcity of fresh water is a potential calamity for societies that are concentrated in urban centers or megastructures. While this turn of events is not in the immediate purview of designers, we must be aware of the possibility in order to help shape the delicate equilibrium between the natural environment and modern man. With an increase in population and an ever greater range of age groups concurrent in the work force, a radical change in societal behaviors is to be anticipated (see population and life expectancy diagrams on pages 176 and 177). Achieving this change must be design's primary goal.

Design is both a rational and an intuitive exercise, a composite form of the arts and sciences. It drives human progress and must be palliative at all times, so that we may continue to honor our human roots:

> The world has now become aware of the impasse to which we have been led through an overemphasis on purely rational thought. We have again become conscious of the limits of logic and rationality. We again realize that the principles of form are based on more profound and significant elements than rigid logic. We know that things are not simple, and that, even when we wish to, we are unable to cut ourselves off abruptly from the whole of our past: it continues to live on in us.[16]

Recognizing design as the means by which we survive and as the creative engine of human adaptation, we must now attempt to restore these "more profound" and "significant" elements to the process. Designers must endeavor to capture heightened experiences, generating trust, dignity, respect, and pride in ourselves and our world; to reinvent comfort so that it becomes a platform for successful human interaction; and to provide the responsible foundations of living upon which humanity may continue to progress. Let the initial sense of security and the exhilaration our ancestors felt when they first entered the cave begin anew. By recapturing that earliest sense of discovery, we will design the environments of the future—environments that will bring us delight, pleasure, satisfaction, and the ultimate sense of well-being: the sense of being human.

ENDNOTES

Chapter 1

1 Guy Davenport, "The Geography of the Imagination," title essay in *The Geography of the Imagination* (Boston: David R. Godine Publisher, 1997).

2 J. Walter Fewkes, "The Cave Dwellings of the Old and New Worlds" in *American Anthropologist* 12:3 (1910), 394. Despite its age, Fewkes' account is still one of the most thorough available. Fewkes (1850–1930) was instrumental in the preservation, excavation, and documentation of numerous Native American sites in the southwestern United States and served as director of the Smithsonian Institution's Bureau of American Ethnology. He supervised excavations at Casa Grande, a Hohokam site just outside Phoenix, Arizona, and at Mesa Verde, Colorado.

3 Norbert Schoenauer, *6,000 Years of Housing* (New York/London: W.W. Norton, revised and expanded edition, 2000), 47.

4 Schoenauer, 21.

5 Lawrence Guy Straus, "Caves: A Paleoanthropological Resource" in *World Archaeology* 10:3 (February 1979), 333.

6 Schoenauer, 91. He introduces the idea that many cultures existing today can be studied to give an insight into earlier and preclassical housing patterns. While much evidence exists to the contrary and while he does include Chinese cave dwellings (pages 75–77) he does not include any references to the American Southwest and concludes the chapter somewhat surprisingly, when he writes: "If one applies knowledge acquired from the study of contemporary Stone Age cultures to view prehistoric ones, it is difficult to accept the notion that man was originally a cave dweller. For example, although the Kalahari Desert has many caves suited for shelter, the Bushmen seldom use them for that purpose. [...] Food-gathering nomads are constantly on the move, and the notion of sedentary cave living is inconsistent with this activity. A sedentary lifestyle belongs to a more advanced society."

7 Shelter, n. Definition 1a. OED *The Oxford English Dictionary*, second edition, 1989. OED Online. Oxford University Press.

8 Shelter, n. Definition 2a. OED online.

9 Note the genre of "shelter magazine," a subtle change in nomenclature used to encompass earlier home or ladies' magazines. Wikipedia defines the genre as a "publishing trade term used to indicate a segment of the U.S. magazine market, designating a periodical publication with an editorial focus on interior design, architecture, home furnishings, and often gardening." en.wikipedia.org/wiki/Shelter_magazine

10 Joseph Rykwert's *On Adam's House in Paradise: The Idea of the Primitive Hut in Architectural History* (New York: Museum of Modern Art, 1972) is the definitive work on the long mythology and cultural relevance of the hut—rather than the cave—in architectural history, and its role in shaping our basic expectations of architecture. Rykwert's history, invaluable as a reference on the imagined early history of architecture across a variety of stories and cultures, also asserts the continued relevance of this early history to the present. The book concludes with the following lines, which evoke the same inspiration for perfection that underpins our examinations of origins: "The return to origins is a constant of human development and in this matter architecture conforms to all other human activities. The primitive hut—the home of the first man—is therefore no incidental concern of theorists, no casual ingredient of myth and ritual. [...] The desire for renewal is perennial and inescapable. I believe, therefore, that [the primitive hut] will continue to offer a pattern to anyone concerned with building, a primitive hut situated permanently perhaps beyond the reach of the historian or archeologist, in some place I must call Paradise. And Paradise is a promise as well as a memory." 192.

11 Joseph Gwilt, *The Encyclopedia of Architecture: Historical, Theoretical, and Practical* (originally published London: Longmans, Green, 1867; reprinted New York: Crown Publishers, 1982), 1. It should be noted that this encyclopedia first appeared at a time when architecture was attempting to establish its professional legitimacy, hence the need to cast the historical net as far back in time as possible. Though architecture's professional existence was legally codified in most places through health, safety, and welfare requirements, its giant historical claim to legitimacy was as the art that encompassed and gave birth to all other arts. Gwilt (1784–1863) had published the *Encyclopedia of Architecture* as early as 1842 but the expanded 1867 edition appeared after his death. Coincidentally, he prepared a translation of Vitruvius in 1826.

12 ibid., 1. Gwilt continues: "Such is in various degrees to be found among people of savage and uncivilised habits; and until it is brought into a system founded upon certain laws of proportion, and upon rules based on a refined analysis of what is suitable in the highest degree to the end proposed, it can pretend to no rank of a high class. It is only when a nation has arrived at a certain degree of opulence and luxury that architecture can be said to exist in it."

13 Others are more charitable to the cave as a valid architectural form. For example, the writings of American architect and author Russell Sturgis (1836–1909): *Dictionary of Architecture and Building* offers an relatively even-handed take in his entry on the cave: "CAVE DWELLING. A natural cave occupied by men as a dwelling place. Caves have been so occupied in all ages. In Europe there are caves that were occupied long ago for an extended period; but in America, while numerous natural caves have been inhabited, the duration of the residence within them was comparatively short." However, the definition of architecture offered in this influential volume—as either the "art and the process of building with some elaboration and with skilled labor" or the "modification" of a building "by means which they become interesting as works of fine art"—does not apply to early shelter or found space. *Dictionary of Architecture and Building*, Russell Sturgis, ed. (New York: The Macmillan Company, 1901), 3 vols. References respectively Vol. I, 478, 144.

14 Sir Banister Fletcher, *A History of Architecture on the Comparative Method* (New York: Charles Scribner's Sons, 17th edition, 1967), 1. Intriguingly, this observation is stated more firmly than in the previous editions, which had only stated that architecture "*must have had* a simple origin in the primitive efforts of mankind." (Author's emphasis added.) Indeed, looking farther back to the fourth edition, published in 1901, the opening of the same section reads even more strongly: "The origins of architecture, although lost in the mists of antiquity, must have been connected intimately with the endeavours of man to provide for his physical wants. It has been truly said that protection from the inclemency of the seasons was the mother of architecture." Fletcher (1866–1953) was the son of an eponymously named architect and politician, who was himself an author and practicing architect in London.

15 ibid., 1–2.

16 ibid., 5. Indeed, the point is underlined in the structure of the contents to Fletcher's book. The chapters on primitive architecture are cordoned off in a prologue, separated from his primary history of architecture. The rest of the book is composed of an interpretation of architectural history as a series of succeeding stylistic epochs—an interpretation that echoes the battles over architectural style in the nineteenth and early twentieth centuries.

17 Most famously formulated by Nikolaus Pevsner in his often-cited declaration: "A bicycle shed is a building; Lincoln Cathedral is a piece of architecture." Nikolaus Pevsner, *Outline of European Architecture* (Harmondsworth: Penguin Books, 1942), 3–4. This book became a standard text in many design and architecture schools in the period after World War II in lieu of Fletcher.

18 Fletcher, 5. Histories of the interior also tend to be organized along period lines, often even in more recent publications, for example, Peter Thornton, *Authentic Decor: The Domestic Interior* (London: Weidenfeld and Nicholson, 1984).

19 Marcus Vitruvius Pollio, *De Architectura*, is commonly known in translation as *The Ten Books on Architecture*. Though there may be other ancient references to buildings in older manuscripts, Vitruvius' text appears to be the earliest surviving document devoted exclusively to architecture and building. All references to Vitruvius in the text refer to *Vitruvius: The Ten Books on Architecture* (Cambridge, MA: Harvard University Press, 1914). Translated by Morris Hicky Morgan.

20 *Vitrivius: The Ten Books on Architecture*, 38.

21 Vitruvius describes three types of shelter that primitive men originally constructed: "Some made them of green boughs, others dug caves on mountain sides, and some, in imitation of the nests of swallows and the way they built, made places of refuge out of mud and twigs." ibid., 38.

22 Rykwert makes the point that the "original house" had a "double parentage": "the 'found' volume of the cave and the 'made' volume of the tent or bower in a radically reduced form." One might slightly adapt Rykwert's formulation to posit that the "made" volume of the tent or bower mimicked the found space of the cave; see Rykwert 191–92.

23 Marc-Antoine Laugier, *Essai sur l'architecture* (An Essay on Architecture) 1755 (Los Angeles: Hennessey & Ingalls, 1977), 12. Translated and with an introduction by Wolfgang and Anni Herrmann. The entire account is found on 11–12. Laugier's and Vitruvius' accounts are arguably the two most influential stories of the origin of building in the Western tradition, though Laugier's writings are more far more recent, dating from the Enlightenment. While speculative, the Frenchman's argument carries a conceptual clarity not expected from Vitruvius. Laugier (1713–1769) was a Jesuit priest.

24 ibid., 11.

25 ibid., 11–12.

26 Thomas Hubka, "Just Folks Designing: Vernacular Designers and the Generation of Form" in *Journal of Architectural Education* 32:3 (1979), 27; Bernard Rudofsky, *Architecture Without Architects: A Short Introduction to Non-Pedigreed Architecture* (New York: Doubleday, 1964). For a sequel, see Rudofsky, "Before the Architects" in *Design Quarterly* No. 118–119 (1982), 60–63; here he not only refers back to his earlier book and its acceptance but also discusses "Similarities Between Folk and Modern Design Methods."

27 While cave art generally is perceived to be primarily referring to painting and sculptural activities, it is also extended into other arts, for example, music; see "Stone Age Flutes Are Window Into Early Music," *New York Times* (June 24 , 2008), which describes the existence of musical instruments as far back as 35,000 years ago.

28 See, for instance, Thomas Heyd and John Clegg, *Aesthetics and Rock Art* (Burlington, VT: Ashgate Publishing, 2005).

29 James Marston Fitch and William Bobenhausen, *American Building: The Environmental Forces that Shape It* (New York/ Oxford: Oxford University Press, 1999), 9. This volume reflects ideas that Fitch expressed in similar language in earlier 1948 and 1973 editions of the book. Intriguingly, there is also a direct analogy, in the case of "womb rooms" constructed for premature babies, which are "predicated on the obvious notion that the best place for a premature baby would be the exquisitely complex environment where, in the last three months of gestation, the neural connections in the baby's brain grow exponentially as it curls up in amniotic fluid, listening to the mother's heartbeat, breathing, intestinal gurgling, and pitch of her voice," described by Christine Hauser, "For the Tiniest Babies, The Closest Thing

to a Cocoon," *New York Times* (May 29, 2007). According to the article, there is yet little peer-reviewed evidence for the actual scientific underpinnings of such rooms, even as they have grown in popularity.

30 Frank Alvah Parsons, *The Psychology of Dress* (Garden City, NY: Doubleday, Page & Company, 1921), xxi. Parsons' own idiosyncratic capitalization.

31 Fitch and Bobenhausen, 9.

32 Stanley Abercrombie, *A Philosophy of Interior Design* (Boulder: Westview, 1990), 3. He precedes the remark with: "[W]e know from experience that interiors have a power over us that facades can never have. This is not due to the commonly observed fact that we spend most of our time indoors; it is due instead to the fact that interiors surround us and facades are essentially two dimensional and can only be experienced visually. It is the very reason why interiors treated as a formal space are nothing more than a compilation of facades."

33 *The Columbia World of Quotations* (New York: Columbia University Press, 1996). Accessed online at www.bartleby. com/66/. It is an important argument against building and architecture as a (mostly) visual art, to be seen but not experienced.

34 Rykwert, 140.

35 ibid., 140.

36 Fewkes, 391.

Chapter 2

1 Martin Heidegger, *Poetry, Language, Thought* (New York: Harper Colophon Books, 1917). Translated from the German by Albert Hofstadter.

2 C.G. Jung. *Memories, Dreams, Reflections* (New York: Pantheon Books, c. 1963). Recorded and edited by Aniela Jaffé. Translated from the German by Richard and Clara Winston.

3 For a more recent discussion about design, architecture, and phenomenology see Jorge Otero-Pailos, *Architecture's Historical Turn: Phenomenology and the Rise of the Postmodern* (Minneapolis/London: University of Minnesota Press, 2010).

4 This is not to argue that the external world is not real without human perception, a point of view that some philosophers have espoused, Ralph Waldo Emerson prominent among them. Instead, it is more reflective of the works of recent scientists of cognition who recognize that the brain does not always perceive things as they actually are. The most well known of these scientists over the past 30 years has been Oliver Sacks, who has authored popular works such as *The Man who Mistook His Wife for a Hat* (New York: Summit, 1985) and *Musicophilia: Tales of Music and the Brain* (New York: Knopf, 2007).

5 The second and concluding paragraph of the entry states: "The words interior and exterior can be used for physical and moral uses, and we say that modern architecture is concerned with the distribution, commodity and interior decoration, but it has all but neglected the exterior. It is not sufficient that the exterior must be composed; the interior must be innocent. The Chancellor Bacon titled one of his books on inside the man, from the cave. This title makes one shiver." Denis Diderot and Jean le Rond d'Alembert, eds., *Encyclopédie, ou dictionnaire raisonné des sciences, des arts et des métiers* (Encyclopedia, or a systematic dictionary of the sciences, arts, and crafts) (Paris: 1751–1772), Vol. 8, 829. Translated from the French by Patrick Ciccone; there is no standard published English version for this entry. Available online from the University of Chicago: ARTFL Encyclopédie Projet (Winter 2008 edition), Robert Morrissey (ed.), http://encyclopedie.uchicago.edu/. Diderot's reference to Chancellor Bacon concerns the writings of the Englishman Francis Bacon (1561–1626).

6 "Skin" is now a nearly universal, nonjargony way of referring to the exterior of a building. The term has grown especially popular with the creation of completely smooth building envelopes through advanced curtain wall systems—though such skins are transparent, unlike our own. Similarly, the expression "breathing walls" is commonly used to describe a wall system that has some permeability for air and water vapor, and in more recent times it has been used to contrast characteristics of earlier construction methodologies with airtight building envelopes created today. It could be argued that in our time the word skin referring to buildings has taken on a new meaning as a system of biomorphic enclosures, suggesting a greater ecological awareness of sustainable practices.

7   This argument was made convincingly by Reyner Banham, *The Architecture of the Well-Tempered Environment* (London: The Architectural Press, 1969).

8   Ralph Waldo Emerson, "Works and Days" in *Society and Solitude* reprinted in *The Complete Works of Ralph Waldo Emerson*, Vol. VII (Cambridge, MA: Riverside Press, 1904). The essay opens: "Our nineteenth century is the age of tools. They grow out of our structure. 'Man is the meter [*sic*] of all things,' said Aristotle; 'the hand is the instrument of instruments, and the mind is the form of forms.'"

9   Marshall McLuhan, *Understanding Media: Extensions of Man* (New York: New American Library, 1964).

10 Edward T. Hall, *The Hidden Dimension* (New York: Anchor Books, second edition, 1969), 4.

11 Adrian Forty, *Words and Buildings: A Vocabulary of Modern Architecture* (New York: Thames and Hudson, 2000), 257. Forty writes: "As a term, 'space' simply did not exist in the architectural vocabulary until the 1890s. Its adoption is intimately connected with the development of modernism, and whatever it means, therefore, belongs to the specific historical circumstances of modernism, just as is the case with 'space's' partners, 'form' and 'design.'" He adds: "Much of the ambiguity of the term 'space' in modern architectural use comes from a willingness to confuse it with a general philosophical category of 'space.' To put this issue slightly differently, as well as being a physical property of dimension or extent, 'space' is also a property of the mind, part of the apparatus through which we perceive the world. It is thus simultaneously a thing within the world, that architects can manipulate, and a mental construct through which the mind knows the world, and thus entirely outside the realm of architectural practice (although it may affect the way in which the results are perceived). A willingness to connive in a confusion between these two unrelated properties seems to be an essential qualification for talking about architectural space. […] The development of space as an architectural category took place in Germany, and it is to German writers that one must turn for its origins, and purposes. This immediately presents a problem for the English-language discussion of the subject, for the German word for space, *Raum*, at once signifies both a material enclosure, a 'room,' and a philosophical concept."

12 Qtd. in Forty, 261. Paul Zucker offers an analysis relevant in this context: the rhetoric of space is at least partially adaptable to theories of human perception, since architecture, like the mind, was organized in the same manner, thus mimicked human perception of inside space: "Thus the idea that one must build from inside to outside, from interior to the volume-body (*von innen nach aussen*) actually became an architectural slogan. […] space was the decisive factor and its purposeful (functional) organization only a natural symptom of all human activity." Paul Zucker, "The Paradox of Architectural Theories at the Beginning of the Modern Movement," *The Journal of the Society of Architectural Historians* 10:3 (October 1951), 9. The Wölfflin work cited in the article is by the Swiss art historian Heinrich Wölfflin, *Prolegomena zu einer Psychologie der Architektur* (1886).

13 Dom H. Van der Laan, *Architectonic Space: Fifteen Lessons on the Disposition of the Human Habitat* (Leiden: E.J. Brill, 1983). Translated by Richard Padovan. Van der Laan was a Dutch Benedictine monk and also an architect.

14 ibid., 11. The outside world is not actually a limitless plain set against a vast sky. The natural world contains as many types of space as does the architectural world. Yet reducing the natural environment to this paradigm, as Van Der Laan does, is useful in creating an intriguing theory of what makes the insides of buildings and our relation to them unique. There is another more mystical formulation worth citing, by Oswald Spengler: "All Classical building begins from the outside, all Western from the inside … There is one and only one soul, the Faustian, that craves for a style which drives through walls into the limitless universe of space, and makes both exterior and the interior of the building complementary images of one and the same world-feeling." Oswald Spengler, *The Decline of the West* (New York: Knopf, 1926), qtd. in Peter Collins, *Changing Ideals in Modern Architecture 1750–1950* (London: Faber and Faber, 1965), 292.

15 Van der Laan sees both an emptiness and fullness in space: "This emptiness is as it were subtracted by the space-apart of the walls from the homogenous fullness of natural space, and suspended within it, like a bubble in water.") ibid., 12. He puts into words for our physical environments the sentiments expressed in psychological terms in William Blake's famous lines from *The Marriage of Heaven and Hell*: "If the *doors of perception were cleansed every thing would* appear to man as it is: *Infinite*."

16 He continues: "Precisely because the two space-images are diametrically opposed, they are able to complement each other exactly, like the form of a seal and its imprint in wax. The overall function of the house, the reconciliation of man and nature, is in essence nothing else but this fitting-together of the two space-images: that of the separated space on the one hand, and that of the experienced space on the other." ibid., 12–13

17 From inside to outside is the English translation of the German *von innen nach aussen*, which is a phrase that is used throughout the beginning of the twentieth century and mostly refers to the visual relationship between the inside and outside and thus the transparency of the wall. For a more detailed discussion, see Ulrich Müller, *Raum, Bewegung und Zeit* (Berlin: Akademie Verlag, 2004), 20–21.

18 As summarized in Charles J. Holahan, *Environmental Psychology* (New York: Random House, 1982), 275.

19 Hall, xi.

20 Holahan, 275. Author's emphasis added.

21 French psychiatrist Eugène Minkowski's work offers an intriguing corollary to this concept: "We obviously know the movement of bodies, but we also experience situations where we delineate a path through space without this act or path having something of a material quality to it; in such cases, 'to travel through space' does not have subject properly speaking, it is through its dynamism ['*an a priori dynamism*'] that this space is created." Minkowski, *Vers une Cosmologie: fragments philosophiques* (Paris: Aubier-Montaigne, new edition, 1967), 70, qtd. in Richard Etlin, "Aesthetics and the Spatial Sense of Self," *The Journal of Aesthetics and Art Criticism* 56:1 (Winter 1998), 4.

22 As qtd. in Stanley Abercrombie, *A Philosophy of Interior Design* (Boulder: Westview, 1990), 77. This is a slight paraphrase of Rudofsky's words as they appear in *Behind the Picture Window* (New York/London: Oxford University Press, 1955).

23 The more detailed analysis of the social and functional history is found in Galen Cranz, *The Chair: Rethinking Culture, Body and Design* (New York/London: Norton, 1998).

24 There were interesting attempts to classify the sitting positions of the world's population in the immediate post-World War II era, most notably by Gordon W. Hewes in "World Distribution of Certain Postural Habits," *American Anthropologist* 57:2 (April 1955) 231–44.

25 *Immeuble* in French means all that cannot be moved, from which the French equivalent of real estate, *immobilier*, is derived. The opposite of *immeuble* in French is *meuble* which comprises furniture and all movable objects, including art, within the household. For a good nineteenth-century rendering of these terms and associated French phrases into English, see John Charles Tarver, *The Royal Phraseological English–French, French–English Dictionary* (London: Dulau & Co, 1879). See *immeuble, immobile, immobilier*, 437, and *meuble, meubler*, 520.

26 Hall stated that a fundamental aim of writing *The Hidden Dimension* was "to communicate to architects that the spatial experience is not just visual, but multisensory." Hall, xi.

27 Qtd. in Clare Cooper "The House as Symbol of the Self" in *Environmental Psychology, 2nd Edition: People and Their Physical Settings*, Harold M. Proshansky, William H. Ittleson, Leanne G. Rivlin, eds. (New York: Holt, Rinehart and Winston, 1976), 435–36.

28 Socrates quotes Protagoras as the origin of the idea in the c. 360 BCE dialog *Theaetetus*. For a standard English version, see Plato, *Theaetetus*. Translated by Benjamin Jowett, c. 1892, available online at classics.mit.edu/Plato/theatu.html.

29 The anthropic principle in science is defined as "the principle that theories of the universe are constrained by the need to allow for man's existence in it as an observer." From "Anthropic, a." Definition 1a. *OED The Oxford English Dictionary*. Second edition, 1989. OED Online. Oxford University Press.

30 Though the passage in Vitruvius and Leonardo's rendering of it have been celebrated for centuries, it was Kenneth Clark's *The Nude: A Study of Ideal Art* (New York: Pantheon Books, 1956) which brought wide attention to Leonardo's rendering in the twentieth century, and where the "Vitruvian Man" as a expression in English was popularized.

31 *Vitruvius: The Ten Books on Architecture* (Cambridge, MA: Harvard University Press, 1914), 72. Translated by Morris Hicky Morgan. A different translation of the same quote, along with an interesting analysis, can be found in Joseph Rykwert, *The Dancing Column: On Order in Architecture* (Cambridge, MA: MIT Press, 1998), 97.

32 The complete list provided by Vitruvius follows: "For the human body is so designed by nature that the face, from the chin to the top of the forehead and the lowest roots of the hair, is a tenth part of the whole height; the open hand from the wrist to the tip of the middle finger is just the same; the head from the chin to the crown is an eighth, and with the neck and shoulder from the top of the breast to the lowest roots of the hair is a sixth; from the middle of the breast to the summit of the crown is a fourth. If we take the height of the face itself, the distance from the bottom of the chin to the under side of the nostrils is one third of it; the nose from the under side of the nostrils to a line between the eyebrows is the same; from there to the lowest roots of the hair is also a third, comprising the forehead. The length of the foot is one sixth of the height of the body; of the forearm, one fourth; and the breadth of the breast is also one fourth. The other members, too, have their own symmetrical proportions, and it was by employing them that the famous painters and sculptors of antiquity attained to great and endless renown." *Vitruvius: The Ten Books on Architecture*, 72. These proportions can easily be measured against one's own body, and are often off by significant margins. Performing such an experiment on oneself or on a host of other bodies was not the aim of this system, for it is not a human-centered system but rather an expression of universe.

33 Rykwert, *The Dancing Column*, 99.

34 *Vitruvius: The Ten Books on Architecture, 72–73*

35 Qtd. in Anthony Blunt, *Artistic Theory in Italy 1450–1600* (London/New York: Oxford University Press, 1940; 1968 reissue, unrevised), 18.

36 Rudolf Wittkower, *Architectural Principles in the Age of Humanism* (London: Alec Tiranti, third edition, 1962), 14, 15.

Leonardo da Vinci, who criticized Alberti's methodology and recommended the observation of human difference as the basis for understanding proportion, claimed that otherwise these figures on a "single model" threatened to "all look like brothers." However, even though da Vinci recommended the study of human variation, he still did so to indicate divine proportions. Leonardo's associate, mathematician Luca Pacioli, wrote in the 1509 book *Divina proportione* that man must be considered first when talking about architecture, "because from the human body derive all measures and their denominations and in it is to be found all and every ratio and proportion by which God reveals the innermost secrets of nature." Leonardo da Vinci and Pacioli, both quoted in Blunt, 32.

37 Edmund Burke, *On the Sublime and Beautiful*. Vol. XXIV, Part 2. *The Harvard Classics* (New York: P.F. Collier & Son, 1909–1914). Available online at www.bartleby.com/24/2/.

38 ibid.

39 That phrase is taken from the first English edition of Le Corbusier's 1948 book devoted to the system, *The Modulor: A Harmonious Measure to the Human Scale Universally Applicable to Architecture and Mechanics* (London: Faber and Faber, 1956). The system uses a Fibonacci sequence (in fact, miscalculated) to render the human body in numerical proportion, based on a height from feet to navel of 3½ feet (1.08 meters), later revised to 3⅝ feet (1.13 meters). In the 1955 sequel, published in English in 1958 as *Modulor 2: Let the User Speak Next* (London, Faber and Faber, 1958), Corbusier printed letters of testimony from architects and designers worldwide who claimed to have successfully applied the universal principles of the Modulor to their own designs. The figure of the Modulor man can, of course, be seen in 1:1 scale in Corbusier's later buildings, most notably the Unité d'Habitation in Marseilles.

40 The book was first published in German as Ernst Neufert, *Bauentwurfslehre, Grundlagen, Normen und Vorschriften über Anlage, Bau, Gestaltung, Raumbedarf, Raumbeziehungen: Masse für Gebäude, Räume, Einrichtungen und Geräte mit dem Menschen als Mass und Ziel: Handbuch für den Baufachmann, Bauherrn, Lehrenden und Lernenden* (Berlin: Bauwelt, 1936) and has subsequently been translated into 18 languages. Neufert (1900–1986) served as Walter Gropius' assistant in the 1920s at the Bauhaus and went on to establish his own firm after World War II. During the war he was instrumental in standardizing German industry under Albert Speer.

41 Henry Dreyfuss, *The Measure of Man: Human Factors in Design* (New York: Whitney Library of Design, 1960). Later editions have been retitled *The Measure of Man and Woman: Human Factors in Design*.

42 Dreyfuss recognized there were separate classifications of needs—physical and often psychological—for different groups. Probably the most significant such group is the physically disabled, for whom there are numerous design requirements in local building codes. Similar design criteria for other needs groups will inevitably develop over time.

43 Grant Hildebrand, *Origins of Architectural Pleasure* (Berkeley: University of California Press, 1999)

44 ibid., 9. The book is a synthesis of a large amount of primary research from both within and beyond the province of design. By taking this approach Hildebrand extends the natural selection process to include, among other things, the reward of those who make good homes: "If we are to have a good chance of survival success, we must be highly competent at four basic activities: ingestion, procreation, the securing of appropriate habitation, and exploration."

45 ibid., 22. The terms are not Hildebrand's invention but represent the synthesis of several decades of research on human environmental desires.

46 ibid., 22, quoting D.M. Woodcock, "A Functionalist Approach to Environmental Preference (PhD diss., University of Michigan,

1982). Hildebrand writes: "D.M. Woodcock has introduced a distinction between the characteristics of a setting we actually occupy and those of a setting we could occupy. He calls the conditions of an immediate setting primary refuge and primary prospect; conditions of a setting seen at a distance he terms secondary refuge and secondary prospect." Hildebrand's terms are directly inspired by Jay Appleton's concept of refuge in *The Experience of Landscape* (Chichester, UK: John Wiley & Sons, 1975). There is not a completely secure scientific underpinning for these suppositions—they are largely drawn from the realm of philosophy rather than empirical data.

47 Jane Jacobs, *The Death and Life of Great American Cities* (New York: Random House, 1961), 35.

48 Oscar Newman, *Defensible Space: Crime Prevention through Urban Design* (New York: Macmillan, 1972). The book was released in the United Kingdom under the somewhat more colorful title *Defensible Space: People and Design in the Violent City* (London: Architectural Press, 1973) and was subsequently adapted for design guidelines by the US National Institute of Law Enforcement and Criminal Justice as *Design Guidelines for Creating Defensible Space* (Washington, DC: National Institute of Law Enforcement and Criminal Justice, Law Enforcement Assistance Administration, US Department of Justice: US Government Printing Office, 1976).

49 With Jacobs, one can cite the attempts to replicate—successfully or unsuccessfully—the urban elements of New York City's West Village and Boston's North End in the design guidelines of the Congress of the New Urbanism, arguably the most influential United States urban design movement of the past three decades.

50 comfort, n. *OED The Oxford English Dictionary*. Second edition, 1989. OED Online. Oxford University Press.

51 Reyner Banham, *The Architecture of the Well-Tempered Environment* (London: The Architectural Press, 1969), 8. A wide variety of authors have addressed the concept of comfort; the two most compelling, apart from Banham, are James Marston Fitch, in various editions of *American Building* (see individual notes for bibliographic information), and Witold Rybcyznski in *Home: A Short History of an Idea* (New York: Viking, 1986).

52 Unlike many other airports, New York's JFK was designed as a collection of separate terminals for the individual airlines. Many of these early terminals have since been replaced with newer facilities reflecting the changes in volume and expectations for contemporary airline travel.

53 Ralph Waldo Emerson, "Experience" in *Essays: Second Series* (Boston and New York: Houghton Mifflin, 1889), 56.

54 Marc-Antoine Laugier, *Essai sur l'architecture* (An Essay on Architecture). Translated and with an introduction by Wolfgang and Anni Herrmann, (Los Angeles: Hennessey & Ingalls, 1977), 81.

55 The French term was *convenance*, which does not translate literally as convenience. The term was used in association with *distrubution* from Vitruvius' *distribution*, meaning "the suitable arrangement of all the parts of a building." See especially, J.L. de Cordemoy, *Nouveau traité de toute l'architecture* (Paris: J.B. Coignard, second edition, 1714; Farnborough: Gregg, 1966), 236.

56 Rybcyznski, 31–32.

57 Sigfried Giedion, *Mechanization Takes Command* (New York: Oxford University Press, 1948), 260. A great deal has been written since about the cultural and historical dimensions of the concept of comfort. See, for instance, J.E. Crowley, *The Invention of Comfort* (Baltimore: The Johns Hopkins University Press, 2001) and K.C. Grier, *Culture and Comfort: Parlor Making and Middle-Class Identity, 1850–1930* (Washington, DC: Smithsonian Institution Press, 1997).

58 Indeed, one might remark upon the odd situation where many Americans, during the summer, wear significantly fewer layers of clothing inside air-conditioned environments than they did when environments were not air-conditioned—a disconnect between the formal and the functional roles.

59 It is hard to imagine a more 180-degree view from contemporary thinking, which seeks to restore natural lighting and natural ventilation to the office. Herman Worsham, "The Milam Building" in *Heating, Piping and Air Conditioning* 1 (July 1929), 182, qtd. in Cecil D. Elliot, *The Development of Materials and Systems for Buildings* (Cambridge, MA/London: MIT Press, 1992), 320.

60 Privacy, n. OED online. The full etymology is listed as being "from the Anglo-Norman *priveté, privetee, priveitie, priveité, privité, privitee* and Old French *privé*, Old French, Middle French *privé* secrecy, secret (*c*1170 in Old French), familiarity, intimacy (*c*1170 in Anglo-Norman) < *privé* PRIVY *adj.* + *-té* -TY *suffix*1; compare -ITY *suffix*. Compare post-classical Latin *privitas* intimacy, familiarity (9th cent.), private capacity (1333 in a British source)." In more current discussions the term privacy seems to be applied more to rights with regard to the protection of information from search or other intrusions. The word architecture is also found in that context, but it refers to the architecture of information systems and not buildings.

61 Rybcyznski, 28. He also writes: "Before the idea of the home as the seat of family life could enter the human consciousness, it required the experience of both privacy and intimacy, neither of which had been possible in the medieval hall." ibid., 48.

62 Walter Benjamin, *Reflections: Essays, Aphorisms, Autobiographical Writings* (New York: Harcourt Brace Jovanovich, 1978), 154. Edited and with an introduction by Peter Demetz. Translated by Edmund Jephcott. Benjamin also poses the interior as the opposite of the "private person who squares his accounts with reality in his office and demands the interior be maintained in his illusions." The passage has been frequently quoted in architectural theory and, in the past decade, in writing on interiors.

63 Privacy is, as influentially defined in the 1890 essay "The Right to Privacy," both "the right to be let alone" *and* "the right to one's personality." Though this definition is legal, its connection to the human response to the built environment is relevant: privacy is a psychological reflection of the self rendered in terms of architecture. Samuel Warren and Louis Brandeis, "The Right to Privacy," (1890), qtd. in Judith DeCew, "Privacy" in *The Stanford Encyclopedia of Philosophy* (Fall 2008 edition), Edward N. Zalta, ed., plato.stanford.edu/archives/fall2008/entries/privacy/>. Warren and Brandeis' essay is the foundation of American legal writing about privacy, which is, for the most part, only of passing interest here.

64 Tomas Maldonado, "The Idea of Comfort" in *Design Issues* 8:1 (Autumn 1991), 43. The article is a translation from Italian by John Cullars of an essay in Tomas Maldonado's *Il Futuro della Modernità* (Milan: Feltrinelli, 1987).

65 Benjamin, 154.

66 This terminology represents the criteria that most professional bodies and legal authorities impose upon certification and licensing of design professionals.

67 Edward Diener, "Guidelines for national indicators of subjective well-being and ill-being." http://www.psych.uiuc.edu/~ediener/Guidelines_for_National_Indicators.pdf, 4–6. The Gallup-Healthways Well-Being Index is located at www.well-beingindex.com/.

68 Alain de Botton, *The Architecture of Happiness* (New York: Vintage, 2006), 152. Indeed, the sight of beauty may provoke sadness, rather than happiness, because it forces us to recognize the gap between our daily existence and the object that we observe. De Botton further emphasizes this point: "It is perhaps when our lives are at their most problematic that we are likely to be most receptive to beautiful things." He underlines that those in a passive state of contentment—those whose needs for safety, comfort, and privacy have been fulfilled—are perhaps the least likely to react to aesthetic experience: "Our downhearted moments provide architecture and art with their best openings, for it is at such times that our hunger for their ideal qualities will be at its height." ibid., 150.

69 William Lescaze, *On Being an Architect* (New York: G.P. Putnam's Sons, 1942), 47.

Chapter 3

1 Jean-Anthelme Brillat-Savarin, *The Physiology of Taste* (New York: Knopf, 1971), 33. Translated by M.F.K. Fisher.

2 Not surprisingly, the discipline's exact point of origin is vastly open to interpretation. In some instances, it is argued that the discipline did not come into being until the beginning of the twentieth century, and its existence is conflated with interior decoration. A recent article in the *New Yorker* on decorator Kelly Wearstler, for example, states with a tone of authority: "Interior design as profession was invented by Elsie de Wolfe, an actress from a middle-class family, who catered to the new-money aristocrats of the Gilded Age: Condé Nast, Anne Vanderbilt, Henry Clay Frick." Dana Goodyear, "Lady of the House: Kelly Wearstler's maximal style," *New Yorker* (September 14, 2009), 63.

3 Clive D. Edwards, "History and Role of the Upholsterer" in *Encyclopedia of Interior Design*, Joanna Banham, ed. (London: Routledge, 1997), 1321–22.

4 Ayn Rand, *The Fountainhead* (Indianapolis: Bobbs-Merrill, 1943). Though the novel was primarily a literary exposition of Rand's objectivist philosophy, the character of Roark was modeled—at least in his individualism—after Wright. There is a 1949 film version of the story starring Gary Cooper. The film's director, King Vidor, engaged Wright to design Howard Roark's architectural projects as they would appear in the film, but Warner Bros. executives blocked Wright's participation after balking over his fee of 10 percent of the budget, his standard rate for an architectural commission.

5 C. Victor Twiss, "What is a Decorator?" in *Good Furniture* 10 (February 1918),109. Twiss notes that "The term Interior Decorator is of comparatively recent origin. While the writer is unable to state just when it was first used, he is sure it has not been generally used longer than twenty-five or thirty years," which, by subtraction, dates back to the 1890s. This would seem to confirm the thesis that the concept of interior decoration—which is a more limited practice than interior design, despite the current cultural conflation of the two—is a much more recent phenomenon than interior design, with its history deeply embedded in human evolution. Intriguingly, Twiss says that the interior decorator must "be a student of the principles of psychology so that he will be able to do the right thing for the right person." Twiss was identified in the byline as "C. Victor Twiss, Interior Decorator."

6 There is a substantial body of sophisticated writing on interior decorating from this period. The three most famous figures and their works are Elsie de Wolfe (1865–1950), *The House in Good Taste* (New York: Century, 1913), collected after serial publication in *Good Housekeeping*; Edith Wharton (1862–1937), *The Decoration of Houses* (New York: Charles Scribner's Sons, 1897), co-written with Boston architect Ogden Codman; and Dorothy Draper (1889–1969), *Decorating is Fun: How to Be Your Own Decorator* (New York: Doubleday, Doran & Company, Inc., 1939). The epigraph to Wharton's book from Henry Mayeux, *La Composition decorative* (Paris: A. Quantin, 1885), is particularly intriguing: "*Une forme doit être belle en elle-même et on ne doit jamais compter sur le décor appliqué pour en sauver les imperfections*" (A form must be beautiful in its own right, and applied décor must never be relied upon to save it from its imperfections). Other later publications that extend the analysis of interior decoration include Frank Alvah Parsons, *Interior Decoration: Its Principles and Practice* (Garden City, NY: Page & Company, 1915) and Sherrill Whiton, *Elements of Interior Decoration* (Chicago: Lippincott, 1937), with recent editions incorporating interior design into the title as Sherrill Whiton and Stanley Abercrombie, *Interior Design and Decoration* (Upper Saddle River, NJ: Pearson Prentice Hall, 2008). Parsons started a course in interior decoration in 1906 as president of the New York School of Fine and Applied Art in New York City (now integrated into The Parsons New School for Design); Whiton founded in 1915 what is now the New York School of Interior Design. Many of the earlier introductions to interior design and decorating contain substantial sections dedicated to the various stylistic periods in France and England; it was not until after World War II that modern interiors and planning began to be included in these volumes. See *House and Garden's Complete Guide to Interior Decoration*, Richard Wright, ed. (New York: Simon and Schuster, 1947), for instance, which presents a mixture of traditional and more modern designs and detailing. Contemporary histories of interior design strike a more balanced note. See, for instance, John Pile, *A History of Interior Design* (New York: John Wiley & Sons, 2004). Much has been published about the role of women and their place in the discipline and professional life including architecture and interiors, and the fact it was considered a "suitable" occupation. See, for instance, M.A. Livermore, *What Should We do with Our Daughters?* (Boston: Lee and Shepard, 1883); G.H. Dodge, *What Women Can Earn: Occupations of Women and their Compensation* (New York: F.A. Stokes, 1899); H.C. Candee, *How Women May Earn a Living* (New York: The Macmillan Co., 1900) of which chapter 7 is titled "Architecture and Interiors." The same author, Helen Churchill Candee, published a book titled *Decorative Styles and Periods in the Home* (New York: F.A. Stokes, 1906). Finally, F.E. Willard, *Occupations for Women: A Book of Practical Suggestions for the Material Advancement* (Cooper Union NY, Success Co., 1897). Willard was also deeply involved in other women's issues and the temperance movement. More contemporary sources about the important role of women designers include: Isabelle Anscombe, *A Woman's Touch: Women in Design from 1860 to the Present Day* (New York: Viking Penguin, 1984) and Adam Lewis, *The Great Lady Decorators: The Women Who Defined Interior Design, 1870–1955* (New York: Rizzoli, 2009).

7 This is not to say that demand for professional decorators existed only for domestic clients in the late nineteenth century; at the highest levels of architectural practice, there were firms that specialized in interior decoration in buildings designed by leading New York City firms, as Robert Koch noted in his history of Louis C. Tiffany: "During the early eighties Louis C. Tiffany and the Associated Artists were well on their way to becoming one of New York's top decorating concerns. Only the New York firms of Marcotte and Co. and the Herter Brothers were considered more fashionable, but the Tiffany firm was known as the most 'artistic.' The Associated Artists not only decorated dozens of interiors but produced many of the decorative accessories to go with them. Much of their work came to them from the rapidly growing architectural firm of McKim, Mead, and White, although Stanford White favored La Farge for his interiors until they disagreed in 1888." Robert Koch, *Louis C. Tiffany, Rebel in Glass* (New York: Crown Publishers, Inc., 1964, third edition 1982), 16. Also, "interior design" was used to describe the interior work of architects; see the posthumous estimation of "Richardson as an Interior Designer," *The Art Amateur* (August 1887), 62–63. By the end of the nineteenth and the first quarter of the twentieth century the fascination with French eighteenth-century architecture and interiors led to the replication of these interiors not just in the United States. The work of French decorating firms such as Allard et Fils or Carlhian et Fils, who acted almost in a design–build capacity in close collaboration with the building's architects, is not yet fully explored.

8 William Seale, *The Tasteful Interlude: American Interiors through the Camera's Eye, 1860–1917* (New York: Praeger Publishers, 1975), 11, 19.

9 In the 1840s, Catherine E. Beecher, sister of Harriet Beecher Stowe, the author of *Uncle Tom's Cabin*, published her first book, *Treatise of Domestic Economy, for the Use of Young Ladies at Home and at School* (Boston: T. H. Webb, 1842), later reprinted numerous times. After the Civil War, the sisters authored the equally popular *American Woman's Home, or Principles of Domestic Science, being a guide to the formation and maintenance of economical, healthful, beautiful, and Christian homes* (New York: J.B. Ford, 1869). The subject of home economics became deeply embedded in education, ranging from degrees offered at colleges to high school curricula. The widespread popular interest in the beauty and the efficiency of the home is also reflected in the appearance of what could be could considered early versions of what we would call shelter magazines today, including *Ladies' Home Journal* and *Practical Housekeeper* (1888), *Architectural Digest* (1920), *Better Homes & Gardens* (1924), and *House Beautiful* (1924).

10 Robert Gutman, *Architectural Practice, A Critical View* (Princeton: Princeton Architectural Press, 1988), 64–65. See also Mary N. Woods, *From Craft to Profession: the Practice of Architecture in Nineteenth-Century America* (Berkeley CA: University of California Press, 1999). Woods observes that, "Beginning in the late nineteenth century, many women interested in architecture were shunted into allied fields like interior design," footnote, 139. For a comprehensive short survey of the role of women in the architectural profession, see Gwendolyn Wright, "On the Fringe of the Profession" in *The Architect: Chapters in the History of the Profession*, Spiro Kostof, ed. (New York: Oxford University Press, 1977), 280–308.

11 The reference comes from an intriguing letter to the editor by American lexicographer Frank H. Vizetelly that appeared in 1935 in the *New York Times*, under the heading "Embellishers: Name Offered to Describe Interior Decorators". *New York Times* (June 30, 1935), E9. Vizetelly challenges the claims by the American Institute of Decorators, published in a previous article, that "not a single one of all the thousand dictionaries in existence gives a proper definition of what these people (decorators) are or what they do." To the contrary, Vizetelly wrote: "For nearly two centuries the word decorator has meant 'one who professionally decorates houses, public buildings, &c., with ornamental painting, plaster work, gilding and the like. In 1787 Sir John Hawkins described James and Kent as 'mere decorators' in his 'Life of Samuel Johnson,' but by 1885 the term had taken a more dignified position in the language, for in the Queen's Bench Division evidence was taken (Law Reports 14) concerning persons who 'carried on the business of upholsters, house painters and decorators.'" The letter concludes by suggesting a new name to substitute for the semantic confusion evident among decorators: "If decorators are not satisfied with the word that they themselves have used as the name of their institution, why not change it and substitute 'embellishers'?"

12 Interior architecture, another term that has gained currency in the past two decades, can be traced back at least to the 1920s, as evidenced in the unsigned article "Interior Architecture: The Field of Interior Design in the United States. A Review of Two Decades: Some Comments on the Present and a Look into the Future" in *The American Architect* (January 2, 1924), 25–29.

13 Codman and Wharton, qtd. in the excellent analysis by Pauline C. Metcalf, "Design and Decoration" in *Odgen Codman and the Decoration of Houses*, Pauline C. Metcalf, ed. (Boston: Boston Athenaeum, 1988), 65–66.

14 Peter Collins' *Changing Ideals in Modern Architecture* (London: Faber and Faber, 1965), a wide-ranging theoretical survey of the origins of modern architecture, ascribes numerous modernist theories to architectural concepts that emerged in the mid-eighteenth century, many of which revolved around the plan and design of interior space. Though interior design is not analyzed in detail in the book, the phrase "interior design" appears in the chapter "The Influence of Industrial Design," where Collins proposes a trio of eighteenth-century French architects as the first designers who can be considered both architects and interior designers in the modern sense: "[Germain] Boffrand was not only one of the greatest architects of his day, but, together with Jean-François Blondel and Robert de Cotte, was one of the first to establish himself as an interior designer." 266.

15 *Distribution*, from Vitruvius' *distributio*, meaning "the suitable arrangement of all the parts of a building." J.L. de Cordemoy, *Nouveau traité de toute l'architecture*, (Paris: J.B. Coignard, second edition, 1714; reprinted Farnborough, UK: Gregg, 1966), 236. Blondel wrote that distribution was directly tied to decoration: "In addition to consisting of arranging well all of the rooms composing a building, there is another sort of distribution, which concerns decoration, both interior and exterior." Jacque-François Blondel, *De la distribution des maisons de plaisance* (Paris: C.A. Jombert, 1737; reprinted Farnborough, UK: Gregg, 1967). See also, Germain Boffrand's 1745 *Livre d'architecture: contenant les principes généraux de cet art, et les plans, elevations et profils de quelques-uns des bâtimens faits en France & dans les pays étrangers* (Paris: Chez Guillaume Cavelier père, rue Saint-Jacques, au Lys d'or, 1745), available in English as *Book of architecture: containing the general principles of the art and the plans, elevations, and sections of some of the edifices built in France and in foreign countries* (Burlington, VT: Ashgate, 2002), edited with introduction and notes by Caroline van Eck, translated by David Britt; and Jacques-François Blondel, *Cours d'architecture, ou, Traité de la décoration, distribution & construction des bâtiments; contenant les leçons données en 1750, & les années suivantes* (Paris: Desaint, 1771–77).

16 For a critical history of the exact role played by architects in eighteenth-century France, see Katie Scott, *The Rococo Interior* (New Haven: Yale University Press, 1995), 65–77.

17 Charles Matlack Price, "Architect and Decorator," *Good Furniture* (1914), 554. Price's notion of the interiors practitioner is far closer to the decorator than to the interior designer as we have laid it out here. He writes that "interior decoration was a profession demanding not only taste but a minute and conscientious consideration of all details of wood-work, ornamental plaster, rugs, tapestries, fabrics, papers, lighting, fixtures, hardware and furniture and the like." ibid., 554. It is important to note that Price was a frequent contributor to various architectural and design magazines at the time.

18 Bobbye Tigerman, "'I Am Not a Decorator': Florence Knoll, the Knoll Planning Unit and the Making of the Modern Office" in *Journal of Design History* 20:1 (2007), 63.

19 ibid., 63.

20 The splinter group that formed the National Society of Interior Designers broke off from the New York chapter of the American Institute for Decorators (AID), which had been formed in 1931. In 1961, reflecting a changing professional environment, AID itself changed its name to the American Institute of Interior Designers while keeping the same acronym. The two organizations merged in 1975 to form the American Society of Interior Designers (ASID). The maturation and development of these professional organizations was mirrored by attempts to develop more standardized interior design education and licensing standards; the Interior Design Educators Council (IDEC) was formed in 1963, and the National Council for Interior Design Qualification (NCIDQ) was formed in 1974. The International Interior Design Association (IIDA) was not formed until 1992.

Endnotes

See Christine M. Petroski, *Professional Practice for Interior Designers* (New York: Wiley-Interscience, 2001), 7–13, for a good summary of the recent history of the interior design professional organizations.

21 In recent years attempts are being made to correlate knowledge obtained in the neurosciences with the design of buildings and spaces. An example is the 2003 initiative by the San Diego Chapter of the American Institute of Architects in creating the Academy of Neurosciences for Architecture. Here scientists and designers are brought together for workshops. A good summary of these various efforts can be found in Emily Anthes, "Building around the Mind" in *Scientific American*, April/May/June 2009, 52–59. The conclusions presented in the article would seem quite apparent to most designers. A more interesting article in the same issue is Vilayanur S. Ramachandran and Diane Rogers-Ramachandran, "The Power of Symmetry," 20–22, which discusses studies of the figure ground and their relationship to the perception of motion.

22 "Psychology, n." OED *The Oxford English Dictionary*. Second edition, 1989. OED Online. Oxford University Press. The term *psychology* combines *psycho-* (of or relating to the soul or spirit) with *-logy* (study of); the word appeared first in post-classical Latin *psychologia* (late sixteenth century, originally in German sources: see note 24); it was adapted as substantially the same word in all western European languages.

23 ibid. Author's emphasis added.

24 "psychology." *Encyclopedia Britannica*. 2009. Encyclopedia Britannica Online. <search.eb.com/eb/article-9061727>.

25 T.H. Huxley, *Hume, with Helps to the study of Berkeley: Essays* (New York: D. Appleton & Company, 1896), 59. The essay itself is from 1879 and was reprinted and quoted in psychology textbooks as early as the following year. Huxley's most familiar public face was as "Darwin's Bulldog"—as the defender and Great Britain's chief popularizer of the Darwinian theory of evolution.

26 The spleen, for example, was regarded as the seat of melancholy or morose feelings, and also (somewhat contradictorily) as the seat of laughter or mirth. The sixteenth-century expression "from the spleen" could be seen as synonymous with what we mean today by "from the heart." We have kept the latter expression, even though we know full well the heart is not the seat of human emotion.

27 Gaston Bachelard, *La Terre et les rêveries du repos* (Paris: José Corti, 1948). Translation appears in Joan Ockman ed., *Architecture Culture 1943–1968: A Documentary Anthology* (New York: Rizzoli/Columbia, 1993), 112–13.

28 Huxley, 60.

29 William James, "A Plea for Psychology as a 'Natural Science'" (1890) in William James, *Collected Essays & Reviews* (New York: Longmans, Green & Co., 1920), 317.

30 William James, *Principles of Psychology* (New York: Henry Holt and Co., 1890, 1918 edition), 468.

31 Except, of course, in a post facto identification that occurs in a book like Jonah Lehrer's *Proust Was a Neuroscientist* (New York: Houghton Mifflin Harcourt, 2007), which argues that writers like Proust were, through literature, already conducting the basic outlines of what we would now recognize as cognitive science.

32 According to the *Encyclopedia Britannica*, "the general assumption [of the logical positivists] was that, insofar as biology is like physics, it is good science, and insofar as it is not like physics, it ought to be. The best one can say of modern biology, in their view, is that it is immature; the worst one can say is that it is simply second-rate." See "nature, philosophy of ." *Encyclopedia Britannica*. 2009. Encyclopedia Britannica Online. <search.eb.com/eb/article-36170>.

33 Different design and research methodologies have been proposed and published, though they all fall short. Most seek to develop basic comparative data as it relates to the factual planning needs of a project. A good example from an architectural perspective is Linda Groat and David Wang's *Architectural Research Methods* (New York: John Wiley & Sons, 2002). On the design end, see Graeme Sullivan, *Art Practice as Research: Inquiry in the Visual Arts* (Thousand Oaks, CA: Sage Publications, 2005). Note should also be made of the *Journal of Interior Design*, published by the Interior Design Educator's Council (IDEC), where many tightly defined experimental and design observation studies and experiments may be found.

34 "science." *Encyclopedia Britannica*. 2009. Encyclopedia Britannica Online. <search.eb.com/eb/article-9066286>.

35 The most significant attempt is Denise A. Guerin and Caren S. Martin, *The Interior Design Profession's Body of Knowledge: Its Definition and Documentation*, first published in 2001 and revised in 2005.

36 Richard Neutra, *Survival Through Design* (New York: Oxford University Press, 1954). A subsequent 1969 edition of the book has an introduction by Raymond Neutra. Intriguingly, Richard Neutra collapsed physiology and psychology into one term, physiopsychology, derived from Wilhem Wundt's *Principles of Physical Psychology*. The young Neutra, it's worth pointing out, knew Freud personally. In a 1967 interview he recounted Freud scoffing at him for having read Wundt: for Freud, "the formative and molding influences of a human mind were primarily human relations." Sylvia Lavin in "Open the Box: Richard Neutra and the Psychology of the Domestic Environment" writes: "On the one hand, it is now taken for granted that the environment has an impact on psychic life and, indeed, seems a banal observation of pop psychology. On the other hand, Neutra's writings have a frenzied and pseudoscientific air that has isolated them from the architectural mainstream. Thus Neutra's ideas have fallen prey twice: first to the idea that they are too popular to be serious and second to the idea that they are too idiosyncratic to have broad cultural significance." Sylvia Lavin, "Richard Neutra and the Psychology of the Domestic Environment," *Assemblage* 40 (December 1999), 8. Lavin has continued to publish about Richard Neutra, most recently, "Form Follows Libido: Architecture and Richard Neutra in a Psychoanalytic Culture" in *Harvard Design Magazine* 29 (Fall–Winter, 2008–2009) 161–64, 167.

37 Richard J. Neutra and Richard Hughes, "Interview with Richard J. Neutra" in *Transition* 29 (February–March, 1967), 22–34.

38 Neutra, *Survival Through Design*, 86

39 Neutra, "Human Setting in an Industrial Civilization" in *Zodiac* 2 (1958), 69–75. Reprinted in Joan Ockman, ed., *Architecture Culture 1943–1968: A Documentary Anthology* (New York: Rizzoli/Columbia, 1993), 287

40 For introduction to the principles of biomimicry, see Janine M. Benyus, *Biomimicry: Innovation Inspired by Nature* (New York: Perennial, 1998); for permaculture, see, for instance, David Holmgren, *Permaculture: Principles and Pathways Beyond Sustainability* (Holmgren Design Services, 2002).

41 Efforts to develop metrics for indoor air quality are being made. See, for instance, *ASHRAE Proposed New Guideline 10, Interactions Affecting the Achievement of Acceptable Indoor Environments* (Atlanta, GA: American Society of Heating, Refrigerating and Air-Conditioning Engineers, April 2010). This is a draft document for public review and comment only, and it is to be expected that a final version will be issued at some future date.

42 Building full-scale mock-ups of parts of buildings is a well-established architectural and interior practice. The construction of a full-scale mock-up of an entire facade is rare but not entirely unheard of. One of the most famous examples is the full-scale mock-ups of a villa for Kröller-Müller Museum *in situ* in Wassenaar, the Netherlands, by Ludwig Mies van der Rohe. The house was never built.

Chapter 4

1   Walter Pater, *The Renaissance* (New York/London: Oxford University Press, 1998), 152; originally published 1873 as *Studies in the History of the Renaissance*.

2   Edgar Kaufmann, Jr., "Nineteenth-Century Design" in *Perspecta* 6 (1960), 61.

3   For an overview see especially Adrian Forty, *Objects of Desire: Design and Society Since 1750* (London: Thames and Hudson, 1992).

4   Sloan brought Earl to GM after the latter's success in creating custom bodies for vehicles in Los Angeles in the 1920s. The Sloan–Earl model of periodic stylistic obsolescence reflected the large-scale adoption of streamlining in 1930s design, as evidenced in the work of such prominent American industrial designers as Norman Bel Geddes, Henry Dreyfuss, Raymond Loewy, and Walter Dorwin Teague.

5   James Marston Fitch, "Physical and Metaphysical in Architectural Criticism" in *James Marston Fitch: Selected Writings on Architecture, Preservation, and the Built Environment*, Martica Sawin, ed. (New York: Norton, 2006), 82.

6   For a general discussion of design thinking, see Peter G. Rowe, *Design Thinking* (Cambridge, MA: MIT Press, 1991); Nigel Cross, *Designerly Ways of Knowing* (Basel: Birkhäuser, 2006), especially the section "Research in Design Thinking," 30–31; *Managing as Designing*, Richard Boland and Fred Collopy, eds. (Stanford: Stanford University Press, 2004), note especially the essay by Jeanne Liedtka, "Design Thinking: The Role of Hypotheses and Testing," 193–97. The origins of design thinking seem to lie in systems analysis and the nascent architecture of computing as formulated in the 1960s, rather than in the traditional practices of design.

7   In the context of design thinking the word "design" is used not only to indicate a creative form-giving process but also to denote a level of competency. The term "user-centered design" describes a level of customization rather than fully individualized work. See, for instance, John Heskett, *Design: A Very Short Introduction* (London/New York: Oxford University Press, 2003), 3.

8   Maslow's hierarchy of human needs, first published in the article "A Theory of Human Motivation" in 1943, identified a five-step pyramid. Starting from the bottom, those needs were: 1. Physiological; 2. Safety; 3. Love/belonging; 4. Esteem; and 5. Self-actualization. Maslow's hierarchy has had a vast influence in popular culture, especially in marketing literature, though the hierarchical construction of human needs has come under fire from subsequent psychologists. For the original text, see Abraham H. Maslow, "A Theory of Human Motivation" in *Psychological Review* 50:4 (1943), 370–96.

9   "The Economic Effects of Design," The Danish National Institute for Enterprise and Housing (September 2003) http://www.ebst.dk/file/1924/the_economic_effects_of_designn.pdf. That ladder has subsequently been adopted in many discussions of design management. While the format of the ladder reflects Maslow's methodology, the actual content of the design ladder does not seem to be directly related to the psychological components of Maslow's hierarchy.

10   It should be noted that the concept of design thinking has not been universally accepted. Museum of Modern Art (MoMA) design curator Paola Antonelli has, for example, criticized the idea that design thinking can be brought in from outside a company—as opposed to growing organically from within. See the interview with Paola Antonelli: "Thinking and Problem Making" on the Design Research Network at https://www.designresearchnetwork.org/drn/content/interview-paola-antonelli:-%2526quot%3B thinking-and-problem-making%2526quot%3B.

11   Rudolf Arnheim, "Sketching and the Psychology of Design" in *The Idea of Design*, Victor Margolin and Richard Buchanan, eds. (Cambridge, MA: MIT Press, 1995), 71.

12   Much of the research-based academic design literature does include publications on experiments and experimental installations. However, many seem not only to miss a clear "testing protocol" but the outcome also seems to have little direct applicability besides showing the participants the importance of the method by which particular phenomena can be manipulated, and too many surprising outcomes. See, for example, much of the case study and studio literature published in the *Journal of Design Education*.

13   Design, n. OED *The Oxford English Dictionary*, second edition, 1989. OED Online. Oxford University Press.

14   Industrial Design, definition in Paolo Portoghesi, ed., *Dizionario Enciclopedico di architettura e urbanistica* (Rome: Ist. editoriale romano, 1968–1969), 61.

15   There is a considerable body of recent literature establishing the relationship between the emergence of process engineering and labor studies and the birth of modern architecture. See, for instance, Mauro F. Guillén, "Scientific management's lost aesthetic: architecture, organization, and the taylorized beauty of the mechanical" in *Administrative Science Quarterly* (December 1, 1997), 682–715, and David A. Hounshell, *From the American System to Mass Production, 1800–1932: The Development of Manufacturing Technology in the United States* (Baltimore and London: The Johns Hopkins University Press, 1984).

16   Edgar Kaufmann Jr., *What is Modern Design?* (New York: Museum of Modern Art, 1950), 5; reprinted in Kaufmann, *Introductions to Modern Design* (New York: Arno Press, 1969). (Kaufmann's italics in the sentence "conceiving and giving form to objects used in everyday life" have been removed). Edgar Kaufmann Jr. was for some years involved with the Museum of Modern Art and its various exhibitions dealing with "design." He was the Director of Industrial Design at the Museum of Modern Art (MoMA) in New York City from 1946 through 1955, where one of his major contributions was the program "Good Design" in cooperation with the Merchandise Mart. For a summary of his involvement at the museum, see Franklin Toker, *Fallingwater Rising: Frank Lloyd Wright, E. J. Kaufmann, and America's Most Extraordinary House* (New York: Alfred A. Knopf, 2004), 371–80. More recently the museum held a "retrospective" of what was seen as good design between 1944 and 1956, the period when Kaufmann was at the museum. See Roberta Smith, "What was good design? MOMA's message 1944–56," *New York Times* (June 5, 2009). For a short summary of Kuafmann's life and career, see Paul Goldberger, "Edgar Kaufmann Jr., 79, Architectural Historian," *New York Times* (August 1, 1989).

17   Rowena Reed Kostellow was present at the creation of the first industrial design faculty in the United States in 1934 at the Carnegie Technical Institute, and helped to found the industrial design department at Pratt Institute in Brooklyn, New York, in 1936. Her husband, Alexander Jusserand Kostellow, was, with Reed, instrumental in formulating basic standards for industrial design education. Her teaching was later compiled into a book, though perhaps that publication does not entirely make clear its relevance to the design of interior spaces. See Gail Greet Hannah, *Elements of Design: Rowena Reed Kostellow and the Structure of Visual Relationship* (New York: Princeton Architectural Press, 2002).

18   Qtd. in Hannah, 100.

19   It is precisely this repetitive and exploratory sketching, searching for three-dimensional form, that is attractive in the design process of visualizing alternative scenarios to arrive at satisfactory problem resolution.

20   John Chris Jones, *Design Methods* (New York: John Wiley and Sons, second edition, 1992), 10–11.

21   Fitch 1973, 313.

22   It is important to note here that Fitch's interest was not just in the formal and historical but also in the environmental, as

witnessed as early as 1948 in his seminal *American Architecture: the Forces that Shaped It*, in which he discusses not only the historical and stylistic developments of American architecture but also shows how environmentally sensitive this same architecture was. James Marston Fitch, *American Architecture: the Forces that Shaped It* (New York: Houghton Mifflin, 1948).

23 Fitch 1973, 314.

24 Albert Borgmann "The Depth of Design" in *Discovering Design: Explorations in Design Studies*, Richard Buchanan and Victor Margolin, eds. (Chicago: University of Chicago Press, 1995), 15. Borgmann coined the term "device paradigm" in his *Technology and the Character of Contemporary Life* (Chicago: Chicago University Press, 1984), referring to the manner in which a technology is perceived by its users.

25 Richard Buchanan, "Rhetoric, Humanism, and Design" in *Discovering Design,* 31.

26 William Lescaze, *On Being an Architect* (New York: G.P. Putnam's Sons, 1942), 28–29. Lescaze himself was essentially a modernist and his early work dating from the 1930s is quite interesting, since he designed not only the buildings but often also the furniture for the interior. See Christian Hubert and Lindsay Stamm Shapiro, *William Lescaze 1896–1969* (New York: Rizzoli/Institute of Architecture and Urban Studies, 1993).

27 Fitch, *American Building* 1973, 314.

28 Qtd. in Hannah, 42.

29 J. Gordon Lippincott, "Industrial Design as a Profession" in *College Art Journal* 4:3 (March 1945):149–50.

30 The important English-language work on the architecture of the Beaux-Arts is by Arthur Drexler, *The Architecture of the École des Beaux-Arts* (New York: Museum of Modern Art, 1977). The book does not, however, focus on the educational ethos behind the Beaux-Arts. An intriguing study of the difference between the two schools' curricula is Harold Bush-Brown's *Beaux-Arts to Bauhaus and Beyond: An Architect's Perspective* (New York: Whitney Library of Design, 1976). The displacement of the Beaux-Arts design curricula with a modernist one occurred over a roughly three-decade span, as stated in the relatively conventional historical summation provided in the *Encyclopedia Britannica*: "Beaux-Arts architectural design has been particularly influential. About 1935 the system of the Paris school began to be displaced by an essentially German curriculum stemming from functionalism and machine-inspired theory taught at the Bauhaus." "Beaux-Arts, École des," *Encyclopedia Britannica*, 2009. Encyclopedia Britannica Online, search.eb.com/eb/article-9014011>. In this context it is interesting to note that women were not admitted to the Ecole officially till 1897 but their numbers remained small. See Meredith L. Clausen, "The École des Beaux-Arts: Toward a Gendered History, *Journal of the Society of Architectural Historians*, Vol. 69 (2 June 2010), 153–61. The first woman to be admitted to the École, in architecture, was the American Julia Morgan. In the United States it was not until the 1940s and 1950s that modernist curricula were installed in most architectural schools. See, for instance, Anthony Alofsin, *The Struggle for Modernism: Architecture, Landscape Architecture, and City Planning at Harvard* (New York: W.W. Norton, 2002). The role of history as a reference and source of inspiration was different for the two schools. Whereas the École des Beaux-Arts was clearly oriented towards a more historical approach, the approach to history in a modernist curriculum was quite different. See, for instance, Winfried Nerdinger, "From Bauhaus to Harvard: Walter Gropius and the Use of History" in *The History of History in American Schools of Architecture 1865-1975*, Gwendolyn Wright and Janet Parks, eds. (New York: Princeton Architectural Press, 1990), 89–98.

31 A.D.F. Hamlin, "The Influence of the École des Beaux-Arts on our Architectural Education" in *Columbia University Quarterly* (June 1908), reprinted from *Architectural Record* XXIII 4 (April 1908), 286.

32 This division between objects and buildings does not address the teaching of the orders as a design element, which was central in many of the Beaux-Arts-inspired design curricula, at least in the United States. But the teaching of the orders was not exclusive to Beaux-Arts education, and had formed a part of formal architectural education in many venues since the mid-eighteenth century.

33 William R. Ware's vision for American architectural education at Columbia University—which was formulated before the popular influence of the Beaux-Arts in America—suggested that students take home plaster casts from a collection to draw in their free time. Whether this ever occurred is a matter of conjecture. William R. Ware, "Architecture at Columbia College" in *The American Architect and Building News* (August 6, 1881), 61.

34 "The Bauhaus in Dessau," Curriculum, 1925, Broadside (November 1925) in *Bauhaus*, 107. This was published on the school's move to Dessau. The other purpose of the curriculum was stated as "practical research into problems of house construction and furnishing. Development of standard prototypes for industry and the crafts."

35 The Deutscher Werkbund was founded in 1907 in Munich, It remained active until the mid-1930s and was reestablished after World War II. The Werkbund organized several exhibitions, the best known of which were held in Cologne (1914) and Stuttgart (1927).

36 "The Bauhaus in Dessau" curriculum (1925) in *Bauhaus*, 107.

37 First Bauhaus Declaration, qtd. in Reyner Banham, *Theory and Design in the First Machine Age* (London: The Architectural Press, 1960), 277. The definitive collection of documents on the Bauhaus in English is Hans W. Wingler, ed., *Bauhaus: Weimar, Dessau, Berlin, Chicago* (Cambridge, MA: MIT Press, 1969). See also Leah Dickerman, "Bauhaus Fundaments" in *Bauhaus 1919–1933, Workshops for Modernity*, Barry Bergdoll and Leah Dickermann, eds. (New York: Museum of Modern Art, 2009), 15–39.

38 Walter Gropius, "Is there a Science of Design?," qtd. in Peter Collins, *Changing Ideals in Modern Architecture* (London: Faber and Faber, 1965), 269.

39 Laszlo Moholy-Nagy, "New Approach to the Fundamentals of Design" from the periodical *More Business* 3:11 (Chicago, November 1938) in *Bauhaus*,196. The components of the fundamentals course were organized under six workshops: "1. Wood, metal, 2. Textile, 3. Color, 4. Light, 5. Glass, 6. Display."

40 ibid., 196.

41 ibid., 197.

42 From the document "The Municipal Infant-Toddler Centers and Preschools of Reggio Emilia" on the main Reggio Emilia educational site: zerosei.comune.re.it/inter/nidiescuole.htm.

43 Several descriptions of Reggio Emilia are available in English. See *The Hundred Languages of Children: Narrative of the Possible* (Reggio Emilia: City of Reggio Emilia, 1987); Louise Boyd Cadwell, *Bringing Learning to Life: The Reggio Approach to Early Childhood Education* (New York and London: Teachers College Press, 2002); *Making Learning Visible: Children as Individual and Group Learners* (Reggio Emilia: Reggio Children, 2001); Ann Pelo, *The Language of Art: Inquiry-Based Studio Practices in Early Childhood Settings* (St. Paul, MN: Redleaf Press, 2007); and *In the Spirit of the Studio: Learning from the Atelier of Reggio Emilia* (New York and London: Teachers College Press, 2005). In the last publication, particularly in chapters 12 and 13, the importance of space, its organization, and patterns of change are discussed in the context of a school in St. Louis, MO. Most of the written material emphasizes the pedagogical role of the Reggio Emilia method in the development of children, and does not provide a specific "content" to the education. However, in the context of design education, the process of inquiry, and experience as a form of long-term learning is what is most relevant.

44 The account of Reggio Emilia's methods is based on the author's experiences at a conference in Reggio Emilia in 2007.

45 While the primary interest here is not early childhood education, it is important to note that the Reggio Emilia system works within a structure of teamwork and collaboration. Teams always consist of between three and five children. At a very early age they learn how to feel safe, secure, and curious while contributing to creative activities and participating in a helpful manner within a group setting.

46 In most of the Reggio Emilia literature, reference is made to an atelier—a studio-like setting—when discussing creative activities.

47 In the context of architectural schools, there is a great deal of discussion about the value and culture of the studio teaching method that is ingrained in their educational process. Many design schools have already begun to explore a more diversified studio model with frequent reference to the word "laboratory." However, most of them seem to focus on exploring particular design ideas, representation, or fabrication rather than the experiential.

48 For a description of one of the examples of this process, see "The Ideo Cure: De Paul Health Center" in *Metropolis* (October 2002), 3–10.

49 David Woodruff Smith, "Phenomenology," *The Stanford Encyclopedia of Philosophy* (Summer 2009 edition), Edward N. Zalta, ed., http://plato.stanford.edu/archives/sum2009/entries/phenomenology/.

50 That essay, titled "*Der Versuch als Vermittler von Objekt und Subjekt*," was not published until three decades later, however, with the printing of Goethe's six-volume "Scientific Notebooks" (*Naturwissenschaftliche Hefte*), from 1817–1824. The essay is available in English translation at http://pages.slc.edu/~eraymond/bestfoot.html.

51 Johann Wolfgang von Goethe, *Theory of Colours* (originally published London: John Murray, 1840; reprinted Cambridge, MA and London: MIT Press, 1970), iiv.; trans. Charles Lock Eastlake. The book first appeared in German in 1810.

52 Neil Ribe and Friedrich Steinle, "Exploratory Experimentation: Goethe, Land, and Color Theory" in *Physics Today* (July 2002), 44. See also Dennis L. Sepper, *Goethe Contra Newton: Polemics and the Project for a New Science of Color* (Cambridge: Cambridge University Press, 2003). Goethe's color theories were an integral part of his other scientific explorations. See Karl J. Fink, *Goethe's History of Science* (Cambridge: Cambridge University Press, 1991), 31–44.

53 ibid., 43 The authors contrast this method against Newton's: "Newton's investigations into optics were guided by the metaphysical belief that color was merely a subjective correlate of mechanical properties of light rays. He therefore abstracted from the complex world of normal visual perception, working in a dark chamber illuminated only by a single sunbeam. [...] His mathematization of light and color could best take flight from a few particular effects. But the price paid was that his experiments had only limited relevance to color as usually perceived."

54 Lois Swirnoff, *Dimensional Color* (New York: W.W. Norton & Company, 2003). Where Josef Albers in his *Interaction of Color* (New Haven: Yale University Press, 1963) explores color primarily as a series of two-dimensional exercises, Swirnoff's work concerns all three dimensions.

55 Serra's own description of *Tilted Arc* from a PBS interview available at www.pbs.org/wgbh/cultureshock/flashpoints/visualarts/tiltedarc_a.html, part of the website companion to the arts program *Culture Shocks*.

56 *Tilted Arc* was removed in 1989 after extended litigation that began shortly after the sculpture's installation. See Michael Breason, "The Messy Saga of 'Tilted Arc' is Far From Over," *New York Times* (April 2, 1993). Serra has proposed a similar installation for the Loris Malaguzzi International Centre in Reggio

Emilia, Italy. See "An invitation for....Richard Serra," *Rechild, Reggio Children Newsletter* (December 2006), 12.

57 Turrell's three-dimensional achievements are reminiscent of the skies of the painted ceilings of the seventeenth and eighteenth century (albeit these were full of gods and cherubs), and also recall some of the effects experienced in the atmospheric theaters of the 1920s, when, in addition to the scenery, steam would be blown across a painted sky to simulate clouds. A good monograph on Turrell's work, with extensive discussion of skyscapes, is *Rencontres 9: James Turrell* (Paris: Almine Rech/Images Modernes, 2005). For some of his earlier work, try the exhibition catalog *James Turrell: The Other Horizon* (Vienna: MAK Austrian Museum of Applied Arts, 1999).

58 From the transcript of a TV interview with Turrell, available at www.pbs.org/wnet/egg/215/turrell/interview_content_1.html, from the television program *EGG: The Arts Show*.

59 Madeleine Grynsztejn "(Y)our Entanglements: Olafur Eliasson, The Museum, and Consumer Culture" in *Take Your Time: Olafur Eliasson* (San Francisco and London: San Francisco Museum of Modern Art/Thames and Hudson, 2007), 15. The experience is analogous to many of the phenomena that Goethe described for the first time. Goethe described the reverse experience: "If we look at a dazzling, altogether colourless object, it makes a strong lasting impression, and its after-vision is accompanied by an appearance of colour." Goethe, 16.

60 Grynsztejn., 15.

61 See, for example, the work of Karen Stephenson, who has surveyed the nature of trust in corporate settings. Her work largely focuses on the networks of trust that exist between workers in a large corporate office. See http://www.drkaren.us and http://netform.com.

62 A preponderance of evidence from the last decade shows that sensory stimulation and exercise are critical to maintaining mental health and physical agility when aging. Sensory stimulation is also necessary in the workplace but should not be confused with concerns that are being raised about overstimulation and distractions as a result of the various forms of instant communication that are available today. See, for example, the 2008 Lexis-Nexis Workplace Productivity Survey for a discussion of the estimated loss of productivity.

63 It is interesting to note in this context that Goethe's writings about color also included studies of language. See Fink, *Goethe's History of Science*, 31-44.

64 Bergdoll and Dickerman, *Bauhaus 1919–1933*, 27–36. In this section reference is made to "Gesamtkunstwerk Thinking," "The Modern Specialist," "Tactility," and "Commemoration" as headings suggesting some of the themes addressed here.

65 Richard Wagner, *The Art Work of the Future* (1849). Translated by William Ashton Ellis; available at http://users.belgacom.net/wagnerlibrary/prose/wagartfut.htm.

Chapter 5

1 Walter Benjamin, *Reflections: Essays, Aphorisms, Autobiographical Writings* (New York: Harcourt Brace Jovanovich, 1978). Translated and edited by Peter Demetz.

2 A variation, of course, on the Churchill quote in chapter 1.

3 It is easier to define the end of this era—marked by the onset of the Industrial Revolution—than the beginning, because the formation of craft professions was dispersed widely over time and geography. In fact, all three eras overlap, but their delineation has been simplified for greater clarity.

4 Paradoxically, the reinforcement of design as a specialized knowledge has kept, to some extent, the quality of designed objects equal to, or perhaps higher than, the craft objects they replaced, and made them affordable to an ever larger group. The wide availability of relatively high-quality material goods could never have occurred without the specialization of industrial production and the demotion of the role of craft in creating objects.

5 See the section in chapter 2, "Design for Basic Human Needs (Measures of Man)" for more on this point.

6 Marshall McLuhan, *Understanding Media: Extensions of Man* (New York: New American Library, 1964), 67.

7 Interview, Mike Davis, *New Perspectives Quarterly* (Summer 2006), www.digitalnpq.org/archive/2009_summer/16_davis. html. See also Davis, *Planet of Slums* (New York: Verso, 2007).

8 The statistics are fascinating. The world's population is expected to rise from 6.1 billion people in 2000 to 9.2 billion in 2050; at the same time, the percentage of the world's population living in urban areas will rise from just under 50 percent in 2000 to nearly 70 percent in 2050, again with the majority of urban population growth in developing countries according to the United Nations Population Division. The agency's website allows one to produce an array of fascinating comparative tables, by economic divisions, and on a country-by-country or worldwide basis. See http://www.un.org/esa/population/unpop.htm.

9 The height of buildings was the product of many different factors including structural limitations, and lack of any or suitable elevators or fire protection. By the end of the nineteenth century almost all these issues were sufficiently resolved to allow for much taller buildings. By 1913 with the opening of the Woolworth Building in New York City, whose 54 stories and height of 794 feet (242 meters) made it the tallest building in the world for the next 17 years, most of those issues were adequately resolved.

10 Many post-World War II architects developed plans for new cities and megastructures. Constant Nieuwenhuys (generally only referred to as Constant) was a Dutch artist, who throughout his life worked on New Babylon, a utopian anti-capitalist city. See Mark Wigley, *Constant's New Babylon: the hyper-architecture of desire* (Rotterdam: 010 Publishers, 1998). For the work of Cedric Price, see Stanley Mathews, *From agit-prop to free space: the architecture of Cedric Price* (London: Black Dog Publishers, 2007). Both Nieuwenhuys and Price envisioned structural systems where infills could be made to accommodate specific functions or needs without necessarily any regard for exterior appearance. For the work of R. Buckminster Fuller, see the catalog of the exhibition at the Whitney Museum of Art in New York City: K. Michael Hays, ed., *Buckminster Fuller: Starting with the Universe* (New Haven: Yale University Press, 2008).

11 Jon Kolko, "Abductive Thinking and Sensemaking: The Drivers of Design Synthesis" in *Design Issues*, Winter 2010, Volume 26, Number 1.

12 Jeffrey T. Schnapp and Michael Shanks, "Artereality (Rethinking Craft in a Knowledge Economy)" in *Art School (Propositions for the 21st Century)*, S.H. Madoff, ed. (Cambridge, MA: MIT Press, 2009).

13 Cornelia Dean, "Ancient Man Hurt Coasts, Paper Says", *New York Times* (August 21, 2009), A20. The article describes how researchers are challenging the idea that primitive hunter-gatherers lived in harmony with nature.

14 William N. Morgan, *Ancient Architecture of the Southwest* (Austin, TX: University of Texas Press, 1994).

15 For a comprehensive survey of the issue surrounding the world's water supply, see UNESCO The 3rd United Nations World Water Development Report: Water in a Changing World (WWDR-3), available at http://www.unesco.org/water/wwap/wwdr/wwdr3/index.shtml. For food (as well as further perspective on water resources) see the Statistics section of the United Nations Food and Agriculture Organization http://www.fao.org/corp/statistics/en/.

16 Sigfried Giedion, *Space, Time and Architecture: The Growth of a New Tradition* (Cambridge, MA/London: Harvard University Press, sixth edition, 1969)

FURTHER READING

Ackerman, Diane, *A Natural History of the Senses*, New York: Random House, 1990

Abercrombie, Stanley, *A Philosophy of Interior Design*, Icon Editions, New York: Harper & Row, 1990

Abercrombie, Stanley, *A Century of Interior Design, 1900–2000*, New York: Rizzoli, 2003

Appleton, Jay, *The Experience of Landscape*, Chichester, UK: John Wiley & Sons, 1975

Albers, Josef, *Interaction of Color*, New Haven: Yale University Press, 1963

Alofsin, Anthony, *The Struggle for Modernism: Architecture, Landscape Architecture, and City Planning at Harvard*, New York: W. W. Norton, 2002

Anscombe, Isabelle, *A Woman's Touch: Women in Design from 1860 to the Present Day*, New York: Viking, 1984

Arnheim, Rudolf, *Visual Thinking*, Berkeley: University of California Press, 1969

Aynsley, Jeremy, and Charlotte Grant, *Imagined Interiors: Representing the Domestic Interior Since the Renaissance*, London/New York: V&A/Harry N. Abrams, Inc, 2006

Bachelard, Gaston, *La Terre et les rêveries du repos*, Paris: José Corti, 1948. Translation appears in Joan Ockman, ed., *Architecture Culture 1943–1968: A Documentary Anthology*, New York: Rizzoli/Columbia, 1993

Banham, Reyner, *Theory and Design in the First Machine Age*, London: The Architectural Press, 1960

Banham, Reyner, *The Architecture of the Well-tempered Environment*, Chicago: University of Chicago Press, 1969

Beecher, Catherine E., *Treatise of Domestic Economy, for the Use of Young Ladies at Home and at School* (Boston: T. H. Webb, 1842)

Beecher, Catherine E. with Beecher Stowe, Harriet, *American Woman's Home, or Principles of Domestic Science*, New York: J.B. Ford, 1869

Benjamin, Walter, *Reflections: Essays, Aphorisms, Autobiographical Writings*, Peter Demetz, ed., New York: Harcourt Brace Jovanovich, 1978

Benyus, Janine M., *Biomimicry: Innovation Inspired by Nature*, New York: Perennial, 1998

Bergdoll, B. and Dickerman, L., *Bauhaus 1919–1933, Workshops for Modernity*, New York: MOMA, 2009

Blake, Peter, *The Master Builders*, New York: Knopf, 1960

Blondel, Jacques-François, *De la Distribution des maisons de plaisance*, Paris: C.A. Jombert, 1737; reprinted Farnborough, U.K: Gregg, 1967

Blondel, Jacques-François, *Cours d'architecture, ou, Traité de la décoration, distribution & construction des bâtiments; contenant les leçons données en 1750, & les années suivantes*, Paris: Desaint, 1771–77

Blunt, Anthony, *Artistic Theory in Italy, 1450–1600*, Oxford: The Clarendon Press, 1940

Boffrand, Germain, *Livre d'architecture: contenant les principes généraux de cet art, et les plans, elevations et profils de quelques-uns des bâtimens faits en France & dans les pays étrangers*, Paris: Chez Guillaume Cavelier père, rue Saint-Jacques, au Lys d'or, 1745; and in English, Caroline van Eck, ed., *Book of Architecture: Containing the General Principles of the Art and the Plans, Elevations, and Sections of some of the Edifices Built in France and in Foreign Countries*, translated by David Britt, Burlington, VT: Ashgate, 2002

Borgmann, Albert, "The Depth of Design" in *Discovering Design: Explorations in Design Studies*, Richard Buchanan and Victor Margolin, eds, Chicago: University of Chicago Press, 1995

Borgmann, Albert, *Technology and the Character of Contemporary Life*, Chicago: University of Chicago Press, 1984

Buchanan, Richard, and Victor Margolin, eds, *Discovering Design: Explorations in Design Studies*, Chicago: University of Chicago Press, 1995

Brillat-Savarin, Jean-Anthelme, *The Physiology of Taste*, M.F.K. Fisher, trans., New York: Knopf, 1971

Burke, Edmund, *On the Sublime and Beautiful*, Vol. XXIV, Part 2, The Harvard Classics, New York: P. F. Collier & Son, 1909–14. Available online at www.bartleby.com/24/2/

Bush-Brown, Harold, *Beaux-Arts to Bauhaus and Beyond: An Architect's Perspective*, New York: Whitney Library of Design, 1976

Cadwell, Louise Boyd, *Bringing Learning to Life: The Reggio Approach to Early Childhood Education*, New York and London: Teachers College Press, 2002

Candee, H. C., *How Women May Earn a Living*, New York: The Macmillan Co., 1900

Candee, H. C., *Decorative Styles and Periods in the Home*, New York: F. A. Stokes, 1906

Clark, Kenneth, *The Nude: A Study of Ideal Art*, New York: Pantheon Books, 1956

Collins, Peter, *Changing Ideals in Modern Architecture*, London, Faber and Faber, 1965

Cooper, Clare, "The House as Symbol of the Self" in *Environmental Psychology, Second Edition: People and Their Physical Settings*, Harold M. Proshansky, William H. Ittleson, Leanne G. Rivlin, eds, New York: Holt, Rinehart and Winston, 1976, 435–6

Cranz, Galen, *The Chair: Rethinking Culture, Body and Design*, New York/London: Norton, 1998

Cross, Nigel, *Designerly Ways of Knowing*, Basel: Birkhäuser, 2006

Crowley, J. E., *The Invention of Comfort*, Baltimore: The Johns Hopkins University Press, 2001

Davenport, Guy, "The Geography of the Imagination," title essay in *The Geography of the Imagination*, Boston: David R. Godine Publisher, 1997

de Botton, Alain, *The Architecture of Happiness*, New York: Pantheon Books, 2006

de Cordemoy, J.-L., *Nouveau traité de toute l'architecture*, second ed., Paris: J.-B. Coignard, 1714; Farnborough: Gregg, 1966), 236

de Wolfe, Elsie, *The House in Good Taste*, New York: Century, 1913

Diderot, Denis, Jean Le Rond d'Alembert and Pierre Mouchon, *Encyclopédie, ou Dictionnaire raisonné des sciences, des arts et des métiers*

Dodge, G. H., *What Women Can Earn: Occupations of Women and their Compensation*, New York, F. A. Stokes, 1899

Draper, Dorothy, *Decorating is Fun: How to Be Your Own Decorator*, New York: Doubleday, Doran & Co., Inc., 1939

Dreyfuss, Henry, *The Measure of Man: Human Factors in Design*, New York: Whitney Library of Design, 1960

Drexler, Arthur, *The Architecture of the École des Beaux-Arts*, New York: Museum of Modern Art, 1977

Dutton, Denis, *The Art Instinct: Beauty, Pleasure, and Human Evolution*, New York: Bloomsbury, 2009

Elliott, Cecil D., *Technics and Architecture: The Development of Materials and Systems for Buildings*, Cambridge, MA: MIT Press, 1992

Emerson, Ralph Waldo, *Nature: Addresses, and Lectures*, Boston: James Munroe, 1849

Emerson, Ralph Waldo, "Works and Days" in *Society and Solitude*, reprinted in *The Complete Works of Ralph Waldo Emerson*, Vol. VII, Cambridge, MA: Riverside Press, 1904

Etlin, Richard, "Aesthetics and the Spatial Sense of Self" in *The Journal of Aesthetics and Art Criticism*, 56:1 (Winter 1998), 4

Fewkes, J. Walter, "The Cave Dwellings of the Old and New Worlds" in *American Anthropologist*, 12:3 (1910), 394

Fink, Karl J., *Goethe's History of Science*, Cambridge, Cambridge University Press, 1991

Fitch, James Marston, *American Building: The Forces that Shape It*, Boston: Houghton Mifflin, 1948

Fitch, James Marston, *American Building: The Historical Forces that Shaped It*, second edition, New York: Schocken Books, 1973

Fitch, James Marston, and William Bobenhausen, *American Building: The Environmental Forces That Shape It*, rev. and updated ed., New York: Oxford University Press, 1999

Fitch, James Marston, and Martica Sawin, *James Marston Fitch: Selected Writings on Architecture, Preservation, and the Built Environment*, New York: W. W. Norton, 2006

Fletcher, Banister, *A History of Architecture on the Comparative Method*, 17th ed., New York: Scribner, 1961

Fletcher, Banister, and J. C. Palmes, *Sir Banister Fletcher's A History of Architecture*, 18th ed., London: Athlone Press, 1975

Forty, Adrian, *Words and Buildings: A Vocabulary of Modern Architecture*, New York: Thames & Hudson, 2000

Forty, Adrian, *Objects of Desire: Design and Society Since 1750*, London: Thames & Hudson, 1992

Gallagher, Winfred, *The Power of Place: How Our Surroundings Shape Our Thoughts, Emotions, and Actions*, New York: Poseidon Press, 1993

Giedion, Sigfried, *Space, Time and Architecture: the Growth of a New Tradition*, 5th ed., Cambridge, MA: Harvard University Press, 1967

Giedion, Sigfried, *Mechanization Takes Command*, New York, Oxford University Press, 1948

Goethe, Johann Wolfgang, *Theory of Colours*, trans. Charles Lock Eastlake, originally published London: John Murray, 1840; reprinted in facsimile Cambridge, MA and London: The MIT Press, 1970

Grier, K. C., *Culture and Comfort: Parlor Making and Middle-Class Identity, 1850–1930*, Washington, DC: Smithsonian Institution Press, 1997

Groat, Linda N., and David Wang, *Architectural Research Methods*, New York: John Wiley, 2002

Grynsztejn, Madeleine, "(Y)our Entanglements: Olafur Eliasson, The Museum, and Consumer Culture" in *Take Your Time: Olafur Eliasson*, San Francisco and London: San Francisco Museum of Modern Art/Thames & Hudson, 2007

Guerin, Denise A., and Caren S. Martin, *The Interior Design Profession's Body of Knowledge: Its Definition and Documentation*, first published in 2001, rev. 2005; available at http://www.careersininteriordesign.com/idbok.pdf

Guillén, Mauro F., *The Taylorized Beauty of the Mechanical: Scientific Management and the Rise of Modernist Architecture*, Princeton: Princeton University Press, 2006

Gutman, Robert, *Architectural Practice, A Critical View*, Princeton: Princeton Architectural Press, 1988

Gwilt, Joseph, and Wyatt Angelicus Van Sandau Papworth, *The Encyclopedia of Architecture: Historical, Theoretical and Practical*, rev. ed., New York: Crown, 1982

Hall, Edward T., *The Hidden Dimension*, first ed. Garden City, NY: Doubleday, 1966

Hall, Edward T., *Beyond Culture*, Garden City, NY: Doubleday, 1976

Hannah, Gail Greet, *Elements of Design: Rowena Reed Kostellow and the Structure of Visual Relationship*, New York: Princeton Architectural Press, 2002

Heidegger, Martin, *Poetry, Language, Thought*, New York: Harper Colophon Books, 1917, trans. Albert Hofstadter

Heskett, John, *Design: A Very Short Introduction*, London/

New York: Oxford University Press, 2003

Hesselgren, Sven, *Man's Perception of Man-Made Environment*, Lund, Sweden/Stroudsburg, Pennsylvania: Studentlitteratur ab/Dowden, Hutchinson & Ross, 1975

Hewes, Gordon W., "World Distribution of Certain Postural Habits" in *American Anthropologist* (April 1955) 57:2

Heyd, Thomas and Clegg, John, *Aesthetics and Rock Art*, Burlington, VT: Ashgate Publishing, 2005

Hildebrand, Grant, *Origins of Architectural Pleasure*, Berkeley: University of California Press, 1999

Hiss, Tony, *The Experience of Place*, New York: Knopf, 1990

Holahan, Charles J., *Environmental Psychology*, New York, Random House, 1982

Holmgren, David, *Permaculture: Principles and Pathways Beyond Sustainability*, Holmgren Design Services, 2002

Hounshell, David A., *From the American System to Mass Production, 1800–1932: The Development of Manufacturing Technology in the United States*, Baltimore and London: The Johns Hopkins University Press, 1984

Hubert, Christian and Lindsay Stamm Shapiro, *William Lescaze 1896–1969*, New York: Rizzoli/Institute of Architecture and Urban Studies, 1993

Hubka, Thomas, "Just Folks Designing: Vernacular Designers and the Generation of Form" in *Common Places: Readings in American Vernacular Architecture*, ed. Dell Upton and John M. Vlach, Athens: University of Georgia Press, 1986

Huizinga, Johan, *Homo Ludens: A Study of the Play-element in Culture*, in the series Humanitas, Beacon Reprints in Humanities, Boston: Beacon Press, 1955

Huxley, Thomas Henry, *Hume, With Helps to the Study of Berkeley: Essays*, New York: D. Appleton, 1896

Jacobs, Jane, *The Death and Life of Great American Cities*, New York: Vintage Books, 1961

James, William, and Ralph Barton Perry, "A Plea for Psychology as a 'Natural Science'" in William James, *Collected Essays & Reviews*, New York: Longmans, Green & Co., 1920

James, William, *Principles of Psychology*, New York: Henry Holt and Co., 1890 (1918 edition)

Jones, John Chris, *Design Methods*, New York: John Wiley and Sons, second edition, 1992

Jung, C. G., *Memories, Dreams, Reflections*, New York: Pantheon Books, c. 1963. Recorded and edited by Aniela Jaffé; trans. Richard and Clara Winston

Kaufmann Jr., Edgar, *What is Modern Design?*, New York: Museum of Modern Art, 1950, reprinted in Kaufmann, *Introductions to Modern Design*, New York: Arno Press, 1969

Kentgens-Craig, Margret, *The Bauhaus and America: First Contacts, 1919–1936*, Cambridge, MA: MIT Press, 1999

Koch, Robert, *Louis C. Tiffany, Rebel in Glass*, New York: Crown Publishers, Inc., 1964, third edition, 1982

Kopec, David Alan, *Environmental Psychology for Design*, New York: Fairchild, 2006

Kostof, Spiro, ed., *The Architect: Chapters in the History of the Profession*, New York: Oxford University Press, 1977

Laugier, Marc-Antoine, *An Essay on Architecture*, trans. by Wolfgang and Anni Herrmann, Los Angeles: Hennessey & Ingalls, 1977

Le Corbusier, *The Modulor: A Harmonious Measure to the Human Scale Universally Applicable to Architecture and Mechanics*, London: Faber and Faber, 1956

Le Corbusier, *Modulor 2: Let the User Speak Next*, London, Faber and Faber, 1958

Leatherbarrow, David, *Uncommon Ground: Architecture, Technology, and Topography*, Cambridge, MA: MIT Press, 2000

Lehrer, Jonah, *Proust Was a Neuroscientist*, New York:

Houghton Mifflin Harcourt, 2007

Leroi-Gourhan, André, *Gesture and Speech*, Cambridge, MA: MIT Press, 1993

Lescaze, William, *On Being an Architect*, New York: G.P. Putnam's Sons, 1942

Lewis, Adam, *The Great Lady Decorators: The Women Who Defined Interior Design, 1870–1955*, New York, Rizzoli, 2009

Livermore, M. A., *What Should We do with Our Daughters?*, Boston: Lee and Shepard, 1883

Margolin, Victor, and Richard Buchanan, *The Idea of Design, A Design Issues Reader*, Cambridge, MA: MIT Press, 1995

Mathews, Stanley, *From Agit-prop to Free Space: The Architecture of Cedric Price*, London: Black Dog, 2007

McKellar, Susie, and Penny Sparke, *Interior Design and Identity, Studies in Design*, Manchester/New York: Manchester University Press, 2004

McLuhan, Marshall, *Understanding Media: The Extensions of Man*, second ed., New York: New American Library, 1964

Metcalf, Pauline C., ed., *Ogden Codman and the Decoration of Houses*, Boston: Boston Athenaeum, 1988

Minowski, Eugène, *Vers une Cosmologie: fragments philosophiques*, new ed., Paris: Aubier-Montaigne, 1967

Moholy-Nagy, Laszlo, *Vision in Motion*, Chicago: P. Theobald, 1947

Moholy-Nagy, Laszlo and D. Hoffmann, *The New Vision and Abstract of an Artist, The Documents of Modern Art*, New York: George Wittenborn, Inc., 1947

Morgan, William N., *Ancient Architecture of the Southwest*, Austin: University of Texas Press, 1994

Müller, Ulrich, *Raum, Bewegung und Zeit*, Berlin: Akademie Verlag, 2004

Nerdinger, Winfried, "From Bauhaus to Harvard: Walter Gropius and the Use of History" in *The History of History in American Schools of Architecture 1865–1975*, Gwendolyn Wright and Janet Parks, eds., New York: Princeton Architectural Press, 1990

Neufert, Ernst, *Bau-Entwurfslehre, Grundlagen, Normen und Vorschriften über Anlage, Bau, Gestaltung, Raumbedarf, Raumbeziehungen: Masse für Gebäude, Räume, Einrichtungen und Geräte mit dem Menschen als Mass und Ziel: Handbuch für den Baufachmann, Bauherrn, Lehrenden und Lernenden*, Berlin: Bauwelt, 1936. Subsequently published in English as *Architects' Data*

Neutra, Richard J., *Survival Through Design*, New York: Oxford University Press, 1954

Newman, Oscar, *Defensible Space: Crime Prevention through Urban Design*, New York: Macmillan, 1972

Ockman, Joan, *Architecture Culture 1943–1968: A Documentary Anthology*, New York: Rizzoli/Columbia, 1993

Otero-Pailos, Jorge, *Architecture's Historical Turn: Phenomenology and the Rise of the Postmodern*, Minneapolis/London: University of Minnesota Press, 2010

Opulent Interiors of the Gilded Age: All 203 Photographs from "Artistic Houses," New York: Dover, 1987; first published as *Artistic Houses*, New York: D. Appleton, c. 1883

Panero, Julius, and Martin Zelnik, *Human Dimension & Interior Space: A Source Book of Design Reference Standards*, New York: Whitney Library of Design, 1979

Parsons, Frank Alvah, *Interior Decoration: Its Principles and Practice*, Garden City, NY: Page & Company, 1915

Pater, Walter, *The Renaissance*, New York/London: Oxford University Press, 1998; originally published 1873 as *Studies in the History of the Renaissance*

Pelo, Ann, *The Language of Art: Inquiry-Based Studio Practices in Early Childhood Settings*, St. Paul, MN: Redleaf Press, 2007

Petroski, Christine M., *Professional Practice for Interior Designers*, New York: Wiley-Interscience, 2001

Further reading

Pevsner, Nikolaus, *Outline of European Architecture*, Harmondsworth: Penguin Books, 1942

Piedmont-Palladino, Susan, *Tools of the Imagination: Drawing Tools and Technologies from the Eighteenth Century to the Present*, New York: Princeton Architectural Press, 2007

Pile, John, *A History of Interior Design*, New York: John Wiley & Sons, 2004

Plato, *Theaetetus*, Benjamin Jowett, trans. c. 1892, available online at classics.mit.edu/Plato/theatu.html

Portoghesi, Paolo, *Dizionario enciclopedico di architettura e urbanistica, Collana di dizionari enciclopedici di cultura artistica*, Rome: Ist. editoriale romano, 1968

Prak, Niels Luning, *The Language of Architecture: a Contribution to Architectural Theory*, The Hague/Paris: Mouton, 1968

Price, Charles Matlack, "Architect and Decorator" in *Good Furniture*, 1914

Proshansky, Harold M., William H. Ittelson and Leanne G. Rivlin, *Environmental Psychology: People and Their Physical Settings*, second ed., New York: Holt, Rinehart and Winston, 1976

Pulos, Arthur J., *The American Design Adventure, 1940–1975*, Cambridge, MA: MIT Press, 1988

Rand, Ayn, *The Fountainhead*, Indianapolis: Bobbs-Merrill, 1943

Rice, Charles, *The Emergence of the Interior: Architecture, Modernity, Domesticity*, London/New York: Routledge, 2007

Rowe, P. G., *Design Thinking*, Cambridge, MA: MIT Press, 1991

Rudofsky, Bernard, *Streets for People: A Primer for Americans*, Garden City, NY: Doubleday, 1969

Rybczynski, Witold, *Home: A Short History of an Idea*, New York: Viking, 1986

Rykwert, Joseph, *On Adam's House in Paradise: The Idea of the Primitive Hut in Architectural History*, New York: Museum of Modern Art, 1972

Rykwert, Joseph, *The Dancing Column: On Order in Architecture*, Cambridge, MA: MIT Press, 1996

Sacks, Oliver, *The Man who Mistook His Wife for a Hat*, New York: Summit, 1985

Sacks, Oliver, *Musicophilia: Tales of Music and the Brain*, New York: Knopf, 2007

Schoenauer, Norbert, *6,000 Years of Housing*, New York: W. W. Norton, 2000

Scott, Katie, *The Rococo Interior*, New Haven: Yale University Press, 1995

Seale, William, *The Tasteful Interlude: American Interiors through the Camera's Eye*, 1860–1917, New York: Praeger Publishers, 1975

Seamon, David, and Robert Mugerauer, *Dwelling, Place and Environment: Towards a Phenomenology of Person and World*, Malabar, FL: Krieger Publishing Company, 2000

Sepper, Dennis L., *Goethe Contra Newton: Polemics and the Project for a New Science of Color*, Cambridge: Cambridge University Press, 2003

Sternberg, Esther M., *Healing Spaces: The Science of Place and Well-Being*, Cambridge, MA/London: The Belknap Press of Harvard University Press, 2009

Straus, Lawrence Guy, "Caves: A Paleoanthropological Resource" in *World Archaeology* 10:3 (February 1979), 333

Sturgis, Russell, *A Dictionary of Architecture and Building: Biographical, Historical, and Descriptive*, New York: Macmillan & Co., 1901

Sullivan, Graeme, *Art Practice as Research: Inquiry in the Visual Arts*, Thousand Oaks, CA: Sage Publications, 2005

Swirnoff, Lois, *Dimensional Color*, New York: W. W. Norton, 2003

Tarver, John Charles, *The Royal Phraseological English–French, French–English Dictionary*, London: Dulau & Co, 1879

Taylor, Mark, and Julieanna Preston, *Intimus: Interior Design Theory Reader*, Chichester: Wiley-Academy, 2006

Thornton, Peter, *Authentic Decor: The Domestic Interior, 1620–1920*, first US ed., New York: Viking, 1984

Tigerman, Bobbye, "'I Am Not a Decorator': Florence Knoll, the Knoll Planning Unit and the Making of the Modern Office" in *Journal of Design History* 20:1, 2007

Toker, Franklin, *Fallingwater Rising: Frank Lloyd Wright, E. J. Kaufmann, and America's Most Extraordinary House*, New York: Alfred A. Knopf, 2004

U.S. National Institute of Law Enforcement and Criminal Justice, *Design Guidelines for Creating Defensible Space*, Washington, DC: National Institute of Law Enforcement and Criminal Justice, Law Enforcement Assistance Administration, US Dept. of Justice: US Government Printing Office, 1976

Van der Laan, Dom H., *Architectonic Space: Fifteen Lessons on the Disposition of the Human Habitat*, Richard Padovan, trans., Leiden: E. J. Brill, 1983

Veitch, Russell, and Daniel Arkkelin, *Environmental Psychology: An Interdisciplinary Perspective*, Englewood Cliffs, NJ: Prentice Hall, 1995

Vitruvius Pollio, Marcus, *De Architectura*, trans. by Morris Hicky Morgan as *Vitruvius: The Ten Books on Architecture*, Cambridge, MA: Harvard University Press, 1914

Wagner, Richard, *The Art Work of the Future* (1849), William Ashton Ellis, trans., available at http://users.belgacom.net/wagnerlibrary/prose/wagartfut.htm

Ware, William R., *An Outline of a Course of Architectural Instruction*, Boston: J. Wilson & Sons, 1866

Wharton, Edith, *The Decoration of Houses*, New York: Charles Scribner's Sons, 1897

Whiton, Sherrill, *Elements of Interior Decoration*, Chicago: Lippincott, 1937

Wigley, Mark, *Constant's New Babylon: The Hyper-architecture of Desire*, Rotterdam: 010 Publishers, 1998

Willard, F. E., *Occupations for Women: A Book of Practical Suggestions for the Material Advancement*, Cooper Union NY, Success Co, 1897

Wingler, Hans W., ed., *Bauhaus: Weimar, Dessau, Berlin, Chicago*, Cambridge, MA: MIT Press, 1969

Wittkower, Rudolf, *Architectural Principles in the Age of Humanism*, New York: Random House, 1965

Wölfflin, Heinrich, and Jasper Cepl, *Prolegomena zu einer Psychologie der Architektur: mit einem Nachwort zur Neuausgabe von Japser Cepl*, Edition Ars et Architectura, Berlin: Mann, 1999

Woodcock, D.M., "A Functionalist Approach to Environmental Preference," PhD diss., University of Michigan, 1982

Woods, Mary N., *From Craft to Profession: The Practice of Architecture in Nineteenth-Century America*, Berkeley: University of California Press, 1999

Worsham, Herman, "The Milam Building" in *Heating, Piping and Air Conditioning*, 1 (July 1929), 182

Wright, Frank Lloyd, *The Natural House*, New York: Horizon Press, 1954

Wright, Gwendolyn, and Janet Parks, eds, *The History of History in American Schools of Architecture 1865–1975*, Princeton: Princeton University Press, 1990

Wright, Richard, ed., *House and Garden's Complete Guide to Interior Decoration*, revised and enlarged edition, New York: Simon & Schuster, 1947

Yaneva, Albena, *Scaling Up and Down: Extraction Trials in Architectural Design*, Thousand Oaks, CA: Sage Publications Ltd., 2005

Zevi, Bruno, *Architecture as Space: How to Look at Architecture*, New York: Horizon Press, 1957

Further reading

ARTICLES

Anon., "Interior Architecture: The Field of Interior Design in the United States. A Review of Two Decades: Some Comments on the Present and a Look into the Future" in *The American Architect* (January 2, 1924), 25–29

Anthes, Emily, "Building around the Mind" in *Scientific American*, April/May/June 2009

Attfield, Judy, "Beyond the Pale: Reviewing the Relationship between Material Culture and Design History" review in *Journal of Design History* 12 (4): 373–380, 1999

Biester, Charlotte E., "Catherine Beecher's Views of Home Economics" in *History of Education Journal* 3 (3): 88–91, 1952

Briggs, Martin S., "Architectural Models—I." in *The Burlington Magazine for Connoisseurs* 54 (313): 174–183, 1929

Briggs, Martin S., "Architectural Models—II." in *The Burlington Magazine for Connoisseurs* 54 (314): 245–252, 1929

Buchanan, Richard, "Rhetoric, Humanism, and Design" in *Discovering Design*, 31

Clausen, Meredith L., "The École des Beaux-Arts: Toward a Gendered History" in *Journal of the Society of Architectural Historians* 2 June (Vol. 69, 2010): 153–161

Collins, Peter, "The Eighteenth-Century Origins of Our System of Full-Time Architectural Schooling" in *Journal of Architectural Education* 33 (2) (November 1979): 2–6

Dean, Cornelia, "Ancient Man Hurt Coasts, Paper Says," *New York Times* (August 21, 2009), A20

Deforge, Yves, and John Cullars, "Avatars of Design: Design before Design" in *Design Issues* 6 (2): 43–50, 1990

Eames, Charles, "Language of Vision: The Nuts and Bolts" in *Bulletin of the American Academy of Arts and Sciences* 28 (1): 13–25, 1974

Eames, Charles, and Ray Eames, "The Eames Report April 1958" in *Design Issues* 7 (2): 63–75, 1991

Edwards, Clive D., "History and Role of Upholsterer" in *Encyclopedia of Interior Design*, Joanna Banham, ed., London: Routledge, 1997

Etlin, Richard A., "Le Corbusier, Choisy, and French Hellenism: the Search for a New Architecture" in *The Art Bulletin* 69 (2) (June 1987): 264–278

Goodyear, Dana, "Lady of the House: Kelly Wearstler's Maximal Style" in *New Yorker* (September 14, 2009)

Guillén, Mauro F., "Scientific Management's Lost Aesthetic: Architecture, Organization, and the Taylorized Beauty of the Mechanical" in *Administrative Science Quarterly* (December 1, 1997): 682–715

Hamlin, A. D. F., "The Influence of the École des Beaux-Arts on our Architectural Education" in *Columbia University Quarterly* (June 1908), reprinted from *Architectural Record* XXIII: 4 (April 1908), 286

Hays, Michael, ed., *Buckminster Fuller: Starting with the Universe*, New Haven: Yale University Press, 2008

Hayward, Stephen, "'Good Design Is Largely a Matter of Common Sense:' Questioning the Meaning and Ownership of a Twentieth-Century Orthodoxy" in *Journal of Design History* 11 (3): 217–224, 1998

Hewes, Gordon W., "World Distribution of Certain Postural Habits" in *American Anthropologist* 57 (2): 231–244, 1955

Hewes, Gordon W., "The Domain Posture" in *Anthropological Linguistics* 8 (8): 106–112, 1966

Howarth, Thomas, "Background to Architectural Education" in *Journal of Architectural Education* 14:2 (Autumn 1959): 25–30

Kaufmann, Edgar, Jr., "Nineteenth-Century Design" in *Perspecta* 6: 56–67, 1960

Kelley, C. F., "Architectural Models in Miniature" in *Bulletin of the Art Institute of Chicago* (1907–1951) 31 (5): 65–68, 1937

Kirkham, Pat, "Humanizing Modernism: The Crafts, 'Functioning Decoration' and the Eameses" in *Journal of Design History* 11 (1): 15–29, 1998

Kolko, Jon, "Abductive Thinking and Sensemaking: The Drivers of Design Synthesis" in *Design Issues* 26 (1), Winter 2010

Lavin, Sylvia, "Richard Neutra and the Psychology of the Domestic Environment" in *Assemblage* No. 40 (December 1999), 8

Lavin, Sylvia, "Form Follows Libido: Architecture and Richard Neutra in a Psychoanalytic Culture" in *Harvard Design Magazine* (Fall–Winter, 2008–2009), n. 29, 161–164, 167

Ley, David, untitled review in *Annals of the Association of American Geographers* 64 (1): 156–158, 1974

Lippincott, J. Gordon, "Industrial Design as a Profession" in *College Art Journal* 4: 3, 1945

Maciuika, John V., "Adolf Loos and the Aphoristic Style: Rhetorical Practice in Early Twentieth-Century Design Criticism" in *Design Issues* 16 (2): 75–86, 2000

Maldonado, Tomas, "The Idea of Comfort" in *Design Issues* (Autumn 1991) 8: 1, 35–43

Margolin, Victor, "A World History of Design and the History of the World" in *Journal of Design History* 18 (3): 2005, 235–243

Maslow, Abraham H., "A Theory of Human Motivation" in *Psychological Review* 50 (4): 370–396, 1943

Moholy-Nagy, Laszlo, "New Approach to the Fundamentals of Design" from the periodical *More Business* 3:11 (Chicago, November 1938) in *Bauhaus*, 196

Moholy-Nagy, Sibyl, "The Indivisibility of Design" in *Art Journal* 22 (1): 12–14, 1962

Muschenheim, William, "Curricula in Schools of Architecture: A Directory" in *Journal of Architectural Education* (1947–1974) 18 (4): 56–62, 1964

Neutra, Richard J., "Human Setting in an Industrial Civilization" in *Zodiac* 2 (1958): 69–75; reprinted in Joan Ockman, ed., *Architecture Culture 1943–1968: A Documentary Anthology*, New York: Rizzoli/Columbia, 1993, 287

Puetz, Anne, "Design Instruction for Artisans in Eighteenth-Century Britain" in *Journal of Design History* 12 (3): 217–39, 1999

Purser, Robert S., "The Historical Dimension of Environmental Design Education" in *Art Education* 31 (4): 13–15, 1978

Ramachandran, V. S. and D. Rogers-Ramachandran, "The Power of Symmetry" in *Scientific American*, April/May/June 2009, 20–22

Ribe, N. and F. Steinle, "Exploratory Experimentation: Goethe, Land, and Color Theory" in *Physics Today* (July 2002), 44

Robinson, Julia W., "Architectural Research: Incorporating Myth and Science" in *Journal of Architectural Education* 44 (1): 20–32, 1990

Smith, Roberta, "What was Good Design? MOMA's Message 1944–56," *New York Times* (June 5, 2009)

Twiss, C. Victor, "What is a Decorator?" in *Good Furniture* 10 (February 1918)

Vizetelly, Frank H., "Embellishers: Name Offered to Describe Interior Decorators," *New York Times* (June 30, 1935)

Ware, William R., "Architecture at Columbia College" in *The American Architect and Building News* (August 6, 1881), 61

Weigley, Emma Seifrit, "It Might Have Been Euthenics: The Lake Placid Conferences and the Home Economics Movement" in *American Quarterly* 26 (1): 79–96, 1974

Wigley, Mark, "White-out: Fashioning the Modern [Part 2]" in *Assemblage* (22): 7–49, 1993

Woodruff Smith, David, "Phenomenology" in *The Stanford Encyclopedia of Philosophy* (Summer 2009 Edition), Edward N. Zalta, ed., http://plato.stanford.edu/archives/sum2009/entries/phenomenology/

Wright, John Henry, "The Origin of Plato's Cave" in *Harvard Studies in Classical Philology* 17: 131–142, 1906

Young, Gregory, Jerry Bancroft, and Mark Sanderson, "Seeking Useful Correlations between Music and Architecture" in *Leonardo Music Journal* 3: 39–43, 1993

Zucker, Paul, "The Paradox of Architectural Theories at the Beginning of the Modern Movement" in *The Journal of the Society of Architectural Historians* 10: 3 (October 1951), 9

Further reading

INDEX